Environmental Policy: A Global Perspective for the Twenty-First Century

Donald T. Wells
West Georgia College

PRENTICE HALL, Upper Saddle River, New Jersey 07458

Library of Congress Cataloging-in-Publication Data

WELLS, DONALD T.
  Environmental policy: a global perspective for the twenty-first
century / Donald T. Wells.
    p.   cm.
  Includes bibliographical references and index.
  ISBN 0-13-400219-9 (pbk.)
  1. Environmental policy.   2. Environmental protection.   3. Man—
Influence on nature.   I. Title.
GE170.W46   1995
363.7 ' 056—dc20   95-30135
                                                        CIP

Printed on Recycled Paper

Editorial/production supervision, interior design,
  and electronic page makeup: Kari Callaghan Mazzola
Acquisitions editor: Mike Bickerstaff
Editorial assistant: Anita Castro
Cover design: Anthony Gemmellaro
Buyer: Bob Anderson

© 1996 by Prentice-Hall, Inc.
Simon & Schuster/A Viacom Company
Upper Saddle River, New Jersey 07458

Printed in the United States of America
10 9 8 7 6 5 4 3 2 1

ISBN 0-13-400219-9

PRENTICE-HALL INTERNATIONAL (UK) LIMITED, London
PRENTICE-HALL OF AUSTRALIA PTY. LIMITED, Sydney
PRENTICE-HALL CANADA INC., Toronto
PRENTICE-HALL HISPANOAMERICANA, S.A., Mexico
PRENTICE-HALL OF INDIA PRIVATE LIMITED, New Delhi
PRENTICE-HALL OF JAPAN, INC., Tokyo
SIMON & SCHUSTER ASIA PTE. LTD., Singapore
EDITORA PRENTICE-HALL DO BRASIL, LTDA., Rio de Janeiro

This book is dedicated to Jake, Sam, Charles, Jessie, Hannah, Sidney, Christopher, Josh, and Katie—nine beautiful reasons for a grandfather to be concerned about the intergenerational consequences of human actions.

Contents

Chapter 3   Air Quality: It's More Than What We Breathe   43

Chapter 4   The World's Great Water Systems and the Sources of Their Pollution   63

Chapter 5   Chemical Dependency and Environmental Degradation   84

Preface

If ever a book was the product of a lifetime of observing, teaching, and studying, this one is. My interest in the environment was formed when I was a boy growing up on a farm in North Carolina. Like so many farms in the area, the farm that my father leased from Duke Power Company bore the visible signs of past abuse—overcultivated land resulting in a loss of topsoil, erosion that formed gullies, and the like. There was substantial emphasis at that time on conservation. The idea was that the productive capacity of the soil had to be preserved if the well-being of future generations was to be protected. I well remember representatives of the Department of Agriculture talking earnestly with my father about conservation. He listened and he acted on the basis of a conservation ethic. Equally vivid are images of the "CCC boys," as they were affectionately called—units of the Civilian Conservation Corps who planted trees, constructed terraces, and took the many other actions necessary to protect the soil.

These early images are the sources of two important themes in this book. The first theme is that environmental protection is not a choice; it is a necessity. Protecting the ecological basis of life, to me, most closely approximates the earthly content of what Immanuel Kant called the "categorical imperative." The second theme formed from these early images is that of the intergenerational nature of human actions. Just as soil conservation actions are necessary to ensure the well-being of future generations, so are environmental quality actions. Indeed, our trust may very well be preservation of the ecological basis of life for future generations.

Very little was taught relative to the environment during the years that I was a student. My field of study in graduate school was public administration and public policy. I was fortunate to have the opportunity to write my doctoral dissertation on a "conservation" topic—one aspect of the programs of the Tennessee Valley Authority—and the dissertation was supported by Resources for the Future, Inc. That experience sealed my academic interest in the environment at the same time that it familiarized me with one of the most responsible and influential think tanks on environmental issues: Resources for the Future, Inc. I have taught and conducted research on the environment ever since.

Two questions have guided my teaching and research and the writing of this book: What is happening to the ecological basis of life? What do these things mean and what significance do they hold? The first question involves trying to separate fact from fiction, to establish a base from which reasoned conclusions can be drawn. Unfortunately, this process still has a long way to go. One of the problems in thinking about the environment is that we simply do not know what is happening in many of the most fundamental aspects of the environment. It is startling that in a day characterized by the "information explosion" we do not have information on some of the most basic requirements for sustaining the ecological basis of life. We drown in numbers, many of them collected on irrelevancies, while we inch ever closer to drowning in our own sewage. I have tried to deal honestly with the absence of data. I do not believe that we should fill in the blanks of an inadequate environmental data set with guesses or opinions. Neither do I believe that we should gloss over inadequacies in data by proceeding to draw conclusions that are not warranted by what we know to be the case. If we are to fulfill the categorical imperative of preserving the ecological basis of life, we must begin with the facts as best as we can establish them.

The second question involves interpreting what we know, making sense out of it, and determining its significance for human actions. This is the process of deriving meaning from what is known. I recognize that even the very nature of meaning is the subject of much dispute among philosophers, psychologists, and scientists, and I do not claim to be able to resolve that dispute. But I do believe that a search for the meaning of environmental data involves three important elements: First, there must be the recognition that environmental quality is a good in itself. It has intrinsic value and does not need justification. Such a recognition, however self-evident it should be, is not a part of the perceptual apparatus of millions of people. Second, there must be the capacity to accept the possibility that we are in danger of losing environmental quality, or, put differently, there is the possibility of the erosion of the ecological basis of life. I attempt to address the issue of the possible infinite deniability of this fact and try to show how meaning is lost when denial occurs. On the other hand, meaning is lost if there is a mechanical assumption that everything that is done poses a mortal threat to the ecological basis of life. Neither the naysayers nor the doomsdayers give us much assistance in attaching meaning to what we know. Third, we must search for ways to restore environmental quality and sustain it if we are to find meaning. This is the prescriptive aspect of the process and is the area in which most disagreement can occur. I approach prescription with the assumption that there are many ways to accomplish an objective. We must look seriously at alternatives, particularly those that have been subject to testing in the crucible of the policy process itself. Consequently, I believe that the best approach to any policy area is a cross-national approach. Nations can and should learn from each other, especially in the environmental policy area. Thus a third theme of the book is that we must engage in cross-national analysis.

A book of this length requires serious choices as to what should be included. In short, there is much about environmental policy that is not discussed. For example, there is no attempt to identify those policy actors and groups who generally oppose environmental policy; such an analysis is appropriate for a book on environmental politics. The objective here is to present a comprehensive overview of environmental policies. To that end, the selection was guided by the following question: If a person wants to be informed on environmental policy, what should he or she know?

Just as the book is the product of a lifetime, it has benefited from my interaction with many people over many years. It is literally impossible for me to list all the individuals from whom I have benefited in my thinking about and study of the environment. Hundreds of students with thousands of comments in various classes have helped shape and direct my thinking. Colleagues in the institutions with which I have been affiliated, particularly at Arkansas State University and West Georgia College, have affected my thinking deeply. In the actual writing of the book, no individual could have had better graduate research assistants than I had in David Haskin and Jefferson Reynolds. They combine great intelligence with an authentic commitment to environmental quality. The world is better for such individuals. The tedious task of producing the manuscript was accomplished cheerfully and competently by Rhonda Waddell, Secretary Extraordinaire, and her assistants, Michelle Bledsoe, Michelle Crosby, and Stephanie Deese. And for this project in particular I owe a debt beyond description to Jewel, companion in things of the mind as well as companion in life.

All of these individuals contributed to making the book better; none contributed to any errors or omissions in it, which are entirely my responsibility. Environmental policy is a highly complex and dynamic area, and we can all benefit from the thoughts of one another. I welcome your comments and reactions to the book.

Donald T. Wells

Chapter 1

The Environment as a Public Policy Issue

Environmental policy is set apart from other policy areas by a simple but very important fact. Environmental policy has to do with sustaining the ecological basis of life. Other policy areas have to do with the quality of life and are certainly important for that reason. For example, transportation policy is concerned with how to move people effectively and efficiently from one place to another. The environment, however, is the milieu within which we survive as biological creatures. Only health policy approximates environmental policy in terms of relating to the basis for human life itself. In many ways, environmental policy and health policy are inextricably intertwined.

Many policy analysts view public policies as paradoxes (Stone 1988:1). Environmental issues certainly contain elements that are seemingly contradictory. The effects of environmental problems are simultaneously direct and indirect, immediate and long term, personal and impersonal. For example, ingesting a toxic chemical residual affects the individual directly while a change in a production process toward more clean technology may have an indirect effect. In regard to immediate versus long term effects, the ingestion of toxic chemical residuals may abruptly cause nausea or it may cause cancer after many years. In terms of personal and impersonal, it is hard to imagine a more personal effect than nausea resulting from drinking contaminated water, but many of the forces that produce that contaminated water are out of the control of individuals. In addition, all these impacts may paradoxically be perceived or unperceived, catastrophic or minor, measurable or unmeasurable.

Since environmental policy contains contradictory elements, how do we talk civilly and think effectively about it? For example, many people believe that the statement that environmental policy has to do with sustaining the ecological basis of life is alarmist or sensationalist. In public discussions about environmental policy worldwide there are references to "environmental rhetoric" and "environmental hype." But the accusation of hype is itself a form of hype (creating another paradox). Certainly the statement that "the impulse of many environmentalists is to vilify and simplify" (Samuelson 1992) is rhetorical, if we mean by rhetorical the modern implication of super grandiose language. But the need is not for balance in our language. The need is for civility in language and for accurate description. The most important issue is not who is guilty of hype and rhetoric, but rather how the environment should be viewed. In Deborah Stone's (1988:4) words, "How can we make sense of a world where paradoxes occur?" Through what conceptual lens should we look? What perspective best allows us to see the world as it really is and to ensure that conditions in the world become what we want them to be?

The basic argument of this book is that the conceptual lenses through which we look determine to a large extent what we see and what we do. Conceptual lenses differ in their power to illuminate reality. In some perspectives on the environment, individuals are "looking through a glass darkly." While our purpose is not to attack the views of others, observing through a truncated and limited set of concepts yields a truncated and limited portion of reality. On the other hand, as all scientists know, no set of conceptual lenses allows us to see all of reality. What is needed, then, is continual development of the conceptual underpinnings of the way we look at the environment. Through continuous refinement of our concepts, we can see more and more of the environment and understand better the dynamics that take place within it.

The conceptual lenses through which we look also determine to a large extent what we will do. Different well-meaning individuals can hold very different views as to what should or should not be done. It is important in an area filled with so many conflicting views to be respectful and tolerant of others. But sincerity and a desire for furthering the common good, as important as these virtues are, are not enough. There must be effective prescription, based in concepts powerful enough to inform us what ought to be and then illuminate for policy how to bring that condition into being. Among other things, this means that the conceptual lenses through which we look must include an ethical component. A perspective that would blind us to the ethical implications of our actions or that would vilify those with a sense of moral urgency is an inadequate basis for public policy. There must be concepts powerful enough to illuminate the "oughts" of environmental action and to identify alternative ways of realizing those ethical imperatives.

CONCEPTS FOR UNDERSTANDING THE ENVIRONMENT

The themes in this book are based on analysis from a specific conceptual perspective. While we do not claim that this perspective allows the observer to see fully and to prescribe perfectly, we do believe that it provides the observer a more powerful descriptive and prescriptive tool than is found elsewhere.

The first proposition in our conceptual perspective is that human beings are biological creatures living in a single, complex, and interrelated environment. Since the system is a single one, what happens in any given part of it affects the whole. Changes in the tropical rain forest, for example, cannot be approached in isolation from the rest of the ecosystem. This feature of the ecosystem has resulted in what many refer to as the "globalization of the environment." It is no longer possible to think of environmental contamination as a local phenomenon. It has global implications wherever it occurs. Thus it is not possible to think of local solutions either. Solutions also must have global aspects.

 ### The Planet Earth

The earth is an irregularly shaped sphere with a diameter of about 8,000 miles and a circumference of about 25,000 miles, resulting in a surface area of about 200 million square miles. Not all this surface is habitable by humans in the ordinary sense of that word. About 70 percent of the earth's surface is covered with water. In addition, considerable portions of the ground surface are either so dry or so frosty that they are inhospitable to human habitation.

While the great natural systems of the world are divided into categories for geographical studies, the most important fact about the planet is its essential global unity. For example, the oceans are divided into the Atlantic, Pacific, and so forth, but in point of fact, these great bodies are uninterrupted and consist of one ocean. Unfortunately, the interrelationships of the earth's natural systems are not well-known. We are only beginning to scratch the surface in our understanding of the ocean as the great regulator of the earth's climate system. Now that the artificial categories of the earth's natural system have been mapped and studied in detail, attention should be turned to a study of global unity and the dynamics of Planet Earth.

The second proposition is that an understanding of environmental problems and policy requires a cross-national mode of analysis, largely because the environment is a single, interrelated phenomenon. Environmental problems are not encapsulated within national borders, and so what happens in one nation affects the environment of us all. The need for multinational cooperation is clear. Additionally, nations can learn from each other. Each nation should examine and evaluate the experience of other nations. It is a strange anomaly that in the United States we argue that different approaches should be tried while at the same time neglect to take the experiences of other countries seriously as the basis for our decision making. Whether we like it or not, environmental degradation does not honor our borders and environmental isolationism is too limited a view.

The third proposition in our theoretical perspective involves the time horizon. Our argument is that effective environmental policy requires an intergenerational mode of thinking. Intergenerational sensitivity is not a new concept. An important body of law written several millenia ago expressed the concept this way: "For I the Lord thy God am a jealous God, visiting the iniquity of the fathers upon the children to the third and the fourth generation of those who hate me" (Exodus 20:5). Thus the concern for the intergenerational consequences of action is quite old indeed. But something very important happened to this concern on the way to the twenty-first century. One line of thought led to the belief in individual accountability for individual actions. The prophet Jeremiah voiced this view: "In those days they shall no longer say: The fathers have eaten sour grapes and the childrens' teeth are set on edge. But everyone shall die for his own sin: Each man who eats sour grapes, his teeth shall be set on edge" (Jeremiah 31:29–30). Coupled with the extreme individualism of Western civilization and of American society in particular, this view meant that modern Western man virtually lost sensitivity to intergenerational issues. Among the most obvious (bleak?) lessons to be learned from observations of the environment is that decisions and actions have significant intergenerational consequences. Indeed, with the halflife of most carcinogens, particularly nuclear wastes, the time frame associated with the "third and fourth generation" seems short and seriously in error.

Our fourth proposition is that environmental policy is inherently intergovernmental. Humans live in different nations with different cultures, laws, and policies relative to the environment, so the relationships between governments is an important component of environmental policy (Porter and Brown 1991).

The intergovernmental nature of environmental policy must be considered on two levels. The first is the national level, involving the relationships between nations. Some of these are direct, one-on-one relations, such as the acid rain agreement between the United States and Canada. Others are within the framework of the institutions of the global community or of regional organizations such as the European Community. In most instances, the actions of individual governments are understandable only in the context of these intergovernmental relationships.

The second intergovernmental level is that of the national policy system, involving actions at all levels of government. This is particularly true of federal systems, in which the relationships between the national government and the states are critical to all policy areas (Hamilton and Wells 1990:2). But it is also true of unitary systems with more centralized governments; here relationships between the central government and regional or local agencies are often critical for policy outcomes. To look at the actions of one level of government in any country, then, distorts what actually is happening in the policy system.

These four themes—a single, interrelated environment; the cross-national mode of analysis; intergenerational sensitivity; and an intergovernmental mode of analysis—are the skeletal elements of our theoretical perspective. We believe that they allow us to see the environment relatively fully and clearly, and, it is hoped, will allow us to prescribe policy actions that achieve a sustainable future.

DESCRIBING THE BEAST: WHAT IS MEANT BY POLLUTION

Analysts and decision makers seem to have the greatest difficulty defining those things that are most fundamental to our well-being. For example, in 1974 the United Nations convened a Special Committee on the Question of Defining Aggression. The Committee issued a report identifying objective criteria for aggression, but the world community has not adopted that report. Aggression remains basically undefined for public policy purposes. The same is true for environmental degradation or pollution. While various domestic laws and regulations and international conventions set criteria for specific forms of pollution, no general agreement has been reached on a comprehensive and unifying definition.

The absence of a definition is a critical problem. A definition is the meaning that is assigned to a situation and thus the mold through which all decisions are cast. The definition also partially defines what an individual will believe about reality. It is really a value statement about the nature of the problem and, by implication at least, a prescription for the solution. The struggle over definition, then, is really the struggle over ideas and values. The definition process in this sense is the most political of all policy processes.

Like other problems, the environmental problem has many definitions, each one producing its particular set of policy prescriptions. It is not our intention here to review and critique the various definitions. Rather, we offer a view of the environment from a particular perspective in the belief that it offers a more complete understanding of the environmental problem and a more effective basis for policy.

We define environmental policy as actions governments take with the objective of protecting the ecological basis of life in all its forms. The first thrust of environmental policy would be toward maintaining what is referred to as environmental quality. The second thrust of environmental policy would be toward preventing or ameliorating environmental degradation. An effective environmental policy must do both: It must seek to maintain environmental quality and it must clean up or neutralize contamination that has already occurred.

The issue of what constitutes pollution is the most controversial aspect of definition. Following our definition of environmental policy, we define pollution as any addition to the environment that damages the ecological basis of life. The damage usually results from a contaminant from either natural or human sources. Contaminants from natural sources are such things as volcano activity, forest fires caused by lightning, or background radiation. Human sources can be either inadvertent or willful.

A major source of contaminants are an inadvertent result of human activity. The environment is a complex, interrelated system that people do not totally understand. Modern societies have developed high levels of technology and sophisticated economic, social, and cultural systems whose impact on the environment cannot be fully determined. Recent years have seen a number of reversals of actions or withdrawal of products thought to be environmentally benign and later found to have adverse effects. DDT was hailed as the basis for an agricultural revolution, before its full toxicity became evident. Even when dramatic reversals do not occur, there are limits to technology. Accidents too are inadvertent causes of contamination. Accidents do happen, of course, but the problem is to determine what is accident and what is negligence. Was Union Carbide's release of toxic gas in Bhopal, India, accidental or negligent? In most instances this question is difficult or impossible to answer.

Contamination can occur also as a result of the willful actions of individuals and groups. There are two important theories to explain why and how willful pollution occurs. The first is the conspiracy theory and the second involves the tragedy of the commons enunciated by Garrett Hardin.

Conspiracy theories refer to the pursuit of maximum personal economic gain. In street language, there are "fat-cat" polluters who dump contaminants into the environment for the single purpose of maximizing profits. A Milwaukee *Journal* cartoon once portrayed fat-cat polluters standing in toxic waste covering the United States, singing "Oh beautiful for spacious waste, For ample savings gained." While this is a caricature, all nations have abundant anecdotal evidence of decisions resulting in environmental degradation. Thus conspiracy theories do partially explain willful contamination.

If anything, conspiracy theories are not general enough. Perhaps what is needed is an NDG or "no-damn-good" theory. That is, it may be that most individuals do not have sufficient moral capacity to act responsibly relative to the environment. The effort to get people in the United States to take recycling seriously is an illustration of this phenomenon. Some members of environmental organizations (Environmental Clubs on college campuses, for example) nevertheless stubbornly refuse to recycle aluminum cans. They know recycling is the right thing to do but lack the moral capacity to carry through on this principle.

Garrett Hardin's *tragedy of the commons* explains willful pollution as a result of the rational pursuit of self-interest. *Tragedy* means the remorseless working of things, and a *commons* is an asset or value that is open to all individuals. Hardin asks that we picture a pasture that is open to anyone who wishes to graze cattle. Each herdsman will seek to maximize his gain and will thus want to keep as many cattle on the commons as possible. By adding an additional animal to his herd, the herdsman will gain—in the value of the additional animal—and lose—in the effects of overgrazing on his herd. Hardin demonstrates that the gain will be larger than the loss. Thus the sensible course for each is to continue to add animals to his herd. But when all herdsmen follow that rational action, the commons is overgrazed and ruin comes upon all. Hardin concludes: "Each man is locked into a system that compels him to increase his herd without limit in a world that is limited. Ruin is the destination toward which all men rush, each pursuing his own best interest in a society that believes in the freedom of the commons" (Hardin 1968:1244). The individual can continue to justify the gain by denying the ultimate truth of the effects of his or her action on society.

The tragedy of the commons works slightly differently in the environment. Instead of taking something out of the commons, pollution puts something into it. However, the calculation of gains and losses is similar. The polluting firm finds that its cost of releasing wastes into the environment is less than the cost of purifying or controlling the waste. At the individual level, the cost to the individual in terms of inconvenience is higher than the benefit from recycling.

Because of the problems associated with defining pollution and identifying sources, environmental policy faces what is known as an uncertain production function. That is, no general agreement exists as to what we are trying to accomplish in the policy arena. Cross-national analysis should be helpful in this regard. In considering the experiences of other countries, we should attempt to identify both what they are trying to accomplish and how they are attempting to do so. In this way, we can give operational meaning to the definition of environmental policy as those actions designed to protect the ecological basis of life.

THE LOGIC OF AND NEED FOR COLLECTIVE ACTION

For much of human history, individuals could go about without concern for the effect of their actions on the ecosystem. Human actions seemed to be in "harmony with nature" and humans were comfortable with being an inherent part of nature. But as societies became more complex and science and technology advanced, humans encountered the need for ever greater controls on the environment. As Lynton Caldwell pointed out, to be civilized, humans had to modify and control the natural environment (Caldwell 1963:100). So the problem is not inherently in the control and manipulation of the natural environment, but rather in those actions that alter the environment in a way that endangers the ecological basis of life. Which of those harmful actions should government address? How is government action justified in a society with a market economy full of individuals with an entrepreneurial spirit?

 Key Components of the UN Declaration on the Human Environment

---

Man is both creature and molder of his environment which gives him physical sustenance and affords him the opportunity for intellectual, moral, social and spiritual growth... [A] stage has been reached when through science and technology, man has acquired the power to transform his environment in countless ways and on an unprecedented scale....

The protection and improvement of the human environment is a major issue which affects the well-being of peoples and economic development throughout the world; it is the urgent desire of the peoples of the whole world and the duty of all governments....

Man has the fundamental right to freedom, equality, and adequate conditions of life, in an environment of a quality which permits a life of dignity and well-being, and bears a solemn responsibility to protect and improve the environment for present and future generations.

The natural resources of the earth including the air, water, land, flora and fauna and especially representative samples of natural ecosystems must be safeguarded for the benefit of present and future generations through careful planning and management as appropriate.

Source: UN Conference on the Human Environment, Stockholm, June 16, 1972.

In many ways, one of the oldest justifications for collective action through government is one of the best for environmental policy. Aristotle argued that politics is largely about how individuals live together in community. In a world consisting of isolated individuals living in harmony with nature there would be no need for government. But Aristotle also said that people do not and cannot live that way. Humans live in community. Government to Aristotle was a legitimate instrument for the accomplishment of collective purposes, among which was the control of individual behavior required for community well-being. If self-interest or the feeling of moral obligation were not strong enough to elicit the desired behavior, then the coercive power of government through rules and sanctions was justified.

In modern policy terminology, Aristotle's view would be called the *command-and-control* strategy. It has resulted in a large body of rules and regulations enforced through complex institutional structures. Sanctions vary from mild reprimands (notices) to fines and imprisonment to punishment by death. As we shall see, levels of enforcement vary substantially in nations where such strategies are in effect, particularly in the United States. But whatever their level of enforcement, rules and regulations are designed to maintain those conditions required for persons to live together in community. This does not mean that all rules and regulations are wise or effective. It simply means that regulations can be justified on the basis of Aristotle's arguments.

Modern public finance offers two additional justifications for governmental action in the environment. The first involves the concept of *pure collective goods*, those goods whose supply is indivisible and whose demand is not individual. Pure collective goods cannot be sold to some and withheld from others, and conversely, if they are provided for one they are provided for all. National defense is the usual example. If a nation is made secure for one, it is made secure for all. Traditional public finance has assumed that government provides or delivers pure collective goods in much the same way that the market provides private goods. The purest of all collective goods is the ecosystem, our environmental commons. In this view, government action in the environment would produce a pure public good called *environmental quality*. In the American constitutional system, no other kind of action is as clearly directed toward providing for the general welfare.

The second justification for collective action inherent in traditional public finance is the phenomenon of externalities. *Externalities* are those actions that affect someone who is not a part of the decision to act. A negative externality imposes a cost on others and a positive externality results in a benefit to others. In the environmental area, a negative externality would be found in a municipality that dumps its inadequately treated sewage into a stream, imposing the cost of the polluted water on individuals downstream. A positive externality would be an individual's retrofitting an automobile with emission controls. Negative externalities exist because individuals or firms do not bear the full cost of their operation; rather, it is transferred to others, who subsidize the operations of the polluter. Positive externalities occur much less frequently. Individuals responsible for positive externalities do not reap the full and exclusive benefit of their action. So the motive for positive externalities is found in something other than a self-interest calculus.

The justification for collective action, then, is found in the need to protect the ecosystem within which communities exist, to safeguard the purest of all collective goods, the ecosystem, and to prevent some individuals or firms from imposing involuntary costs on others. Once agreement is reached on the need for collective action, decisions must be made relative to its scope and strategies.

One caveat is in order. Government action is also a part of the environmental problem, in two ways. First, governments themselves are both inadvertent and deliberate polluters. Like individuals and private firms, they inadvertently pollute because of technology and through accidents. In many respects, the materials that governments handle and the operations in which they engage have the potential for higher—even catastrophic— levels of contamination. Governments are also deliberate polluters. In fact, if all levels of U.S. government are put into the equation, government may be the nation's largest polluter. For example, the Rocky Mountain Arsenal near Denver was called "the most contaminated square mile on earth" by the Army Corps of Engineers (Turner 1991:10). Many dramatic instances of deliberate pollution by government have come to light as a result of the dissolution of the Soviet Union. What would be unthinkable in most advanced societies, such as the excavation of the basin for lakes by nuclear devices, were a part of Soviet practice.

A second way that government is a part of the problem involves its economic growth policies. One of the consequences of economic growth in the past has been high levels of environmental contamination. Economically advanced nations consume a disproportionate share of the world's resources and energy, and as a result, they enjoy a disproportionate standard of living. In the process, they also contribute disproportionately to the pollution problem. For Third World countries, public policy must address the twin problems of providing subsistence for an ever-increasing population while devoting resources to economic growth that will increase the standard of living. Policy makers in Third World countries are sometimes resentful of the policies of economically advanced nations, whom they see as enjoying a high standard of living at the expense of the environment. Is not what is good for the goose also good for the gander?

Environmental policy needs to face squarely the question of whether environmentally responsible action retards economic growth. Is there an environmental quality/economic growth tradeoff? We address that question in the discussions on policy subsets (Chapters 3–9), with a synthesis of the argument in the concluding chapter. It is helpful in following this theme to remember something that is often forgotten in such discussions: the proposition that humans are changeable elements in their own environment. Individuals' perceptions of what constitutes economic growth vary from images of the belching smokestacks of traditional industry to the trend toward the small cottage production process. Perceptions of what constitutes the good life vary substantially as well. It is in this context that the concern for a changing consciousness in the environmental movement takes on particular importance. There is a common position to which all must come in regard to economic growth and its attendant good life: that a clean and esthetically attractive environment that protects the ecological basis of life is the most fundamental element in an ethically defensible concept of sustainable growth and the good life.

Once the need for governmental action is recognized, policy makers must determine the most appropriate level for action, at whatever scope and using whatever strategies. This is the problem of service boundaries—within what area will policy be implemented? Environmental policies involve some complex service boundary problems.

Since the natural environment is involved, it is tempting to think only in terms of naturally defined service boundaries—areas based in the identification of natural regions such as a river basin or an air shed—and to implement policy on the basis of conditions within that region. In the United States, air quality policy relative to emission controls on automobiles varies substantially on the basis of conditions existing in the various air sheds. This approach, however, presents many problems. First, it is difficult to establish the boundaries of the natural regions. Hazardous waste policy, for example, does not involve natural regions since there is no natural dump zone for commercially produced chemicals. In emission control policy, the air sheds involved are usually the boundaries of metropolitan areas, which are commercial or governmental institutional arrangements rather than natural regions.

Some analysts downplay the importance of natural regions and emphasize institutional regions instead. One group of authors concluded that "it is less important that the boundaries of the region include all of the residuals dischargers and all those affected by changes in ambient environmental quality than that the boundaries represent some region or area for which there is an institutional arrangement which can be made responsible" for policy management (Basta and Bower 1982:7). They recognize that factors such as tax policy and price of factor inputs are frequently more important than regional institutions in the effectiveness of environmental policies.

Service boundaries for environmental policy, then, are associated with political and commercial institutions. The essential question is: At what level of political institutions? Should environmental policy be exclusively internal to each nation? Is there a role for transnational and international policy? In practical terms, environmental policy presently is both domestic and transnational.

In summary, environmental policy is plagued with the problem of uncertain service boundaries. Since it is difficult to define "natural regions," various nations reflect different models for the implementation of their internal policy. Service boundaries reflect political or sometimes commercial institutional arrangements, which are often the result of political decisions made long ago and have little relevance for a rational implementation of environmental policy. At the same time, the international community has institutional arrangements for dealing with global problems. The instruments of cross-national cooperation vary between policy subsets and often lack the apparatus necessary for effective implementation. One of the areas for fruitful cross national cooperation would be a search for a more rationalized service delivery mode.

THE IMPORTANCE OF THE TIME HORIZON

Environmental policy makers function in a state of constant tension between the present and the future. Some policy makers are future oriented and are willing to give up present consumption for a quality environment in the future. Others are present oriented and are unwilling to forgo present consumption. How individuals and societies posture themselves relative to the present and the future is extremely important.

In the Western tradition, both the future orientation and the present orientation have long histories and effective advocates. The generational sensitivity cited earlier is certainly an illustration of the future orientation in the religious heritage of the West. The present orientation is equally old with equally effective advocates. The Epicurean motto of "Eat, drink, and be merry" is well-known. It is probably not as well-known that the ultimate in present enjoyment to the Epicureans was quietness apart in the garden, not raucous celebrating on the order of a fraternity party. The present orientation gained its greatest philosophical support in recent times in the form of existentialism.

So how are the competing appeals of the two orientations to be evaluated relative to environmental policy? The best device yet found for converting future value to present value is the discount rate. Finding the proper discount rate can be one of the most important choices an analyst can make.

What is needed in the environmental area is a similar concept that we call the *cultural discount rate* (CDR). The CDR, as we define it, is the implicit interest rate a society uses to determine value in the future. A society with a low CDR places high value on future activity. In essence, such a society would value resources for present consumption at low levels in favor of the value created by alternate use of those resources to realize future objectives. A society with a high CDR, in contrast, is more present oriented. Such a society would place a high value on the use of resources for present consumption and a relatively low value on future conditions. So viewed, the CDR is a measure of the time horizon a society uses in making its decisions.

Two characteristics of the CDR are especially important. The first is that the CDR is society specific; that is, it differs from society to society in the same time period. On a global scale, it could be argued that Third World countries are forced by necessity to a high CDR. The need to provide basic essentials such as food, housing, and medical care are so pressing that these nations have to commit their energy and resources to present needs. This fact explains in significant part the posture of the Third World leadership on environmental questions. It was certainly given forceful articulation at the Rio Conference in June 1992.

A second characteristic of the CDR is that it is time specific; that is, it varies over time in the same society. The United States illustrates this principle clearly. Thomas Jefferson's decision to purchase the Louisiana Territory hardly solved immediate problems facing the fledgling United States. Rather it was aimed at the expected future requirements of a more developed country. By contrast, the 1980s reflected a very high CDR. The suggestion that the government sell off natural resource assets to minimize the federal deficit represented a very short-range view. Doing so would deprive future generations of the public use of the country's natural resources. More fundamentally, target dates for the accomplishment of key environmental objectives were pushed into the future or ignored, all under the guise of "preserving jobs in the present." In essence, there was a fundamental shift to a high cultural discount rate in the 1980s as a result of a distinctly present orientation.

The cultural discount rate can guide and inform discussion of environmental problems in at least three important ways. First, it can assist in a more realistic determination of the overall hazards resulting from environmental contamination. For example, research in other countries, particularly Great Britain, has established rather definitively that certain types of contaminants in the air affect the genetic structure of plants and "higher animals." Can these findings be extrapolated to man?

There is mounting evidence that they can but we do not know. With a high CDR we are unlikely to make the investment necessary to find out.

Second, a low CDR would almost certainly lead to the investigation of the possible effects of environmental degradation on lifestyle. The U.S. lifestyle tends to include a heavy dosage of outdoor activities. What will be the effect of continued ozone depletion on that lifestyle? A high-ranking member of the Reagan administration suggested that Americans could simply wear hats and put on extra thick sunscreen as adaptation behavior. But is this an acceptable alternative to Americans? How else will lifestyles have to change in adapting to other forms of environmental degradation? Again, with a high CDR, it is unlikely that this type of question will receive serious consideration.

Third, a low CDR would facilitate informed discussion on the social disorientation that might result from prolonged environmental degradation. What about an environment so poisoned that entire societies have to live inside bubbles? What about population growth? The Club of Rome, in *The Limits of Growth,* predicted sudden and uncontrollable decline in well-being if the present trends in world population continue. Can our institutions and social structures withstand the effects of this kind of crisis? With a high CDR, we are not likely to make a serious effort to seek answers to these questions.

On a more immediate level, the cultural discount rate would be a valuable tool for understanding and assessing risk. A hazard is a danger that exists externally to the individual. Risk is the probability that harm will result from the hazard. The usual illustration of hazards and risks involves crossing the Atlantic Ocean. Whatever the mode of crossing, the hazard is the same, but the risk is quite different. The risk is much lower if the crossing is made on the *Queen Mary* than if it is made in a homemade sailboat. What level of risk is acceptable for public policy purposes?

Without guidance from a concept like the cultural discount rate, the levels of risk considered acceptable have varied widely over time. During a period with a high CDR (present orientation) policy makers will raise the level of risk, increasing the degree of exposure to the hazard. During a period with a low CDR (future orientation) they will lower the level of risk, decreasing the degree of exposure to the hazard. This phenomenon has produced rather marked policy cycles in the United States. Until political systems can develop and agree upon a cultural discount rate for environmental policy, there is likely to be a waxing and waning of commitment to environmental quality. An established cultural discount rate would not only help bring consistency to environmental policy over time, it would also result in a more realistic assessment of risk.

The social discount rate would also be an important element in the development of an ethics of the environment. How can an ethical system emerge in a society with a high CDR? The commitment to immediate consumption erodes the basis on which any meaningful ethics of the environment can emerge. In large part, we do not know what we ought to do in relation to the environment because we do not see over time the effects of our actions. One of the elements in an ethics of the environment is the imperative to avoid overvaluing the present and undervaluing the future. The social discount rate provides the tool through which we can convert that ethical imperative into practical policy.

The absence of a concept like the cultural discount rate, then, means that environmental policy has had to deal with a high degree of uncertainty relative to the time horizon. This uncertainty has permeated all policy, from the very definition of the hazard to the determination of specific threshold exposure levels to toxic materials (Brookfield 1992). Our basic proposition is that environmental policy is inherently intergenerational. The social discount rate is the analytical device by which we can understand intergenerational effects and prescribe policy for future generations.

ENVIRONMENTAL POLICY IN A CONTEXT OF UNCERTAINTY

There are four basic themes that underlie the discussion throughout the book. The first is that environmental policy is global in scope. This is true because of the inherent unity of the ecosystem. Since there is a single interrelated ecosystem, the second theme is that environmental policy must be cross-national in nature. However, since policy must be implemented through national institutions, this proposition results in substantial uncertainty and inadequacies in service boundaries. The third theme is that environmental policy is inherently intergenerational in outcomes. With the difficulty of developing analytical concepts such as the cultural discount rate, this proposition means that there is substantial uncertainly relative to the time horizon of environmental policy. The fourth theme is that environmental policy is inherently intergovernmental, made and implemented through a dynamic and complex interrelationship between all levels of government. This too adds to the level of uncertainty relative to service boundaries. Within this complex intergovernmental system, both domestic and transnational decision makers have been unable to agree upon what constitutes environmental quality and environmental degradation. This inability to agree upon the nature of the problem creates an uncertain production function.

Perhaps a fifth theme of the book, therefore, is that environmental policy functions in a context of uncertainty: uncertain service boundaries, an uncertain time horizon, and an uncertain production function. As a result, all statements relative to the environment are subject to deniability. It is possible simply to deny that there is an "environmental problem" (*New American*, June 1, 1992).

We do not view this uncertainty as altogether negative, however. Uncertainty can be a powerful motivation to search for understanding; certainty can be the cloak for ignorance. Uncertainty can be an energizing force in the life of an individual or nation; certainty can be the mask for laziness. Uncertainty can result in a powerful thrust toward the development of moral consciousness; certainty can be the rationalization for outright evil. Our references to uncertainty therefore are not intended to produce despair. Rather they are realistic assessments of the situation with the hope that the recognition of these uncertainties will be a motivator to think seriously about the environment.

In the remaining chapters we will attempt to bring the best of policy analysis to an understanding of environmental problems and policy. That is, we will attempt to clarify and alleviate some of the problems in environmental policy. The discussion will be based on the belief that an understanding of environmental policy should include not only policy as it is, but more important, policy as it ought to be.

Chapter 2

Institutions, Strategies, and Actors

The Context within Which Environmental Policy Occurs

A policy, once it is soundly based theoretically and has clearly defined objectives, requires the additional elements of institutional structures, policy strategies, and policy actors. These three elements constitute the context within which environmental policy is developed and implemented. They profoundly affect environmental policy outcomes.

Policy scientists have been deeply divided over what roles institutions play in the policy system. In the view of some, institutions mean very little. Most students of public administration are familiar with the couplet from Alexander Pope to the effect that "For forms of government let fools contest; whatever is best administered is best." In this view, institutions are almost neutral conduits within which the critical actions of individuals and groups take place. A second and more recent view is referred to as the "new institutionalism" (March and Olsen 1984:738). In this view, institutions play a semi-autonomous role in the policy system as political actors in their own right, and so the achievement of policy objectives depends in part on the design of these institutions. This view seems especially important for environmental policy.

Also important in the policy process are policy strategies, or the means by which policy objectives are accomplished. Policy strategies are among the most political of all aspects of the policy process. Certainly, they are subject to much debate, a process that leads to a great deal of change in strategies.

Identifying and tracking the importance of the actors in environmental policy is not the simple task that it might appear to be. We have already seen that institutions are semi-autonomous actors. Beyond that, the influential actors in the policy process often are not visible but ply their trade "behind closed doors," as power structure studies have consistently found. Given these problems, it is important to know the major actors at both the international and national level.

INSTITUTIONS IN ENVIRONMENTAL POLICY

Institutions function in several ways as semi-autonomous actors in the environmental policy arena. One way is in the distribution of resources. Some of these resources are tangible, such as money and human resources. Some are intangible, the most important of these being information. Institutions convey access to information to some and deny it to others. Information is power; denying access to information is a means of keeping an individual powerless.

A second way institutions function semi-autonomously is by determining or modifying individual preferences through control of an extraordinarily wide range of symbols, myths, and rituals. Some of them are true, some false, and some partly both. The important point is not whether they are true or false but whether they are believed. Some of society's most important symbols are numbers (Stone 1988: 129). Issues become policy problems in part because we count or measure them and determine that there is a "problem" of sufficient importance to justify a policy response. Since numbers imply the direction action should take, some level of measurement becomes the standard for a "solution." Institutions by and large control the numbers.

Third, institutions define the rules of the game. They form the action channels within which policy takes place (Allison 1971). The action channels preselect the major players, determine the player's point of entrance into the policy process, distribute advantages and disadvantages for each game, and determine who "gets a piece of the action." Anyone who has dealt with a regulatory agency in any country can testify to the efficiency of institutions in establishing and maintaining these action channels.

Fourth, institutions function semi-autonomously by imposing order on a policy area. In environmental policy, it is hard to avoid the conclusion that policies are designed to ensure that events and behaviors take place in regular and prescribed ways. That orderly process is often equated with protecting the environment when in fact it may have little to do with policy outcomes. All of these functions make institutions critical elements in environmental policy.

International Institutions

International organizations have become increasingly important actors in the environmental policy area. There are a large number of these organizations with a wide variety of objectives. Since it is impractical to examine all international agencies that affect environmental policy, we will identify only the most active of them. Of the multiple-purpose international agencies, the United Nations Environment Programme, the World Bank, the International Monetary Fund, and the United Nations Educational, Scientific, and Cultural Organization are the most important to environmental policy.

The primary purpose of the United Nations Environment Programme (UNEP) is to facilitate international cooperation on all matters relative to the environment. Policies of the UNEP are determined by a Governing Body made up of 58 members allocated among nations on a regional basis. Its Secretariat is located in Nairobi, Kenya, and has a budget of just under $40 million annually. The organization of the Secretariat reflects the three main objectives of UNEP. First, the environmental assessment section consists of the Global Environment Monitoring System, the International Referral System for Sources of Environmental Information, and the International Register of Potentially Toxic Chemicals. This section has produced some of the most valuable data on the condition of the global environment. Second, the environmental management section addresses such concerns as terrestrial ecosystems, technology and the environment, industry and the environment, oceans, coastal areas, and desertification control. Finally, the support section consists of such programs as environmental education, public information, developmental planning, and environmental law.

Pursuing its mission of facilitating international cooperation, UNEP has served as an important catalyst in several international agreements. Conventions that have been sponsored by UNEP include the Convention on International Trade in Endangered Species of Wild Fauna and Flora, the Convention on the Conservation of Migratory Species of Wild Animals, the Convention for the Protection of the Ozone Layer, the Convention on the Control of Transboundary Movements of Hazardous Waste and Their Disposal, the Convention on Regional Seas program, and the Montreal Protocol on Substances that Deplete the Ozone Layer. Pursuing its monitoring and assessment objectives, UNEP has established Earthwatch, an early warning system designed to inform governments on events that pose serious environmental risks. Pursuing its environmental management and support objectives, UNEP has sponsored or conducted more than 1,000 projects addressing a wide range of environmental concerns. As a result of all these activities, UNEP has established a reputation as a responsible and effective international institution for accomplishing environmental objectives.

The World Bank and the International Monetary Fund are important in the environmental area because of their funding activities. The primary purpose of the World Bank is to provide capital for projects that help raise the standard of living in developing countries. Environmental considerations are a part of the decision-making process, especially when the projects have to do with energy, industry, infrastructure, or agriculture. In fact, the Bank has an Environment Department and four Regional Environment Divisions. It also maintains a close working relationship with the United Nations Environment Programme. For example, the Bank often functions as the implementation agency for providing low-interest loans and grants to developing countries for various environmental projects. The primary purpose of the International Monetary Fund (IMF) is the promotion of international monetary cooperation and stability among monetary systems of the world. One IMF activity that affects the environment is the making of loans to developing countries for projects that contribute to sustainable development. IMF staff members work with other institutions in identifying the interplay between economic development and environmental responsibility.

The United Nations Educational, Scientific, and Cultural Organization (UNESCO), as its name implies, seeks to promote cooperation among nations in education, science, and culture. Many of its activities are designed to promote human rights, a commitment to justice, and respect for the rule of law. However, within these broad activities, UNESCO engages in several important environmental functions. These include providing information and expertise to projects seeking to improve environmental quality, conducting programs to increase member states' capacity to deal with environmental problems, and conducting educational and public awareness programs on the environment. Nearly all of UNESCO's environmental activities are linked to the goal of sustainable development.

There are also a number of specialized agencies whose activities are important for environmental policy. They may be categorized as agencies that work primarily with people and those whose work is directed toward some sector of the environment, such as the ocean.

The specialized agencies that work directly with people concern themselves with population, children, agriculture, food, and health. The United Nations Population Fund promotes research on population and family planning and assists developing nations in projects designed to relieve population problems. It has developed a set of guidelines, "Population and Environment," for ensuring the integration of environmental objectives with population activities. The primary objective of the United Nations Children's Fund (UNICEF) is to promote the survival and development of children. The Declaration and Plan of Action adopted by the UNICEF World Summit for Children included a number of goals that are significant for the environment, among them a reduction in infant mortality rates, universal access to safe drinking water, sanitary means of excreta disposal, and an improvement in literacy rates. UNICEF assists governments in developing countries with projects designed to accomplish these objectives.

Several specialized agencies conduct programs in the area of agriculture and food. The Food and Agricultural Organization is committed to freedom from hunger for all humanity. Within this broad objective, it assists in projects to improve the production and distribution of food. Additionally, it advises governments on a wide range of environmental protection activities, including soil degradation, water resource management, pest management, and fertilizers. The World Food Programme (WFP) is specifically charged with assisting the most vulnerable peoples. As a result, it often provides essential emergency relief. Since many of the world's most vulnerable people live on marginal lands and fragile environments, WFP has been a major provider of grants for reforestation, soil conservation, and sustainable agriculture. This money is contributed by governments and intergovernmental bodies at biennial pledging conferences.

The mission of the World Health Organization (WHO) is to promote human health by providing a wide range of support to participating nations for development of programs to control environmental health hazards. Historically, the most important of these have been water supplies and sanitation facilities. Recently, WHO has placed increasing emphasis on air quality, radiation exposure, and environmental epidemiology. The general objectives of WHO are stated in the document, "Global Strategy for Health for All by the Year 2000."

Along with the agencies whose primary concern is service to people, a second type of specialized agency functions in relation to a particular sector of the environment. The most important of these are the World Meteorological Organization, the International Maritime Organization, and the International Atomic Energy Agency.

The World Meteorological Organization (WMO) is one of the world's most active organizations in the assessment of the state of the global atmosphere. WMO has established the Global Climate Observing System, whose objective is to monitor world climate and detect climate change. Substantial data are derived from a network of climate stations cooperating with WMO. In addition to research activities, WMO works through its members to reduce pollution of the atmosphere.

A similar agency with activities targeted to the ocean is the International Maritime Organization (IMO). The IMO's overall objectives have focused on international cooperation in technical matters relative to shipping and to maritime safety. However, it has been very active in environmental policy and reflects a strong commitment to the prevention of pollution to the ocean. The IMO has sponsored negotiations that led to several important international agreements on ocean pollution: the Convention on the Prevention of Marine Pollution by Dumping of Wastes and Other Matter (The London Dumping Convention of 1972), the International Convention for the Prevention of Pollution from Ships (MARPOL, 1973), the International Convention on Civil Liability for Oil Pollution Damage (1969), the International Convention on the Establishment of an International Fund for Compensation for Oil Pollution (1971), and the International Convention Relating to Intervention on the High Seas in Cases of Oil Pollution Casualties (1969). In addition, the IMO provides information, codes of practice, and recommendations to member nations in order to prevent conflicting standards as nations might proceed unilaterally to develop regulations.

The International Atomic Energy Agency (IAEA) is an independent organization within the United Nations system. One of its more important objectives is supporting research on the peaceful uses of atomic energy. For example, the Agency sponsored a joint program with the Food and Agriculture Organization to develop nuclear applications in agriculture in order to reduce the use of fertilizers and pesticides. The Agency has also been very active in the development of standards relative to all aspects of fissionable materials. One of its earliest efforts in this regard was the development of acceptable regulations on the pollution of the ocean by radioactive materials. Like the WMO, the IAEA has sponsored negotiations that led to significant international agreements. These include the Treaty Banning Nuclear Weapon Tests in the Atmosphere, in Outer Space, and Under Water (1963), the Treaty on the Non-Proliferation of Nuclear Weapons (1968), the Convention on Civil Liability for Nuclear Damage (1963), the Convention on Early Notification of a Nuclear Accident (1986), and the Convention on Assistance in the Case of a Nuclear Accident or Radiological Emergency (1986). A significant part of the Agency's work has been to provide services to member nations in the safe operation of nuclear power plants and nuclear facilities. The Agency's Radioactive Waste Management Advisory Programme provides technical assistance to member nations for establishing radioactive waste management programs.

Regional Institutions: A Supranational Institution and Regional IGOs

In addition to the intergovernmental organizations affiliated with the United Nations, there is one supranational institution and several regional intergovernmental organizations that play important roles in environmental policy. The supranational institution is the European Community.

The European Community is in many ways a unique political institution. It is not a nation since the twelve member nations retain sovereignty even in the pursuit of foreign relations. At the same time it can enter into agreements with other nations, one of the primary characteristics of a sovereign nation. The EC is rightly referred to as a "community," without the full attributes of a nation, yet policy that it adopts can have the same force as national legislation. The EC has used that influence to profoundly affect the environmental policies of Europe (Haigh 1992). An understanding of EC environmental policy is essential for an understanding of the environmental policy of member states.

EC legislation can take several forms. A Regulation is legislation that is enforced directly by national courts. The Directive, on the other hand, is legislation that sets broad objectives but leaves to each nation the determination of how to achieve those objectives. For example, a Regulation sets percentage reductions in the quantity of ozone-depleting substances that are emitted; a Directive limits emissions of sulphur dioxides and nitrogen oxides from power plants but leaves to individual nations the means for accomplishing those limits.

The relationship between the EC and its member nations is more complex with regard to international conventions. The EC can enter into international agreements in those areas where it "has competence." Member nations also have competence to enter into international agreements and are at times signatories to the same agreements to which the EC is a party. A treaty to which both the EC and some or all member nations are parties is called a *mixed agreement*. The general rule is that member nations cannot act independently on matters on which the EC has exclusive competence, even when the EC Council cannot reach agreement on policy. When the EC does not have exclusive competence, the member nations may act independently if they choose to do so.

The most active of the regional intergovernmental organizations is the Organization of African Unity. The OAU sponsored the negotiations that led to the Bamako Convention on the Ban of the Import into Africa and the Control of Transboundary Movement of Hazardous Waste within Africa. This convention branded the transportation into and the disposal of hazardous waste within Africa as "a crime." It has been the instrument on which many African nations have acted to end the irresponsible dumping of hazardous wastes. In addition to the formal convention, the OAU has sponsored a number of forums for the discussion of environmental rules, regulations, and standards most relevant for African nations. It has provided substantial technical assistance to member nations with regard to many of the complex environmental issues. The OAU has cooperated extensively with the United Nations Environment Programme in carrying out a number of projects on the African continent. Certainly other regional intergovernmental organizations, such as the Arab League and the Organization of American States, have been much less active in accomplishing environmental objectives.

National-Level Institutions

When the focus shifts to the national level, the variations in practice are so numerous it is difficult to establish meaningful categories that will encompass all national practices. At the most general level, three patterns of national institutions are found. The first is a centralized agency with general jurisdiction for environmental policy. This pattern is most often found in countries with unitary systems of government. The second pattern is one of decentralization, with policy prerogatives vested in provincial or regional governments. This pattern most frequently occurs in countries whose central governments tend to be weak and the provincial governments relatively strong. The third pattern is the one associated with federal systems. Here jurisdiction over policy is dispersed between the central and state governments. Usually there is an agency with responsibility for environmental policy at both levels. In the United States, for example, there is a national Environmental Protection Agency and also an environmental protection agency within each state. The relationship between the two levels is complex and it varies, as does the relation between environmental policy subfields.

In evaluations of national-level institutions, most comparisons have been made between central institutions and decentralized or federal institutions. Lennart Lundqvist did a perceptive study of environmental policy outcomes in the Swedish centralized system and the American decentralized system. He found advantages in both approaches. The advantages of the centralized approach were summarized as consistency, efficiency, expertise, continuity, and a different character to the issues. In the decentralized pattern he found legitimacy, democracy, local experience, continuity, and a different character to the issues (Lundqvist 1974:63). Issues in the centralized systems tend to have a national character while issues in decentralized systems tend to have a local character. Weighing the relative merits of a centralized versus a decentralized system is a difficult task.

Lundqvist is understandably cautious in his assessment. The general conclusion is that both countries " have experienced some success in fighting air pollution" (Lundqvist 1974:196). He adds that the importance of differences in the two systems "lies in the fact that they provide different political contexts of choice. They provide different sets of political incentives and different sets of political constraints. In short, they provide for different types of clean air politics, different styles of clean air policy choice and change" (Lundqvist 1974:182). The truth of this point will be clear when we examine specific environmental policy areas.

BASIC STRATEGIES IN ENVIRONMENTAL POLICY

A policy that is soundly based theoretically and that occurs within clearly identifiable institutional structures requires the additional element of strategies or policy instruments. In environmental policy, policy instruments are strategies adopted by the international community or by nations to achieve the objective of preserving the ecological basis of life. These instruments vary substantially, particularly the international versus the national instruments.

Multinational Strategies

Most of the instruments of transnational cooperation are utilized to accomplish cooperation in the environment. The most basic instrument of international cooperation is the treaty. Unfortunately, the word *treaty* has been applied to all forms of international cooperation except executive agreements. In this context, *treaties* will be understood in the narrower sense as agreements between two or more nations that have the binding force of international law. In fact, treaties are a major source of international law. Additionally, treaties are a part of the supreme law of the land in the United States and take precedence over state constitutions and laws. An *executive agreement* is an agreement between the heads of states of the nations that are party to it. Executive agreements are not legally binding, as are treaties, but are seen as agreements between the executive authorities of the signatory nations. *Conventions* have the same character as treaties but usually deal with more specific and technical subjects; therefore, they are important policy instruments in the environmental area. A *protocol* is the official record of a diplomatic conference that shows the agreements arrived at by the participants. Protocols are normally signed by the participants and are often preludes to conventions. *Declarations* are either statements setting forth the agreements reached on certain principles of international law or statements of policy on the part of particular governments. Finally, *nonbinding agreements* are agreements between nations that do not have the force of law.

A complex array of factors are involved in the choice of one or the other of these instruments of multinational environmental policy. Probably the most important factor is the determination of what kind of agreement can be reached with regard to the issue. Consider the use of chlorofluorocarbons (CFCs) as propellants in aerosol cans. What type of agreement is feasible and can be negotiated? A convention would be the most binding, carrying as it does the force of international law. On the other hand, some nations may not want to be bound formally to a certain course of action. Furthermore, in most countries the process of negotiation and ratification of treaties is more complex and fraught with more "veto points" than other forms of international agreement. An example is the requirement for consent by the U.S. Senate, often the occasion for extensive supportive and obstructionist interest-group activity. The protocol and executive agreement have the advantage of involving executive action without the more formal process of a treaty. The executive in most countries can act unilaterally. If secrecy is desired, the protocol and executive agreement processes can be conducted in greater secrecy than the treaty and convention processes. The declaration offers the advantage of clarifying a nation's understanding of the specific meaning of an agreement. A nonbinding agreement is often possible when no other form of agreement is, and so it is a fall-back possibility when all else has failed.

One of the major problems with all forms of international agreement is the problem of enforcement. Any agreement without an enforcement mechanism is subject to being ignored. There are various sanctions that can be utilized to give multinational agreements some effect, such as a boycott or economic embargo. However, such sanctions are seldom applied, particularly in the environmental policy area, and when they are, their effectiveness depends a great deal on the particular circumstances. Accomplishing environmental objectives, then, depends primarily on mutual cooperation between the parties to an agreement. Such cooperation is not easily obtainable, because of the many social, economic, and cultural differences among nations. Among the most important and clearly visible set of difficulties is that between the economically advanced nations and the economically developing world—often referred to in international relations literature as the North/South conflict. No area of conflict is more important for global environmental policy than the one between the North and the South.

Several features of the North/South conflict are particularly intractable. First, the North is the major source of environmental degradation. It has approximately 16 percent of the world's population and emits 48 percent of the greenhouse gases. The 230 million people in the United States are responsible for the same level of greenhouse gases as the 4 billion people who live in the South (Lunde 1990:9). Second, the North uses a disproportionate amount of the world's resources. Leaders in the South are understandably concerned with this imbalance and insist that global environmental policy must accommodate the future economic development of the South. The failure to develop such a policy will mean that the South could become a major contributor to global environmental degradation.

The most far-reaching proposal to enforce global environmental policies is for a world legislative body with the power to impose such policy on nations. This idea was the basis for substantial discussion at the Hague in 1989. New Zealand suggested that the body be called the Environmental Protection Council and be established as a unit of the United Nations. The Hague meeting resulted in the adoption of a declaration calling for the creation of such an institution and empowering it to supersede national authority on matters of environmental policy. Since no such institution exists at the present time, national-level environmental strategies take on added importance.

National-Level Strategies

There are three categories of strategies generally employed by nations in implementing environmental policy. The most extensively used of the three are command-and-control strategies, which use the coercive power of law and regulation. A second type, market-driven strategies, utilize economic inducements, either positive or negative, to achieve environmental objectives. Finally, technology-forcing strategies are based on the assumption of an ever-improving technology; potential polluters find it in their best interest to utilize the improved technology and thereby reduce their pollution. These policy strategies have been vigorously debated in nearly all nations that have an active environmental policy.

Command-and-Control Strategies   Command-and-control strategies consist of traditional environmental regulations. In most nations, such regulations are formulated through a four-stage process. The first stage is the establishment of the policy goal. This is normally done through an act of the nation's legislative body. The goals may be quite specific, such as setting target dates for lowering automobile emission standards, or the goal may be quite vague, such as the U.S. Clean Air Act goal of protecting the public health and safety.

The second stage is the establishment of policy criteria. Criteria are indicators used to determine when to regulate a particular substance. Three categories of criteria are found in national practices. *No-risk* criteria require that substances be controlled to the point where they pose no risk to human health or safety. The problem is that it is virtually impossible to determine when this criterion is reached, because of scientific uncertainty (Lowrance 1976:83). *Margin-of-safety* criteria require that substances be controlled within a reasonable margin of safety. In many instances, what is reasonable is determined by what is practicable. Thus the utilization of "best available control technology," or BACT, functions as the real criterion of reasonableness. Finally, there are *cost-based* criteria. When these criteria are in effect, regulators are required to take costs into account when setting standards.

The third stage in developing regulations is the establishment of standards, that is, the maximum levels of pollutants that will be allowed in the air, water, soil, or workplace. *Personal exposure* standards specify the levels of pollutants to which humans can be exposed. Radiation exposure standards are important examples of such standards. *Ambient composition* standards prescribe the levels of pollutants that are allowed in a specified "encompassing environment." Air quality standards are examples. *Product composition standards* control the makeup of certain products. Food additives is a good example of something controlled by product composition standards. *Product performance* standards require certain performance levels of various products in emitting pollutants. Automobile emission standards were among the first such standards to be developed. Finally, *packaging* standards regulate the composition of various packaging products. The utilization of styrofoam in food packages is an example of this standard. While there are other standards in use among the policy systems of the world, these are the most frequently imposed and the most important ones for their environmental outcomes.

The fourth stage in command-and-control strategies is enforcement. In some nations, enforcement strategies are very rigid and leave the administrator with little flexibility. In other nations, the administrator is given discretion to bargain with the polluter to achieve maximum reduction in emissions. More important, levels of enforcement vary substantially from nation to nation. Some nations vigorously enforce regulations while others are very lax in enforcement.

The issue of level of enforcement is especially important where there are federal systems. The problem is well illustrated by the experience of the United States, which has both a central Environmental Protection Agency and decentralized state-level environmental protection agencies. U.S. command-and-control strategies are frequently carried out through an instrument known as *partial preemption*. This is the policy instrument employed in the Clean Air Act, the Clean Water Act, and the Resource Conservation and Recovery Act (chemical residuals). The doctrine of *preemption* relates to those policy areas in which both the national government and the states can act. In *Gibbons* v. *Odgen* the Supreme Court ruled that a valid exercise of national power emptied that policy area from state action. This doctrine of preemption is the basis for the policy instrument of partial preemption. The "partial" component opens the way for state action. The initial step is for the national government to take action, such as through the passage of the Clean Air Act, which authorizes the national government to accomplish national objectives in the area of clean air. But this legislation also provides for state action which can supplant national action. In essence, the legislation provides that if the states act, then the national government will not, but if the states do not act, then the national government will. Since the states have a strong interest in the policy area, it is almost certain that the states will act. As a result of partial preemption, separate state programs in the United States accomplish the objectives of clean air, clean water, and the control of toxic chemical wastes.

Utilization of the partial preemption strategy raises the question of the extent of state discretion. Are states simply convenient administrative agencies of national policy or do they have significant discretion in establishing standards and determining enforcement levels? In this question, there is a clear example of the importance of how an individual looks at a situation. Looked at from the "top down," that is from the perspective of national legislation and administrative action, there is the definite appearance of substantial national determination of policy. Clearly, the intent of the Clean Air Act, the Clean Water Act, and the Resource Conservation and Recovery Act (RCRA) is that the responsible official in each policy area is the Administrator of the national Environmental Protection Agency.

When examined from the "bottom up," that is from the perspective of state implementation, a very different conclusion is reached. A bottom-up view suggests wide state discretion that results in substantial policy variation among the states. Five characteristics enhance this state discretion. First, states have adopted standards different from those prescribed as "baseline" standards by the EPA (National Conference of State Legislatures 1982). Second, political, economic, and social factors combine within states to produce varying state levels of enforcement and program activity (Lester, Franke, Bowman, and Kramer 1983). Third, there are no clear and consistent performance audit trails in the environmental policy area. In part, this lack is due to cutbacks in EPA funding, inadequate national office staff, and weak national commitment to enforcement in the 1980s. Fourth, the quality of information provided by states varies widely. The environmental data base in some states is impressive, in others it is minimal. Finally, the EPA is in somewhat of a dependency relationship with the counterpart state agency. In essence, if the RCRA, the Clean Air Act, and the Clean Water Act are to be implemented, the EPA must have the cooperation and support of the responsible state agency. These factors combine to suggest wide discretion for states in environmental policy areas utilizing the partial preemption strategy.

Market-Driven Strategies   Market-driven strategies utilize economic factors such as inducements or penalties to accomplish environmental objectives. The most commonly used market-based strategies are marketable emission credits, full costing mechanisms, and either negative or positive incentives. It is important to emphasize that these strategies have not had wide application as yet. Their advocates, however, propose them as alternatives to the dominant command-and-control strategies.

The most significant application of the marketable emission credits strategy in the United States involved the 1990 Clean Air Act Amendments designed to reduce the level of sulfur dioxide emissions. Under the terms of the Act, implementation begins with the identification of a definable air shed. Policy makers then draw an imaginary "bubble" over that region (Tientenburg 1985:8). The total level of sulfur dioxide emissions that are considered to be within acceptable risk in that air shed is calculated. Each producer of sulfur dioxides is then allocated a certain level of emission, usually through formulas based on the firm's percentage of total production in the area and negotiation with the EPA. If a firm generates less sulphur dioxide than it is allocated, the firm may sell that surplus to another firm. Conversely, a firm may generate more sulfur dioxide than it is allocated if it is able to purchase emission credits from another firm. In any case, the total volume of sulfur dioxide emissions remains at the level established. The assumption is that this strategy will provide incentives for all firms to reduce sulfur dioxide emissions.

Evaluation of marketable emission credits is difficult, given the limited experience with their use. First of all, there are almost no data on the use of such strategies. Perhaps more important, application of this strategy has actually involved a mixture of the incentive and command-and-control strategies—the issuance of the permit is a command-and-control strategy, while the ability to market unused portions is an economic incentive—and separating the impact of one strategy from that of the other is a nearly impossible task (Bower, Barre, Kuhner, and Russell 1981:3). Additionally, persons living in the vicinity of the high emission firm do not breath the air of the general "air shed," but only the air with high concentrations of pollutants purchased under this policy. So the question is what is being traded—people's health or pollution rights?

Full costing mechanisms charge the full cost of a service under the assumption that such action will reduce pollution. Seattle's solid waste plan is a good example. Rather than a flat fee for garbage collection regardless of the volume, Seattle charges by the can. The objective is to encourage individuals and firms to reduce their garbage levels through such tactics as recycling. Results of the plan have been impressive.

The third market-based strategy involves the provision of either negative or positive incentives. When negative incentives are employed, the system is most commonly referred to as an *effluent charge system*. When positive incentives are employed, reference is generally to *tax incentives*. There are at least four variations of the effluent charge system (Bower, Ehler, and Kneese 1977). A charge can be placed on the units of residual discharges. For example, a five cent charge per kilogram of sulphur dioxide could be imposed. Second, a charge can be placed on the unit of related input. For example, the European Community has proposed a $5 per barrel tax on oil, coal, and other carbon fuels as a means of combating global warming. Also, the charge could be on the basis of units of output. An example would be a charge per unit of horsepower on automobiles. Finally, the charge can be placed on some related activity. An example of this would be a surcharge on downtown parking fees to encourage the use of mass transit.

A similar variety exists with regard to tax incentives. A tax subsidy can be placed on each unit of discharge reduction. For example, there might be a five cent tax subsidy for each kilogram of reduction in sulfur dioxide emission. Second, the subsidy could be placed on unit reduction in input use. Here the tax subsidy could be given for each kilogram reduction in pesticide use. Third, the subsidy may be placed on unit reduction of related output. In this instance, the tax subsidy could be placed on the kilogram reduction in package weight. Finally, the tax subsidy could be targeted to a related activity. An example would be a tax reduction for farmers who engage in soil enrichment activities as a means of reducing fertilizer applications. Negative and positive incentives are often used in combination.

As with marketable credits, evaluation of incentives is very difficult. The most ambitious attempt was a study of the French national system for water quality management and of the German system for management of the river basins of Nordrhein-Westfalen (Bower, Barre, Kuhner, and Russell 1981). These two programs were chosen because they are often cited as examples of the effluent charge system. In their findings, the authors argue first that the term "effluent charge system" is something of a misnomer and understates the richness and complexity of the French and German approaches. The strategy, they argue, is not really an effluent charge strategy, but rather represents complex mixed systems with elements of both the command-and-control and the market-driven strategies. Therefore the two systems were found to have little in common with incentive schemes proposed in the United States. Finally and perhaps most important, the authors found that the setting of effluent charges is an extraordinarily difficult task ˋ   because of the difficulty in identifying the damages resulting from pollution of any kind, although there has been significant effort to "price" the damages resulting from air pollution (Smith 1976). Thus the authors concluded that industries in these studies were moved to act because of regulations and available subsidies, not because of the effluent charges.

Technology-Forcing Strategies   The final strategy for accomplishing environmental quality objectives is the technology-forcing strategy. This strategy is based on the assumption of an improving technology that is in the discharger's interest to utilize. The interest served can range from greater efficiency in the production process to enhanced capacity to comply with command-and-control regulations.

Obviously, a distinction has to be made between improvement in technology that results from forces within the economic system and improvement in technology that results from deliberate policy choice to change technology. Those nations that have adopted a technology-forcing strategy have relied primarily on research grants to develop new technology followed by demonstration projects to inform potential users of the technology's advantages. The most serious application of these strategies is found in Europe and particularly within European chemical waste policy. These applications will be examined in the chapter on chemical waste.

Ironically, the North has a distinct opportunity to utilize a variation on technology-forcing strategies to encourage environmentally responsible economic development in the South. For example, India and China have resisted until recently the ban on the use of chlorofluorocarbons. In essence, the two countries forced a technology sharing agreement with the North as a condition of accepting the Montreal Protocol. But the reverse is possible. The North can and should share technology with the South as a means of encouraging environmental responsibility in economic development. Appropriate means of technology sharing, then, would become an essential ingredient in a policy of sustainable development.

ENVIRONMENTAL POLICY ACTORS

In many ways, the dynamics that fuel environmental policy are the various actors in the policy process. Along with the institutions discussed earlier, important actors in the policy process are nongovernmental organizations (NGOs), interest groups, grass roots organizations, and scientists.

Nongovernmental Organizations (NGOs)

Nongovernmental organizations are of much the same character as love—difficult to define precisely but known by nearly everyone who experiences it. The Green Globe Yearbook provides the best definition of NGOs: organizations that "are multinational and have a substantial part of their activities within both environment and development... [and are] reasonably independent of governments" (Bergesen, Norderhaug, and Parmann 1992:14). The wide variety of these groups makes it difficult to identify the most important of them for global environmental policy. Recognizing that any grouping of NGOs is arbitrary, it is useful to think of NGOs in three general categories: those that are basically alliances of other groups, those that engage in direct action, and those whose primary activities are educational and informational in nature.

Of the NGOs that are alliances, some are alliances of environmental groups while others are alliances of groups that have a different primary purpose but a strong environmental emphasis. The most important alliances of environmental groups are the African NGOs Environment Network, the Alliance of Northern People for Environment and Development, the Asia-Pacific People's Environment Network, and the European Environmental Bureau. The African NGOs Environment Network consists of over 530 member NGOs in 45 African countries. Its primary purpose is to facilitate communication and cooperation between its member NGOs. It also provides advice, information, and training in the areas of its primary policy interests—water management, renewable energy, deforestation, sustainable agriculture, and wildlife resources. A similar alliance for North America and Europe is the Alliance of Northern People for Environment and Development. It seeks to provide communication links and facilitate cooperation among NGOs in its primary areas of interest—a holistic approach to environment and development, human rights, social and ecological justice, democracy, and peace. The Asia-Pacific People's Environment Network provides informational and communication services to its member NGOs in 18 Asian countries. Its policy emphases are development and the environment, climate change, the marine environment, and protection of rain forests. The European Environmental Bureau consists of 126 NGOs in 12 European Community countries. This organization puts emphasis on conservation, land use planning, transportation, energy, and agriculture. Like the other alliances of NGOs, it seeks to accomplish its objectives through education, communication, and the provision of advice and information.

Other NGOs are alliances of groups whose primary objectives are not the environment but who have a strong environmental orientation. The most important of these are the International Council of Voluntary Agencies, the International Confederation of Free Trade Unions, and the International Organization of Consumer Unions. The International Council of Voluntary Agencies promotes the development, growth, and improvement of voluntary agencies. Its membership consists of 86 organizations in 34 countries. To accomplish its objectives, it primarily provides information, advice, and assistance to interested parties. The International Confederation of Free Trade Unions has member unions in 108 countries and a total membership of over 100 million individuals. While its primary purpose is to promote the union movement, it is also interested in sustainable development and has made environmental issues important parts of various conferences that it has sponsored. The International Organization of Consumer Unions is a confederation of 175 organizations in 68 countries. Its primary purpose is to promote consumer rights, and it includes among these rights the right to a safe and healthy environment. It has also emphasized the consumer's responsibility to be sensitive to the effect of consumption patterns on the environment and thus has become a major proponent of ecological awareness.

A second major grouping of NGOs engages in direct action. These organizations sponsor projects, engage in direct environmental activities, or mobilize individuals to engage in such activities. For illustrative purposes, Earthwatch, Friends of the Earth International, Greenpeace, the Green Belt Movement, the Sierra Club International, and the World Wide Fund for Nature represent this group of NGOs well.

Earthwatch is both a research and direct action organization. Its Center of Field Research receives donations from foundations, corporations, and individuals to fund significant research projects on environmental problems. In regard to direct action, Earthwatch has a unique program of volunteers who carry out over 140 projects in more than 50 countries. The volunteers pay a share of the costs of their accommodations and food.

Friends of the Earth International in many ways resembles the alliances discussed earlier. It has been instrumental in creating alliances of environmental, consumer, and human rights organizations. However, it also attempts to coordinate the direct action of member groups in lobbying for environmental objectives relative to climate change, rain forests, ozone depletion, and marine conservation. It maintains observer and consultative status in a number of international organizations. Greenpeace International, which has over 4.5 million individual members in 143 countries, has been an active lobbyist for various environmental objectives. The major emphases of Greenpeace are stopping whaling and preventing toxic and nuclear waste dumping and river and sea pollution. The focal point of The Green Belt Movement is the tree. This organization stresses such environmental problems as desertification, the fuel wood and food crises, overpopulation, and the general mismanagement of resources. The Green Belt Movement has established over 1000 tree nurseries and conducted projects in which over 7 million trees were planted. Its membership consists of 1.5 million individuals in 13 African nations. The Sierra Club International engages in extensive lobbying for environmental legislation, primarily in the areas of clean air and water, control of toxic chemicals, and the designation of wilderness areas. It is the international arm of the Sierra Club, an important interest group in the United States. Presently, it has over 500,000 members in 27 countries. One of the most active sponsors of environmental projects is the World Wide Fund for Nature. Since its founding in 1961, it has spent over $300 million on more than 10,000 projects in over 130 countries. The Fund supports a wide range of projects, from the banning of trade in ivory to a reduction in greenhouse gases.

The final group of NGOs consists of organizations whose purposes are primarily educational and informational. They sponsor conferences, publish materials, establish communication networks, and encourage educational activities for young people. Examples of this group include the European Youth Forest Action, the International Solar Energy Society, and the Society for International Development. The primary purpose of the European Youth Forest Action is to teach young people about environmental problems. It sponsors an extremely effective summer camp called "Ecotopia," at which young people are saturated with information on environmental problems. All of the organization's educational programs are designed to teach young people how to act against polluters and how to work for better governmental environmental policies. The International Solar Energy Society promotes education on all aspects of solar energy. Among the more important of its activities is a biennial International Congress on Solar Energy to provide a meeting ground for those interested in the development and utilization of solar energy. The Society for International Development uses a similar strategy, a triennial World

Conference, on sustainable development. In addition to its educational activities, the Society supports research and publication on sustainable development and alternative development strategies.

NGOs accomplish important functions in the global environmental policy process. In a very perceptive case study of NGOs and marine policy, Stairs and Taylor found that NGOs contribute to the international policy-making process in four ways (Stairs and Taylor 1992:134). First, they enhance the legitimacy of the decision-making process. In essence, NGOs provide the mechanism though which people affected by a pending decision can present their views. Second, NGOs improve the quality of decisions. They are the source of facts and perspectives that would not be available otherwise. Third, they help balance access to decision makers. Decision making is often an insider's game with some interests better represented than others. NGOs help balance that representation. Fourth, NGO participation helps foster public education. Since they are involved in many decision situations, NGOs are able to report to their members information that would not be reported in the press. They serve as "watchdogs" for national delegates. In these ways, NGOs have emerged as major actors in the environmental policy process.

Environmental Interest Groups

Environmental interest groups are similar to NGOs and, in fact, are often treated in the literature as NGOs. Interest groups are national-level organizations with the most significant part of their activity within the environment. In most respects, then, the primary difference between an NGO and an interest group is that the former is multinational and the latter is national in scope of operations.

On a global basis, the variety of environmental interest groups is almost staggering. Unfortunately, no comprehensive analysis has been done on these groups from a global perspective. Considerable analysis has been done, however, on environmental interest groups in the United States. Given the richness of the data on U.S. environmental groups, it is useful to use the American experience as a prototype of what can occur within these organizations.

Environmental organizations in the United States, a diverse group representing a broad spectrum of styles and ideologies, have become important forces in the policy system. Much of their influence can be traced to a spurt in growth which they enjoyed in the 1980s. Most of that growth was a result of growing public commitment to environmental objectives, the anti-environmental stance of some Reagan administration officials that provoked "crisis" type confrontations, and the utilization of modern technologies for recruiting members (Dunlap and Mertig 1992). While membership in environmental organizations overlap, the number of Americans who belong to these organizations probably exceeds 7 million. This membership is scattered among many groups, but seven large organizations have the preponderance of memberships and financial resources. Table 2.1 presents the 1990 membership and annual budget of these seven organizations. In total, the Big Seven have 6,663,000 members and over $416 million dollars annual budget.

Environmental organizations in the United States have used three basic strategies in pursuing their objectives: education, direct action, and policy reform (Dunlap and Mertig 1992:19). All of the Big Seven and most other groups engage in educational activities of some kind. Many publish regular magazines, such as the highly regarded *National Wildlife* magazine published by the National Wildlife Federation. The Federation also publishes a Big Backyard series for small children and a Ranger Rick series for older children. Education efforts often have a specific policy interest. An example of this type of campaign is the Natural Resources Defense Council's efforts against the use of Alar on apples. Many organizations go beyond sharing information and are actively engaged in research on a variety of environmental questions.

Table 2.1   **The Seven Largest Environmental Organizations in the United States**

Name	1990 Members	1990 Budget (millions of $)
Greenpeace U.S.A.	2,300,000	50.2
National Wildlife Federation	975,000	87.2
World Wildlife Fund	940,000	35.5
National Audubon Society	600,000	35.0
Nature Conservancy	600,000	156.1
Sierra Club	560,000	35.2
The Wilderness Society	370,000	17.3
Total	6,663,000	416.5

Source: Data in Dunlap and Mertig 1992: pp. 13, 18.

Second, a wide range of direct action strategies are available to environmental organizations. The most formidable in terms of money is the land purchase program of the Nature Conservancy. The Conservancy purchases and then manages land it considers important for ecological reasons. Since 1953 the Conservancy has acquired over 5.5 million acres of land. Various market-based strategies have been used by other organizations, including boycotts of the products of firms that are deemed to be irresponsible toward the environment and shareholder actions to effectuate a change in corporate policy. Greenpeace U.S.A. is probably the most active direct action organization. Its nonviolent strategies include plugging pipes that carry toxic industrial emissions and placing inflatable boats between whaling ships and whales. Litigation is an increasingly important strategy. The Sierra Club Legal Defense Fund has as its primary purpose litigation against polluters. Finally, some environmental organizations advocate "ecotage" or the damaging of property to accomplish environmental objectives. Among these are Earth First! with 200,000 members and the Sea Shepherd Society with nearly a half million members. Ecotage tactics include such actions as sabotaging bulldozers to protect wilderness and sinking whaling ships to protect marine mammals.

Policy reform, the third strategy, is an attempt to get policy adopted or to strengthen existing policy. In this regard, environmental organizations have utilized many of the traditional strategies of interest groups generally. In the past, contributing money to political candidates was disdained by most environmental groups—only the League of Conservation Voters used the technique. Today, most of the Big Seven provide significant financial support for environmentally sensitive candidates. In many ways, the preferred tactic of environmental groups is lobbying Congress and administrative agencies such as the EPA, but it is important to note that this represents a significant shift in the strategy of environmental groups. Before Earth Day, only two lobbyists were retained by environmental organizations. In 1975 twelve organizations employed 40 lobbyists. By 1985 the number of registered lobbyists for environmental organizations had increased to 88 (Mitchell 1989). Lobbying has become such an important emphasis of some organizations that some analysts divide environmental interest groups into two categories, lobbying and nonlobbying.

Measuring the effectiveness of environmental groups in the United States or any other country is a difficult task. However, it is clear that they perform important functions in regard to policy. In the first place, they perform what political scientists call *interest definition*. For most people environmental degradation is essentially invisible. Interest groups help give visibility to environmental problems. This function leads to the charge that such groups "create the issue." In a sense, that charge is correct. Interest groups do assist in developing consciousness about a problem. Once consciousness is developed, interest groups help translate the sense of being affected by a problem into a proactive stance. However, in the sense that the charge "creating an issue" implies the manufacture of an artificial concern the accusation is essentially groundless. Second, interest groups help mobilize individuals and resources toward solving a problem. This function is usually referred to as *interest-group mobilization*. While a lone individual may certainly affect public policy, the policy process in most nations is primarily a group process. Interest groups mobilize like-minded individuals in pursuit of their common goals. In this respect, environmental interest groups are particularly affected by the "free rider problem," that is, the benefits from any given public policy will accrue to a much wider range of individuals than those who have worked to bring about the policy. If clean air is provided for one individual in a community it is provided for all, regardless of how few individuals worked to accomplish clean air. Since environmental organizations cannot, and indeed would not, limit the benefits of a clean environment to those who worked to accomplish that objective, such organizations are particularly vulnerable to the free rider problem. As a result, most national-level organizations seek to offer selective benefits to its participants, such as magazines, field trips, periodic policy updates, and various logo type paraphernalia.

Third, environmental interest groups provide *interest articulation*. That is, they present the position of the membership to government decision agencies. Most groups have expanded their efforts to include appearances before the legislatures and the courts in addition to the traditional effort to influence administrative and regulatory bodies. Through interest articulation, environmental interest groups provide representation beyond what would be accomplished through the formal system.

Grass Roots Organizations

Grass roots organizations are nongovernmental organizations that work at the community level. They are an extremely diverse group. Some are large organizations, most are small and lack significant resources. Some have rather broad objectives, most are single-issue organizations. Some have very high success rates while for others the hope of success is quite low. Some develop sophisticated organizational structures, such as the Pesticide Action Network of over 300 grass roots organizations. Most are loosely organized and very participatory in nature. The concern that triggers the formation of a grass roots organization may vary substantially between and within nations. What links the groups is a common concern for the environment. The perspective of most groups is reflected in the motto, "Think globally, act locally."

One of the strongest motivations for the formation of a grass roots organization is the NIMBY syndrome. NIMBY is an acronym for "Not In My Back Yard," reflecting the intense negative reaction to an attempt to locate any undesirable facility in a community. The reaction can occur with regard to any locally unwanted land use (referred to by the delightful acronym LULU). Thus the proposal to build a prison in a community can provoke the NIMBY reaction. The reaction occurs also when environmental facilities are LULUs. A chemical hazardous waste facility would most certainly provoke the NIMBY reaction. Ironically, the NIMBY reaction can be provoked by proposals for facilities with which people almost unanimously agree. For example, Americans are strongly in agreement with recycling, but the proposal to establish a recycling center to serve the entire city may provoke a NIMBY reaction in the affected neighborhood.

The NIMBY phenomenon illuminates a critical problem with regard to environmental facility siting. All environmental facilities concentrate the risks and disperse the benefits. The easiest way to understand this problem is to consider the example of a hazardous chemical waste facility. Clearly there are benefits from such a facility. As we shall see in a later chapter, the United States faces a serious problem in the inadequacy of facilities for the environmentally benign disposal of chemical waste. Consequently, the benefits accruing to the siting of waste facilities are dispersed to the nation as a whole. Additionally, producers of chemical wastes must have some place to dispose of their residuals. Again, however, these benefits are dispersed among the producers in the so-called "dump zone," while the risks are concentrated in the local area of the site. Locals therefore become obstructionists, often very effective ones, in the siting process. The NIMBY phenomenon is a powerful motivation for the creation of grass roots organizations in the developed countries.

A number of organizations come into being for reasons other than the NIMBY phenomenon. Grass roots organizations sometimes form out of a mutual concern for policy reform. Most often those common concerns are about threats to human health derived from environmental problems. The common concern might also be for racial justice or for respect of cultural heritage. The motivations behind formation of grass roots organizations are as diverse as the organizations themselves.

In the United States there have been attempts to provide some coordination and support for these organizations. The Institute for Conservation Leadership provides training for the leaders of grass roots organizations. Additionally, regional and national environmental interest groups provide support and coordination. The Environmental Support Center helps grass roots organizations obtain pro bono legal advice, raise funds, and obtain scientific information. Often national environmental interest groups, or their state affiliate, will join the grass roots organization in the effort to accomplish objectives.

In economically developing nations, grass roots organizations most commonly form out of a concern for sustainable development. Within this broad concern, local groups tend to emphasize a local problem or attempt to meet a local need. They provide credit or link the individual to credit agencies, engage in production support services to farmers and local entrepreneurs, conduct educational and informational projects, and deliver health services to local residents (Bratton 1989:570–571). Grass roots organizations often provide an extremely important stimulus for locals to participate in projects. In this regard, they are especially important as agencies for mobilizing community support. In some cases they are the most important channel of communication with the poor in a community. Since their contacts with locals are much closer than those of international agencies, grass roots organizations often bring a different perspective to problems. They understand local mores and customs and incorporate them into development plans. As a result, they sometimes offer alternative development plans that are more effective than those of international agencies. In all these respects, grassroots organizations in economically developing countries make significant contributions to both sustainable development and environmental policy.

Scientists

Scientists present special problems in the environmental policy process simply because their perspectives are not as neutral or their findings as exact as is popularly believed.

Affecting their neutrality is the reality that scientists are products of their environment and are influenced by it. They have opinions that affect their judgments on issues. For example, most scientists have at least some vague notion as to how government should function in the economy; support or opposition to a proposed regulation may be the result of this preexisting opinion. Scientists are influenced by social and economic forces. One of these forces, institutional affiliation, has been subject to considerable analysis in the United States and has been found to be an important determinant of the scientist's position. Scientists employed in industry are more politically and socially conservative than those who work in universities, government, or environmental interest groups. For example, a study of 136 scientists relative to risk assessments for carcinogens found that industry scientists favored premises and judgments in the research process that made regulation of a substance less likely (Lynn 1986). Even more to the point, another study found that when scientists became involved in policy issues, say as advisors to government agencies or in testifying before Congress, there was a noticeable weakening of their scientific perspective and a strengthening of ideologically based perspectives (Dietz and Rycroft 1987:17). This means simply that scientists stopped acting like scientists and began acting more like politicians or political activists. Scientific neutrality is often one of the first casualties in policy debates.

Scientific findings also are not as exact as is popularly believed. The major reasons are found in the inherent complexity of most environmental problems and the reluctance of funding institutions to support state-of-the-art advances in environmental research. Environmental problems are so complex that scientists are divided over the most fundamental questions relative to the approach and methods to be used in studying phenomena. And once basic methodological decisions are made, there are many points within the methodology where differences over approach can develop. For example, there are over 50 points in a routine risk assessment where choices have to be made, involving both technical and value issues. It is not easy to get any two individuals to agree on all choices. Thus the "findings" of any two individuals doing the same risk assessment and making slightly different choices will vary.

What are the results of these characteristics of scientists as policy actors? One result is that environmental "facts" and "solutions" are subject to infinite deniability. Sometimes this deniability is cloaked in grandiose polemics. Consider this denial of the problem of carbon dioxide buildup in the atmosphere

> ...the rising CO2 content of the earth's atmosphere is not the grave threat to humanity it is typically made out to be. Quite the opposite, it is one of the better things that could happen to our planet. For CO2 is, literally, the elixir of life, providing the primary molecular link between the atmosphere and the food chain of the entire biosphere. In its absence, life as we know it would be impossible. In abundance, it can lift the biological activity of the planet to heights never before dreamed possible. (Idso 1992:10)

The author refers to scientific experimentation with carbon dioxide augmentation in greenhouse production of plants as his evidence.

A second result of the limited neutrality and the inexactitude of science is difficulty in establishing standards. There is a great range of scientific questions involved in setting standards for any given environmental regulation. Policy makers generally are not scientists. Faced with a wide range of scientific issues, they look to scientists for guidance. But scientists may disagree or supplant their scientific judgment with ideological perspectives. Warren G. Harding is reputed to have evaluated his problem as president as follows: "I listen to one side and they seem right, and then I talk to the other side, and they seem just as right, and there I am where I started.... God, what a job." Any official working in the environmental policy system could echo the same frustration. If the experts cannot agree, how are policy makers to arrive at decisions?

A third result is "advocacy science," the practice of using science in an attempt to influence the provisions of a particular policy. It is used by industry groups opposing various environmental regulations. For example, the tobacco industry fields substantial scientific information and respected scientists in its efforts to dispute the dangers of passive cigarette smoking. Environmental organizations have discovered advocacy science in recent years, and have developed a "counterscience" capability. That is, they use their own scientific capabilities to evaluate the basis of environmental policies and refute the scientific claims of opposing groups (Mitchell, Mertig, and Dunlap 1992:22). Scientists affiliated with environmental organizations frequently hold significantly different positions than their counterparts in industry and the two groups are often adversaries in the policy process.

The general result of all these factors is that science has limited capabilities in the environmental policy process. This is not to denigrate the role of science. Scientists are important actors. But it should be emphasized that in any public policy system, information is never complete. It is "interpretive, incomplete, and strategically withheld" (Stone 1988:21). It is therefore important to understand that much of the efforts of actors in the environmental policy process, including the activity of scientists, is directed toward affecting what information is used and how people in the process interpret that information. This means that information is deliberately kept secret at times—what Stone calls "strategically withholding" information. And it certainly means that policy makers, like all decision makers, must content themselves with making the most informed decision possible in a context of uncertainty.

Chapter 3

Air Quality

It's More Than What We Breathe

Air pollution is the release of waste into the air at a faster rate than the air can clean itself. The carrying capacity of the air—that is, the amount of pollutants that it can cleanse through natural processes—varies according to the type of pollutant. For example, the amount of natural CO_2 released into the air is about 700 billion tons a year. In fact, so much carbon dioxide is released through natural processes that CO_2 is not usually classified as a pollutant. However, carbon dioxide is an unavoidable by-product of the burning of carbon fuels. Thus human activities release 24 billion tons each year, and only about half of this is being cleansed. Joined with other gases in the air, carbon dioxide becomes an important polluter.

As the experience with carbon dioxide suggests, there are both natural-based and human-based sources of air pollution. The list of natural-based sources is long. Anyone who has sneezed in the spring because of pollen in the air has experienced one. There are many other airborne viruses, bacteria, and spores that occur naturally and can be regarded as pollutants. Some naturally based pollutants are sources of great beauty. The haze over the Blue Ridge Mountains is the result of plant decay. Depending on one's esthetic taste, others are not so pretty, including volcanic dust and ash, meteoric dust, particulate matter from burning forests, and salt spray from the ocean. Many of these natural pollutants are recycled into useful material, as is carbon dioxide in the photosynthesis processes of plants. Others are simply returned to earth. Volcanic ash, for example, naturally falls back to earth or is carried back to earth by rainfall. Some join with human-based emissions to form the pollutants that remain in the air.

Human-based air pollution consists of particulate matter and gaseous substances. There are five general types that are most important for an understanding of air pollution. First, particulates consist of unburned residues from the firing process or the dust produced by the grinding and drying of industrial products. The most commonly observed particulate emission is the black smoke from the exhaust of an automobile. Second, sulphur dioxide is the result of burning fossil fuels in both industry and the home. While there has been a special emphasis on coal, sulphur dioxide results from the burning of all fossil fuels. Carbon monoxide, the third important human-based pollutant, is produced by burning carbon with insufficient air. Adjusting the air intake on an automobile carburetor, for example, affects the production of carbon monoxide. Smog reactants are the fourth type of air pollution. These are gaseous substances—hydrocarbons, nitrogen oxides, and nitric oxide—that react in the atmosphere to form photochemical smog. Ultraviolet energy from the sun "cooks" the elements into photochemical smog. Auto emissions are the primary source of smog reactants. Finally, there are the total oxidants. Ozone is the most dangerous element in air pollution. In the United States it is taken as the indicator to determine when an urban area's air has reached a certain threshold. If the ozone count reaches that level, automobile inspection programs must be mandated.

What are the consequences of these pollutants? We will examine three potential effects: ozone depletion, the greenhouse effect, and acid rain.

THE OZONE LAYER: EARTH'S PROTECTIVE COVER

While ozone is the most dangerous air pollutant at the earth's surface, the layer of ozone in the stratosphere is vital to the earth. It is located between 20 and 30 miles above the surface of the earth and varies in thickness both between regions and over time.

Ozone is a molecule consisting of three atoms of oxygen. Oxygen in all its forms is highly unstable. Ozone, as a triatomic form of oxygen, is susceptible to being "destroyed" as a molecule. The process works like this. Chlorofluorocarbon molecules (CFCs) are present in the stratosphere as a result of commercial activities. Incoming ultraviolet radiation breaks off a chlorine atom from a human-made chlorofluorocarbon molecule. The free chlorine atom then attacks and breaks up the ozone molecule. It is estimated that a single chlorine atom can destroy up to 100,000 ozone molecules. Chlorine is a very efficient catalyst in the chemical reaction that destroys ozone. On the other hand, ozone is eroded each day by chemical reactions whose catalyst is intense sunlight. John Firor described the process this way: "The amount of ozone put into the stratosphere each day is steady—it depends almost entirely on the intense sunlight at that altitude and does not change much from day to day" (Firor 1990:29). If more ozone is destroyed than is created, the result is a thinning of the ozone layer or the appearance of a hole in the ozone layer over Antarctica.

Chlorofluorocarbons have been important components in the lifestyle of advanced nations. The most important application was in air conditioners and refrigerators, but they also had a wide range of applications in such things as plastic foams, solvents, sterilants, aerosols, and the quick freezing of fish and vegetables. Five American companies produced CFCs— DuPont, Allied Signed Corp., Penwalt, ICI Americas Inc., and Kaiser Tech. At the height of CFC use, these companies had annual sales in excess of $28 billion and employed 715,000 people. More was at stake in the banning of CFCs, then, than simply the convenience of aerosol cans.

What is the evidence that the ozone layer is thinning and that chloroflourocarbons are the culprit? Global ozone concentrations are measured in *Dobson units*, named for Gordon Dobson, a Cambridge University meteorologist who devised the instrumentation for measuring stratospheric ozone. The global average is about 300 Dobson units, but with wide fluctuation over time and geographic regions. For example, the ozone concentration thins over the Equator as a result of a number of factors. Ozone concentrations are also affected by naturally occurring phenomena, including volcanic eruptions, which spew hydrochloric acid into the stratosphere, and hurricanes, which diffuse ocean spray with its sodium chloride into the stratosphere. The chlorine released from these elements destroys ozone molecules. Given such wide annual and regional fluctuations and the impact of naturally occurring climatic phenomena, is the ozone layer actually thinning and are CFCs responsible?

A number of major efforts have been directed to studying the ozone layer. The United States has sponsored two American National Ozone Expeditions (NOZE I and NOZE II). The Airborne Antarctica Ozone Experiment was an international effort which sent airplanes into the ozone hole. Additionally, the National Aeronautics and Space Agency of the American government maintains an Upper Atmosphere Research Satellite which monitors the levels of ozone in the northern hemisphere. Finally, the Ozone Trends Panel consists of a group of scientists who attempt to interpret the large body of data that are now gathered annually from a variety of sources. Two conclusions can be drawn from the reports of these and other sources. The first is that the evidence has increased to the point of being conclusive that human activities, most notably the production and use of CFCs, have been significant in the depletion of the ozone layer. The second is that ozone depletion has been greater over the earth's middle latitudes than had been predicted. This middle latitude includes most of the United States, the former Soviet Union, Europe, and China.

The hazard created by ozone depletion is the increased level of ultraviolet light which penetrates to the earth's surface. This increased exposure has important outcomes. The UN Environment Programme estimated that for every 1 percent drop in ozone levels there would be a 3 percent increase in nonmelanoma skin cancers among light-skinned people. Using that relationship as the basis for its calculations, the U.S. Environmental Protection Agency estimated that 12 million Americans will develop skin cancer and 200,000 will lose their life as a result of ozone thinning. Those who dispute these data claim that oxygen itself serves as a shield for the worst ultraviolet radiation (Dunn 1992). This statement is correct as far as it goes; ordinary oxygen (O_2) does filter ultraviolet radiation of wavelengths shorter than 185 nanometers, the most dangerous wavelength. But it is ozone that filters ultraviolet radiation in wavelengths from 185 to 290 nanometers, the middle range. (Ultraviolet radiation in the range of 290 to 400 nanometers is not filtered and reaches the earth.) Thus ozone performs an important function in screening ultraviolet waves of a particular wavelength. The criticism of the EPA's calculations is a good example of the "infinite deniability" of environmentally related facts and estimations.

Other potential effects of ozone depletion are more subject to uncertainty but no less significant for human welfare. The most severe outcome may be the effect of ultraviolet radiation on the human immune system. High levels of exposure to ultraviolet radiation can weaken or destroy the immune system—a phenomenon already associated with some types of chemotherapy and radiation medical treatments. Ultraviolet radiation also can result in crop loss and forest damage. It is particularly dangerous to cotton, peas, beans, melons, cabbage, and the loblolly pine. With the hole in the ozone layer at Antarctica, some ecologists fear severe ecological damage in the region. The worst case scenario envisions the loss of the entire food chain.

The significant level of risks associated with ozone depletion resulted in a multinational effort to solve the problem. The most important result of this effort was the Montreal Protocol on Substances that Deplete the Ozone Layer. The protocol was signed on September 16, 1987, by 37 parties, including the United States, the former Soviet Union, and the European Economic Community. It required that industrialized nations by 1998 reduce by one-half their use of five CFCs and stop use of three halons. However, the agreement made no mention of two of the most potent and widely used ozone-depleting compounds: methyl chloroform and carbon tetrachloride. Methyl chloroform is one of the most widely used chemical solvents. Carbon tetrachloride is one of the cheapest and most toxic solvents and is more ozone depleting than any of the five regulated CFCs. The

London Accord of 1990 included the goal of total phase-out of carbon tetra-chloride by the year 2000 and of methyl chloroform by 2005.

The problem of Third World participation in the Montreal Protocol is a difficult one. Third World countries face some complex choices relative to the continued use of CFCs. Many of these countries have been making sub-stantial investment in CFC-based technology, especially refrigeration. A phase-out of CFCs would mean that much of that investment would be lost before the technology could be depreciated. Additionally, the cost of CFC replacement chemicals is expected to be high—up to six times the present cost of CFC 11, the most widely used CFC compound. Third World coun-tries generally make the point that the vast majority of ozone-depleting releases are the responsibility of industrialized nations, and restricting Third World use or imposing higher costs on them would be unfair. Without Third World participation, particularly that of India and China, present policy is doomed to failure (Makhijani, Bickel, and Makhijani 1990:183). Clearly, the need to find ways to deal equitably with Third World needs is an important unfinished item on the international agenda.

An initial attempt to strengthen the Montreal Protocol is found in the London Accord. Along with adding carbon tetrachloride and methyl chlo-roform to the substances to be phased out, the London Accord accelerated the phase-out of the regulated CFCs and halons. One of the more contro-versial features of the Accord was the provision to eliminate the use of HCFCs, the most promising short term substitute for CFCs, by no later than 2040 and earlier than 2020 if possible. The Accord also addressed the problem of Third World nations, giving them a grace period of ten years to complete the phase-out of regulated CFCs—the year 2010, as opposed to the year 2000 for industrial nations. The London Accord also authorized the creation of an international fund of $160 million over the 1991–1993 period, to be used to help Third World nations gain access to new alternate technologies and then implement the CFC substitutes. As a result, minis-ters from China and India announced that they would recommend that their governments become parties to the Accords. This is a dramatic step in the direction of reconciling one of the most significant differences concern-ing ozone depletion among national decision makers.

The Montreal Protocol and the London Accord constitute an ambi-tious attempt to apply the command-and-control strategy at the interna-tional level. They do suggest that international agreement on preventive action to protect the ecological basis of life is possible. However, it should be emphasized that the agreements leave enforcement to national regula-tory agencies. Some nations have taken a proactive position in giving the international agreements the force of domestic law. This is particularly true with the U.S. 1990 Amendments to the Clean Air Act and with the European Community's efforts. However, the same cannot be said of other countries. Implementing legislation simply has not been forthcoming in some nations. Thus an important lesson to be learned from the Montreal Protocol is that international environmental agreements are not self-enforcing and there is no permanent international organization for enforcement.

Can the problems of standard setting and enforcement be averted through technology? Considerable research effort is being devoted to finding substitutes for CFCs. HCFC, a molecule containing hydrogen, chlorine, fluorine, and carbon, is currently the only substitute commonly available, but it contributes to chlorine buildup in the stratosphere and to global warming. Helium-based cooling systems are another option. A research team at the Oak Ridge National Laboratories concluded that helium-based refrigerators and freezers could be equal to or better than conventional CFC models.

Two problems are associated with finding substitutes for CFCs. The first is that companies that have expended considerable money on finding substitutes have a strong vested interest in their products, and they pressure regulatory agencies to approve them. The second problem is associated with mandatory phase-out dates. Such dates encourage an accelerated effort to develop substitutes that will come to the market as soon as possible, and these short-term substitutes carry their own risks, as is illustrated by HCFC. What is needed is an acceleration of research on long-term solutions. Unfortunately, there is little evidence that such research is being done. This situation suggests a very high cultural discount rate, with technological and economic factors taking precedence over generational interests.

THE GREENHOUSE EFFECT AND GLOBAL CLIMATE CHANGE

The earth and its atmosphere constitute a complex energy exchange system whose energy source is the sun. A critical element in the energy exchange system is the layer of air that envelopes the earth. Some *trace gases*, so called because they make up less than 1 percent of atmospheric gases, are relatively transparent to incoming short wavelength sunlight but are opaque to longer wavelength energy radiated from the earth's surface. Trace gases that have this effect are called *greenhouse gases* because they allow energy to come into the earth's atmosphere but not escape from it. Greenhouse gases, then, act like the glass on a greenhouse, allowing heat from the sun to enter the earth's surface and trapping it, thus moderating the average temperature of the earth. The result is the establishment of an average temperature at the earth's surface suitable for plant and animal life. The average ocean and land surface temperatures are 63 and 57 degrees Fahrenheit, respectively. Without trace gases in the atmosphere, earth surface temperatures might be as low as -4 degrees Fahrenheit. Ironically, without the greenhouse gases the earth would be uninhabitable for a large number of plants and animals.

What is the source of concern over the greenhouse gases? The trace gases in the atmosphere are a mixture of gases that occur naturally and gases that are traceable to human activities. Human activities have increased the levels of atmospheric trace gases, particularly carbon dioxide, methane, nitrous oxide, and chlorofluorocarbons. Historically, carbon dioxide has been the most important of the greenhouse gases. Methane is a constituent element in natural gas and is lost in the production, transportation, and use of natural gas. Other human activities that produce methane are cattle raising, rice paddies, and trash dumps. Wild animals, wetlands, and termites are the primary natural sources of methane release. Nitrous oxide results from combustion and from various naturally occurring biological processes in the soil. All chlorofluorocarbons result from human activity. Each of these four greenhouse gases are long lived and mix well in the atmosphere.

The essential question is whether the increase in human-based greenhouse gases is producing global climate change. What is the evidence that the greenhouse effect is occurring?

One of the primary sources of support for the greenhouse effect comes from computer modeling. Computer simulations, called *general circulation models*, attempt to duplicate the known workings of the earth's climate system. These models attempt to measure the difference between existing atmospheric conditions and the conditions that would result from a change in various factors, such as an increase in atmospheric carbon dioxide. General circulation models tend to produce consistent and reasonable estimates of greenhouse warming on a global basis. The almost consistent result is that a doubling of carbon dioxide in the atmosphere will be associated with global warming of about 7 degrees Fahrenheit.

The problem with the climate model experiments is that the climate system is complex and there is much that is not known. For example, the ocean is one of the major determinants of climate but its interrelationship with the climate system is little known. Additionally, there are a number of feedbacks that would occur as a result of global warming that will affect the system. For example, it will lead to more evaporation from the ocean, and water vapor can trap heat. Also, with warming there will be less ice and snow, which are reflectors of heat; presumably, then, more heat would be retained at the surface. There is also the question of the carbon dioxide absorption system. In order to determine the CO2 absorption rate of plants under various conditions, some researchers have examined the effect of plants in a CO2 enriched environment. The U.S. Water Conservation Laboratory in Phoenix, Arizona, has conducted the longest experiment in CO2 enrichment. Findings suggest that CO2 enrichment increases productivity in substantial amounts, perhaps up to ten times that of nonenriched plants. Would a similar effect occur globally with an increase in atmospheric CO2 concentrations?

Thus there is considerable uncertainty surrounding the results of the general circulation models. Two conclusions do seem justified, however. First, regular monitoring of the earth's atmosphere does establish that the concentrations of greenhouse gases are increasing. For example, prior to the Industrial Revolution with its heavy utilization of fossil fuels, carbon dioxide concentrations were approximately 280 parts per million. In 1990 concentration had reached 360 ppm, or about 25 percent more than 100 years ago. Projections accepted even by those who reject the idea of the greenhouse effect suggest that concentrations will reach over 600 ppm in the early part of the twenty-first century.

Second, the models are supported by other evidence. Three meteorological phenomena give some indication of this evidence. First, snow has been disappearing from the high Arctic a little earlier each spring. In the 1940s snow near Barrow, Alaska, melted in mid-June, and in the 1980s in late May. Second, the ice cap in the Dry Valleys area of Antarctica has been thinning each year. There was a six-foot decrease in the thickness of the cap between 1978 and 1988. Third, the United States experienced five of the hottest years recorded in the past 100 years in the 1980s. This hot weather was accompanied by a severe drought in 1988.

The problem with evidence of this kind is that there are well established climatic cycles, and the meteorological events taken as indicators of the greenhouse effect can be explained by reference to these cycles. Additionally, there are significant regional variations in climate. In 1988, for example, most of the world experienced cooler temperatures than normal and was free of drought. So while these events do provide some supporting evidence, they are not proof that global warming is occurring.

Global warming presents in the starkest form the problems of policy making in the face of uncertain knowledge. How should international and national policy systems respond to the prospect of global warming?

The most important international agency responsible for climate change policy is the Intergovernmental Panel on Climate Change (IPCC). Organized in 1987 by the World Meteorological Organization and the UN Environment Programme, the IPCC was given the responsibility for assessing the scientific information and formulating strategies for the management of climate change. In May 1990 the IPCC issued an important report that constitutes a balanced and reasoned policy approach to the problem of global climate change.

The Panel's most important conclusion was that, notwithstanding scientific and economic uncertainty, all countries should take immediate steps to reduce greenhouse gases. It concluded that it is now technically feasible and cost effective to reduce carbon dioxide emissions in all countries in the range of 20 percent by the year 2005. This reduction can be accomplished through a combination of three strategies: to use energy more efficiently, to employ alternative fuels, and to plant more forests. The Panel predicted that without such actions, global warming will increase between 2 and 5 degrees centigrade over the next century. Such global warming would be unprecedented in the last 10,000 years. Finally, if the warming does occur, the Panel predicted significant adverse effects on the ecological basis of life.

A second objective of the Panel was to assess the environmental, economic, and social impacts of climate change. Assuming the global warming predicted to occur in the absence of preventive strategies, the effects can be summarized in four categories: sea level, agriculture, forests, and water resources.

First, warming on the order predicted by the Panel would result in a rise in sea level of between 35 and 65 centimeters. Consequences would include the flooding of low-lying areas, the regression of coastal barrier islands and beaches, the flooding of wetland habitats, and the upstream movement of saline water. The losses associated with such a development could be catastrophic and the cost to mitigate the impact is likely to be high. Various sea level impact studies have been made. A 1989 EPA study of the United States suggested a cost of between $50 billion and $75 billion to mitigate the effect on houses and roadways alone of a 1 millimeter rise in sea level. Adding bulkhead construction and sand pumping increased the cost to $100 billion (Smith and Tirpak 1989). A more specific study predicted a cost of $334 million to reclaim all of California's flooded islands and $298 million to reclaim the thirteen most valuable ones (Logan 1990). The country with the most experience in sea level management is the Netherlands. Estimates in that country for new defense measures in the event of a sea level rise are $3 billion over 50 years (Heakstra 1989). Mitigation costs in all countries, then, would be substantial.

The prospect of high mitigation costs raises an important question which has not received the attention it deserves. What is the marginal difference between costs of mitigating the adverse effects of climate change and costs of reducing environmental degradation? Much emphasis is placed on the latter costs without regard to the former. What is needed is a concept of full system costing that reflects the marginal difference between compliance and mitigation costs.

Second, global warming will have significant effects on agriculture, particularly in regional production patterns. In short, there would be a climate-induced shift in the regions in which various crops are grown. Unfortunately, unlike their consistent estimates of greenhouse warming, the general circulation models have rather high degrees of uncertainty with regard to predicting regional dislocations in climate. Whatever the accuracy of the models, regional changes in crop production are almost certain to occur, with substantial cost to farmers for new equipment and technologies. This problem is particularly acute in the United States, since the commodity price support policy of the American government encourages select crop production in fixed locations.

The impact of global climate change on forests, the third category, is more complex. In earlier analysis, it was assumed that the various species of trees would simply migrate to new areas. However, more recent study suggests that trees do not migrate to follow favorable climatic conditions. Temperature is only one factor determining where trees will grow. Many other factors are involved, including soil types, topography, and elevation. Thus the migration of tree types to adjust to climate change is unlikely.

Finally, evaluation of the impact of global warming on water resources is the most complex question associated with climate change. Increases in mean global temperature would almost certainly be accompanied by increases in warm weather patterns, which would include higher levels of precipitation and more hurricanes, tornados, and monsoons. However, increases in mean global temperatures would also result in higher demand for water. Most models also predict some disruption in regional weather patterns. Thus it could be possible that the arid areas of the world will become more arid as a result of global warming.

Given the shroud of uncertainty over each of these potential outcomes, what should be the public policy response to global warming? The perspective of the IPCC report is compelling: Even given the scientific uncertainty, the potential effects of global climate change are so pervasive and irreversible that all countries should take immediate steps to reduce greenhouse gases, through technically feasible and cost-effective means. Substantial international effort is taking place to develop a convention implementing the recommendations of the report.

The greenhouse effect stands as something of a test case of the cultural discount rate. Those nations that have taken the recommendations of the Panel seriously and adopted policies to reduce greenhouse gases reflect a low cultural discount rate, placing a high value on the future. These include member nations of the European Community, as well as Australia, Austria, Canada, Finland, Iceland, Japan, New Zealand, Norway, Sweden, and Switzerland. Nations that have not taken action to reduce the greenhouse gases reflect a very high cultural discount rate, favoring present consumption over future value. Among the most notable of these countries is the United States. While the American government supports the IPCC and participates in various international conferences on global climate change, its policy response is best characterized by the words "minimal" and "cautious." The United States did adopt the National Global Change Research Act of 1989, which requires the development of a plan to assess the effect of climate change. However, it is difficult to avoid the conclusion that the primary purpose of this Act is to divert criticism from other countries by the appearance of action. Third World nations generally have been inactive also. Thus the cutting and burning of tropical rain forest, a major contributor to atmospheric CO_2, continues at a high rate. Again it appears that Third World nations do not have the luxury of the long view of things and are forced by necessity to provide for immediate needs.

ACID RAIN

The term *acid rain* was first used in 1872 by Robert Angus, a British chemist, to refer to the increasingly acid precipitation falling on the city of Manchester. Actually, acid precipitation is a more accurate term since snow, hail, fog, mist, and dew can also be involved in air transported pollutants.

Acid precipitation is formed when sulphur dioxide and nitrogen oxide react chemically with hydrogen to form sulfuric and nitric acids. These acids then fall to the earth in precipitation. The measure of acidity is the pH scale or the potential hydrogen scale. A neutral substance has a pH of 7. Substances with a pH lower than 7 are acidic and substances with pH numbers higher than 7 are alkaline. Acid precipitation is in the area of 1.5 to 5.5 pH. By comparison, vinegar has a pH of around 3 and lemon juice a pH of around 2.1. Rain water on a global average is acidic, with an average pH of about 5.6.

Acid rain as an environmental issue has evolved into a rather broad area encompassing many concerns with regard to both water and soil. A panel working in the National Acid Precipitation Assessment Program suggested that the most serious effects of acid precipitation could be on soil. Chemical reactions triggered by acid rain could result in the loss of large amounts of calcium and magnesium in the soil. Additionally, acid rain leaches aluminum from the soil. There is evidence that aluminum is reaching toxic levels in some regions of the United States.

Other study groups have emphasized the effects of acid rain on lakes and forests. The U.S. Congress established a research group, the Interagency Task Force on Acid Precipitation, consisting of representatives from twelve national agencies. This group concluded that acid precipitation from industrial emission was probably the major factor in destroying fresh water lakes in the northeast. The Office of Science within the White House established a panel of scientists to study the problem, and that group concluded that the environmental damage from acid deposition may reach the irreversible stage if action is not taken to ameliorate the effect. The National Academy of Sciences issued a report in 1983 that directly linked acid precipitation in the northeastern United States and Canada with industrial emissions. The study concluded that the problem could be reduced by controls on industrial emissions.

These reports in the 1980s were key elements in breaking the political deadlock on acid rain. The Reagan administration had consistently held that no action should be taken until the problem was studied further. Then the Bush administration proposed amendments to the Clean Air Act which included important new efforts to reduce acid deposition.

The effort to amend the Clean Air Act generated substantial political conflict, and extensive compromise was required before the amendments were passed. The final bill (P.L. 101-549) mandated that by the year 2006 sulphur dioxide be reduced to 10 million tons less than 1980 emissions and that nitrogen oxide be reduced to 2 to 4 million tons less. As we observed in Chapter 2, the Act established marketable allowances, to be determined on the basis of an emitter's average 1985–1987 fuel consumption. The bill then provided for the direct sale of a limited number of allowances at $1,500 a ton. The bill also authorized the auction of more allowances by the EPA under certain circumstances. These provisions constitute one of the most extensive applications of a market-driven strategy for attainment of environmental objectives.

NATIONAL AMBIENT AIR QUALITY PROGRAMS: THE UNITED STATES AND GREAT BRITAIN

On a global scale, substantial effort has been directed toward resolving the problems associated with ozone depletion, the greenhouse effect, and acid rain. There is also a concern for the general quality of the air. This concern has expressed itself in major environmental policies of a number of individual nations. It is instructive to examine the experience of the United States and Great Britain.

In the United States the first effort toward air quality legislation was the Clean Air Act of 1970. The Act utilized the partial preemption strategy, the EPA establishing the air quality standards and the states assuming primary responsibility for implementation. The Act mandated the regulation of seven pollutants: particulates, sulfur dioxide, carbon monoxide, nitrogen oxide, ozone, hydrocarbons, and lead. Primary standards were to be set so that the health of the vulnerable, especially the elderly and children, would be protected with an adequate margin of safety. Presumptively, if the vulnerable were protected then the standards would be adequate to protect the general population. Secondary standards were to be established protecting such things as visibility, buildings, crops, and water. Together the two types of standards constitute what are referred to as National Ambient Air Quality Standards, or NAAQS (the word *ambient* refers simply to an encompassing environment). Deadlines were set for primary standards but not for secondary standards.

The Clean Air Act also required the EPA to set emission standards for new stationary sources and mobile sources. New stationary standards were called New Source Performance Standards and were to be set on an industry basis. The EPA was to take into account the costs, energy requirements, and environmental effects of each standard. Relative to mobile sources, the Act established a detailed but flexible timetable for control of automobile and truck emissions. The EPA was given authority to change the timetables for compliance and has done so on several occasions.

Following the partial preemption strategy, the Act provided that each state create an implementation plan. These state plans were to take into account several factors. The most important was the division of the nation into 247 Air Quality Control Regions, each of which was classified as an attainment or a nonattainment region, according to the levels of regulated pollutants present in the air. States with nonattainment areas were required to order existing stationary source emitters to retrofit their plants with the most reasonable available control technology identified by the EPA. States in nonattainment areas were also required to meet carbon monoxide and ozone standards by 1987 through such techniques as automobile inspections and catalytic converters on new vehicles. Some states in the attainment regions were identified as having especially clean air, and were classified as Prevention of Significant Deterioration regions. In these states all new stationary source emitters were required to install the best available control technology.

The Clean Air Act was passed with the presumption that Congress would amend it on a regular basis as conditions changed. The Act was amended in 1977. After this, action was impossible as a result of the Reagan administration coolness toward national regulation generally and industry opposition to extension of air quality regulation. The political gridlock was broken with the important 1990 amendments to the Act. We have already discussed the provisions of the amendments on acid rain (Title IV) and ozone-depleting substances (Title III).

The major departure from previous law contained in the 1990 amendments (Title I) was the classification of nonattainment areas according to the extent to which the standards are exceeded. Each nonattainment area was placed into one of five classes according to how bad the pollution problem was, and deadlines for the attainment of the standards were then established, as follows: marginal (3 years), moderate (6 years), serious (9 years), severe (15 years), and extreme (20 years). Mandated controls increase in both number and severity with the level of pollution in the area.

Mobile source emissions remain major contributors to pollution, and Title II of the Clean Air Act Amendments imposes more stringent standards on tailpipe emissions. It calls for a reduction in hydrocarbon levels by 35 percent and of nitrogen oxide levels by 60 percent over 1990 emissions by the year 1996. A second phase of reductions may be imposed in the year 2003, depending on need and available technology. The Act limits alternative fuels to fleet application. Since California law requires 150,000 low-emission vehicles by 1996, the state is exempt from this requirement.

Other states may adopt low-emission policies for individual vehicles but may not set standards different from those in California.

Title III of the amendments addresses the highly contentious issue of toxic air pollutants. Whereas the Clean Air Act of 1970 had identified only seven substances, the amendments identify 189 chemicals as hazardous air pollutants. The EPA was to identify and categorize emission sources of the chemicals and issue standards for emission. The standards were to require installation of maximum achievable control technology, with cost being taken into account. Standards for 41 of the categories were to be in effect by 1992 and the remaining ones by 2000. If significant health risks remain after installation of maximum achievable control technology, the EPA is to strengthen the standards to achieve an ample margin of safety to protect the public health. Title III further provides for the identification and regulation of stationary "area sources." These are small sources of toxic air pollution, such as dry cleaners, gas stations, and wood-fired heating systems, in a designated area. The EPA is to require the maximum achievable control technology for the 30 most serious area sources, again taking costs into account. Finally, Title III specifies that firms that handle extremely hazardous materials (about 100 are on the list) must publicize the possible risks to the public health. A Chemical Safety Board was created to investigate accidents in handling the chemicals.

One of the more innovative features of the amendments was the establishment of a permitting program. Title I of the Act creates a state-run program requiring permits for the operation of many sources of air pollution, generally those major emitters releasing 100 tons per year of any regulated pollutant, although some stationary and area sources that emit lesser amounts of hazardous air pollutants are also required to have a permit. Each state was required to establish a permitting program and submit it to the EPA by 1993. If a state's plan is not approved within five years, the EPA can administer its own permitting program in the state. States are empowered to collect annual fees sufficient to cover the reasonable costs of the program, but no less than $25 per ton of regulated pollutants. The Act provides that an emitter cannot be held in violation if it is complying with the explicit requirements of its permit.

In summary, the Clean Air Act and its 1977 and 1990 amendments are based in the command-and-control regulatory strategy and utilize partial preemption as the intergovernmental instrument. Thus overall authority is vested in the EPA but there is considerable discretion on the part of the states. Increasing use is made of market-driven strategies, as reflected in the tradeable emission allowances and the fees associated with the permit system. Also EPA is required to take the cost of compliance into account in implementing the nationally established standards.

In Great Britain, responsibility for air quality is vested in the Alkali Inspectorate. The Inspectorate was established in 1863, predating by far the

American EPA. It consists of a headquarters staff, 15 district offices, and "sampling teams" available to the district offices. Much of the organization and procedures of the Inspectorate are the result of the long evolution of the agency.

The standard to be applied by the Inspectorate is associated with the concept of "best practicable means" (b.p.m.). This standard was established in the Alkali Act of 1906 and was made a part of the Health and Safety at Work Act of 1974. The 1974 Act provides that all firms are "to use the best practicable means for preventing the emission into the atmosphere from the premises of noxious or offensive substances and for rendering harmless and inoffensive such substances as may be so emitted." The word "practicable" entails reasonable regard for both the current state of technical knowledge and for compliance costs. The objective is to prevent the release of such substance if possible, and if not, to render them harmless. The Inspectorate relies primarily on "high stacks" to render emissions harmless and "notes on b.p.m." as the means of preventing emissions.

The process for arriving at the "notes on b.p.m." gives an excellent picture of how the Inspectorate functions. It consists of two steps. The first step is a series of private consultations with a wide range of organizations, including industry groups, research organizations, various trade union groups, the national Department of Environment, and the Institution of Environmental Health Officers. The purpose of the consultations is to establish the b.p.m. for each category of source. The process is one of consensual negotiation but with the Inspectorate retaining substantial discretion in setting industry standards.

The second phase is the application of industry standards to individual firms. Here the Inspectorate distinguishes between existing firms and new firms entering the industry. Newly established firms and new process units must comply immediately with the b.p.m. for the industry. Existing plants are permitted to engage in gradual retrofitting to meet b.p.m. requirements. This gradual retrofitting is the product of negotiation between the existing firm and the Inspectorate, a negotiation that is also consensual and largely private.

The Inspectorate has come under substantial criticism on several grounds. As Hill observes, "a key ingredient of criticism of the Alkali Inspectorate has been that it is an inaccessible, secretive and uncommunicative organization" (Hill 1982:171). This factor gives rise to the suspicion that the Inspectorate is a captive agency basically controlled by industry. The Inspectorate, however, maintains that enforcement through private negotiation is much more effective than protracted battles through the courts.A second criticism concerns the size of the Inspectorate—a very small body by American standards, consisting of roughly 40 inspectors in the 15 districts. Such a small group, it is maintained, has to rely on public complaints to initiate action, and many forms of air pollution simply escape public detection because they cannot be seen or smelled.

In summary, the British system is based on a negotiated standard-setting process that is largely private. Statutory-based standards are virtually nonexistent. The private nature of the negotiations means also that both politicians and the public are excluded from the process. On the other hand, the regulated interests are closely involved in both standard setting and enforcement. The Inspectorate also seems sensitive to technological possibilities and economic factors in its decision process.

With major differences in both the institutional arrangements and implementation strategies used for ambient air quality, which of the two countries more effectively accomplishes the objective of clean air? Unfortunately, with present data it is almost impossible to carry out a comparative analysis of national programs. Several conclusions can be drawn, however. The first compares nations with "open enforcement systems" and nations with "closed enforcement systems." The authors of a study of European practice concluded: "Evidence from Switzerland and the U.K. suggests that compared to open systems, countries with closed enforcement processes are more likely to achieve a higher degree of compliance with the license conditions formally stipulated. The close cooperative relationships between the agency and emitter, which are not "disturbed" by public participation, may, paradoxically, even lead to environmentally more favorable results in those cases where energy savings for the firm can be realized at the same time" (Knoepfel and Weidner 1982:112). One of the important points to be underscored in this conclusion is the effect of energy savings to the firm. Other countries might learn from the experience of Great Britain by approaching emission abatement from the standpoint of those technologies that would result in energy savings to emitters and those that would not. A second conclusion is that the effectiveness of air quality efforts, whatever the nature of the system, depends heavily on the level of environmental sensitivity in the country. Italy, with a low level of environmental sensitivity, is ineffective in air quality efforts and Switzerland, with a high level, is effective in regulation. The level of environmental consciousness within a nation appears to be a major factor in program effectiveness.

POLLUTION AND WHERE WE LIVE: THE CASE OF INDOOR AIR POLLUTION

Air pollution represents in dramatic form one of the paradoxical elements of pollution—the fact that the associated risks are both global and individual. To be sure, the effects of global developments are felt by individuals also. A thinning of the ozone layer increases the risk of skin cancer to individuals, not to some generalized amorphous entity called "mankind." In addition to global elements with individual effects, indoor air pollution is an important microscale element in the environment of most people.

The U.S. Environmental Protection Agency ranks indoor pollution at the top of the list of 18 different sources that put the American population at risk of cancer. In spite of the fact that American leisure activities tend to be slanted toward outdoor pursuits, some estimates suggest that Americans spend about 90 percent of their time indoors. For most Americans, then, the risks associated with air pollution may be greater indoors than outdoors. Additionally, the UN Environment Programme estimated that the world's population spend an average of 80–90 percent of their time indoors (UN Environment Programme 1988a:81).

The most important sources of indoor pollution are radon, tobacco smoke, biological contaminants, combustion products, household products, formaldehyde, pesticides, asbestos, and lead. Exposure to any one of these sources may involve significant risks. Moreover, the risks increase as a result of the cumulative effects of exposure.

Radon is a pervasive gas found everywhere at very low levels. The most common source of radon in homes is the uranium in the soil or rock on which the home is built. It enters the home through cracks in floors and underpinnings, dirt floors, or floor drains. Since it is both odorless and colorless, radon is difficult to detect even when concentration builds up to the point where it poses a risk. The EPA estimates that about 10 percent, or about 8 million homes, have radon concentrations above acceptable levels. The only health risk that has been definitely linked to concentrations of radon is lung cancer. While estimates vary, between 5,000 and 20,000 lung cancer deaths per year are attributable to radon in the United States.

U.S. policy response to radon was the passage of the Radon Program Development Act of 1988, an amendment to the Toxic Substances Control Act. The program established under the Act was basically informational. The EPA was not given authority either to establish safe levels of radon in homes or to prescribe radon abatement methods through regulation. The EPA's primary informational tool is a publication entitled "A Citizen's Guide to Radon."

Tobacco smoke is a second source of indoor air pollution. It can result both from sidestream smoke, that is, smoke that comes from the burning end of a cigarette or cigar, and from exhaled smoke. The smoke is a complex mixture of over 4,700 gaseous compounds and particulates. The National Academy of Sciences concluded that tobacco smoke is a cause of lung cancer and heart disease in both smokers and nonsmokers who are exposed to smoke. Young children exposed to smoking at home are more likely to be hospitalized for bronchitis and pneumonia than children in nonsmoking homes. American policy response has been limited to the required warnings on cigarettes that the "Surgeon General has determined that cigarette smoking is dangerous to your health." Increasingly, states are passing regulations requiring smoke-free publicly owned buildings and separate space for smokers and nonsmokers in restaurants. The reduction of exposure to environmental tobacco smoke in the home is entirely voluntary. The physical separation of smokers and nonsmokers in a home reduces but does not eliminate the nonsmoker's risk. The same is true of ventilation. The only effective way to eliminate the risk of exposure to environmental tobacco smoke in the home is to eliminate smoking in the home.

Biological contaminants include such things as bacteria, mold, mildew, viruses, animal dander, mites, cat saliva, cockroaches, and pollen. This wide variety of biologicals come from a number of sources. For example, the ducts for central heating systems can become contaminated with mold, mildew and other biologicals and spread the contaminants throughout the house. It is not a nice thing to think about, but the protein in rat urine is a powerful allergen. When it dries, the urine can become airborne and distributed throughout the house by central air moving equipment. Since there is a wide range of biologicals, there is a wide range of health effects. These include various allergic reactions and infectious diseases. Exposure to allergens alone has been estimated to result in 200,000 emergency room visits a year by asthma patients. There has been no public policy response to biologicals in the United States except the information activities of state and local public health agencies.

Combustion products contaminate the home as a result of unvented or improperly vented space heaters, wood stoves, and fireplaces. The most important contaminants are carbon monoxide, nitrogen dioxide, acid aerosols, and particulates. Like radon, carbon monoxide is an odorless, colorless gas. The symptoms of carbon monoxide poisoning are much like those of the flu, including headaches, dizziness, weakness, nausea, and disorientation. At high concentrations, carbon monoxide can cause unconsciousness and death. Nitrogen dioxide increases the risks of respiratory infection and emphysema. Particulate matter can lodge in the lungs and damage lung tissue. Additionally, other contaminants attach to particles and are carried into the lungs. Public policy response to combustion products in the home has been limited to product-specific safety requirements.

Many household products contain organic chemicals. These include cleaners, disinfectants, paints, varnishes, wax, and some hobby products. All of them release organic compounds when they are used and to a lesser degree when they are stored. The most prevalent of these organic compounds are benzene, perchloroethylene, paradichlorobenzene, and methylene chloride. While some organic compounds are highly toxic, little is known about the health effects of organics in the home. As with chemicals in the macroenvironment, Americans are daily exposed to chemicals in the home with little or no guidance regarding risk. About the only public policy response to organic compounds in the home is the requirement of labeling the product.

Formaldehyde is colorless but it certainly is not odorless. It is a pungent-smelling gas that is used widely in the manufacturing of building products. The most common are various pressed wood products such as particle board, plywood, and paneling. Formaldehyde is also a by-product of combustion, including cigarette smoking. It has been shown to cause cancer in animals and is a suspected carcinogen in humans. Elevated levels of exposure can cause difficulty in breathing and asthma attacks. Public policy response to formaldehyde in homes has been limited to building code requirements. The Department of Housing and Urban Development has required the use of low emission formaldehyde products, as have some state and local building regulations.

Pesticides are used widely in homes. The "active" chemicals in the products are designed to kill pests and are obviously dangerous to humans. What is not so widely known is that the "inerts" in pesticides, while not dangerous to pests, carry health risks to humans. For example, methylene chloride is often used as an inert. Many pesticides, such as chlordane used to control termites, remain active for long periods of time. The EPA estimates that 80 to 90 percent of the exposure to pesticides in the air occurs indoors. Measurable levels of a dozen pesticides are commonly found in American homes. More interesting is the fact that the levels of pesticides found inside the home are larger than can be explained by the amount of pesticide use in the home. That means that the pesticides are entering the home from external applications either by floating in or being tracked in from the outside. Pesticides may cause liver damage, damage to the central nervous system, and cancer. The Toxic Substances Control Act (TSCA) has as its primary purpose the identification and control of toxic chemicals that present an unreasonable risk of injury to health or the environment. The Act gives the EPA general regulatory authority over these substances.

Asbestos was used in building materials as an insulation and fire retardant. Exposure to asbestos can cause lung cancer, cancer of the chest lining, and asbestosis, an irreversible and potentially fatal scarring of the lung. The Asbestos Hazard Emergency Response Act of 1986 attempted to control the level of asbestos in schools. Most exposure of adults to asbestos occurs on the job. Public policy response to asbestos on the job has been limited, involving primarily product-specific safety requirements.

The final specific source of indoor air pollution is lead. Humans experience pervasive exposure to lead, since it can be airborne, carried in drinking water, present in food, and ingested through breathing of contaminated dust. Lead is highly toxic and can cause serious damage to the brain, kidneys, nervous system, and red blood cells. It causes physical and mental development problems in young children. Because of the serious nature of these effects, U.S. policy response to lead has been proactive. Before new cars were required to use unleaded gas, the most important source of airborne exposure to lead was automobile exhaust. Various efforts have been made to reduce lead in drinking water and to prohibit the use of lead in household paints.

IS PURE AIR A PURE PUBLIC GOOD?

Public finance literature defines a pure public good as one that is indivisible. As such, if provided for one person, a pure public good is provided for all. The example traditionally used of a pure public good is air.

Changes have occurred that place this traditional position in serious doubt. The most significant of these changes are deterioration in the quality of air and innovations in air cleaning technology. Deterioration in air quality means that ambient air in some areas of the world is unbreathable within acceptable levels of risks. Because of air-cleaning technology, breathable air can be divided, priced, and delivered to some and withheld from others. The oxygen stations in Mexico City are the most dramatic and visible illustrations of this development. Major innovations associated with ionizing equipment allow the entire volume of air in a room to be purified every five minutes. In essence, this development means that breathable air can be divisible and can be provided for some but not others.

Environmental literature has made a distinction between potable water—that suitable for drinking—and nonpotable water—that unsuited for drinking. Is such a distinction needed for air? Should we now begin to distinguish between breathable and nonbreathable air? Given the levels of pollution in some areas, is breathable air divisible, amenable to pricing and selling to some and withholding from others? It would be irony compounded on irony if breathable air cleaned by air purification equipment is all that remains of air as a "pure public good."

Chapter 4

The World's Great Water Systems and the Sources of Their Pollution

Water pollution may be defined as adding more waste to the water system than the system can purify. The world's water supply is relatively constant but the volume of pollutants and demands on that supply are rapidly increasing. On a regional level, at least, the problem with water is one of quantity and quality. With regard to quality, the issue is both to stop additional pollution and to clean up already polluted waters.

Unlike air, water is a single molecule, the formula for which, H_2O, most schoolchildren know. What is not so well-known is that as a single molecule, water accepts pollution easily. This is the case because the absorption rates of water are very high. Only a few substances, such as oil, are not easily absorbed by water. Pollution occurs as a result of the inability of water systems to cleanse themselves or to neutralize the waste. As an example, one of the processes by which water neutralizes waste is to replenish the oxygen content. One of the important measures of water pollution, then, is the depletion rate of oxygen in the water. The biochemical oxygen demand (BOD) is determined by saturating a sample of polluted water with oxygen at 20 degrees centigrade and then analyzing it after five days to determine how much oxygen has been consumed. The amount of oxygen consumed per liter of water is the BOD. If the BOD is high, there is a high level of oxygen-demanding waste.

The world's water system, like its air, is one great interrelated system. Environmental policy has tended to divide this single system into three categories: surface water, groundwater, and the ocean. *Surface water* consists of continental drainage systems that result in the world's great rivers, such as the Mississippi in the United States, the Amazon in South America, the Danube in Europe, the Nile in Africa, and the Ganges in Asia. *Groundwater* is associated with aquifiers or large underground water systems that exist in most parts of the world.

The *ocean* is the ultimate destination of both surface water and groundwater. While the ocean is divided for purposes of geographical study—the Pacific, the Atlantic, and so on—it is in fact one uninterrupted body of water. Therefore, while it is convenient to categorize the earth's water into three great subsystems, it is important to remember their global unity.

Generally, there are two sources of water pollution. *Point sources* are specific identifiable and measurable sources of pollution. These are emitters such as municipal sewage treatment processes, industrial emissions, agricultural emissions, and maritime vehicles. *Nonpoint source pollution* is diffuse and not easily associated with a specific facility or activity. It consists of such things as runoff from the land, roads, and parking lots. In the United States this distinction has been blurred as a result of the practice in most cities of connecting storm drainage systems to sewers; thus point and nonpoint source pollutants are mixed in the release from municipal sewage treatment plants.

It is difficult to estimate accurately the relative contribution of point source and nonpoint source pollutants to water contamination. In the United States the largest volume of water pollution seems to be from nonpoint sources. The Conservation Foundation did a careful study of the contaminants in the nation's streams and lakes and concluded that 84 percent of the phosphates, 88 percent of the nitrates, and 99 percent of the sediments were from nonpoint sources (Arrandale 1992:69). However, water pollution involves a wider range of waste than these three types.

There are eight types of water pollutants. First, there are oxygen-demanding wastes, measured by the BOD. These are various kinds of organic wastes such as animal waste, human waste (sewerage), and food-processing waste. Disease-causing agents are the second type of water pollutants. These are infectious organisms, many of them associated with city sewage and human and animal waste. Plant nutrients, the nitrogen and phosphorous in fertilizer, are the third type. The presence of these pollutants also poses a problem in regard to point versus nonpoint source distinction. Many plant nutrients simply wash off lawns and gardens and are classified as nonpoint source pollutants. Some are associated with specific agricultural applications and are classified as point source pollutants. Fourth are the many synthetic organic chemicals, the most important of which are detergents, pesticides, and industrial chemicals of various kinds. Inorganic chemicals and mineral substances are the fifth type of water pollutants. These consist of a vast array of metallic salts, acids, solid matter, and mineral compounds. The sixth and one of the most common water pollutants is sediment. This is the soil, sand, and minerals that wash into water systems. Sediment is most visible when a stream becomes muddy or stays muddy, as does most of the Mississippi River. Seventh, radioactive substances constitute a type of water pollution. Radioactive wastes come from a number of sources, including mining ore, nuclear reactors, fallout from various sources, and medical and research applications. Finally, thermal pollution is associated with excessive heat. Increasingly, industries and electric power plants that use water as a coolant construct cooling towers to ensure that the heated water returns to normal temperature before release back into a stream.

Water pollution is complicated by the fact that most human-made waste is a mixture of the eight types of pollutants. Municipal waste is an excellent example. Most municipal waste will have at least oxygen-demanding waste, synthetic organic chemicals, inorganic chemicals, and sediment.

In addition to accepting pollution easily, water has another characteristic that is important for public policy. Although water is pervasive, water use is essentially localized. The Great Lakes, for example, contain one-fifth of the earth's surface supply of fresh water and 95 percent of the surface supply of fresh water in the United States. Utilization of this invaluable source of fresh water, however, is localized to the region of the Lakes. In short, there has been little interbasin transfer of water. As a result of the localized utilization patterns, public policy on water quality has been localized. There has been some transnational activity on ocean policy, but relative to the great surface and underground water systems, such activity has been either by national or subnational jurisdictions. There have been a few cross-national efforts, such as the Great Lakes Water Quality Agreement between the United States and Canada.

SURFACE WATER QUALITY AND POLICY

To most people, surface water contamination is what is meant by water pollution. In large part, this thinking is due to the fact that surface water is both very visible and an important part of their lives. The importance of surface water is attested to by the fact that most water resource management plans and policies have dealt with surface water, usually with the objective of ensuring adequate quantity of water for municipal, industrial, and recreational use. Some of these plans have begun to incorporate concern for water quality as well (see, for example, Schmandt, Merdon, and Clarkson 1988). Water quality policy, the essential concern of environmental policy, has been able to draw on the extensive experience with water resource management.

The major problem for both industrial and nonindustrial nations has to do with human waste. Estimates suggest that about 86 percent of the world's rural population (2 billion people) lack an adequate supply of clean water and that 92 percent lack adequate facilities for waste disposal. In the industrialized nations, municipal waste-treatment facilities have relied heavily on surface water systems to disperse the treated effluent. Obviously, the type and effectiveness of the treatment was a major factor in the resultant quality of surface water. Until the 1950s in the United States, and to this day in many parts of the world, industrial plants dispose of a wide range of pollutants through direct release into surface water systems. Additionally, nations do not effectively regulate point source pollutants from agricultural applications.

In the United States the primary legislation dealing with surface water pollution is the Clean Water Act. Originally passed in 1948, the Act has been amended nine times, most significantly in 1972 and 1987. The 1972 amendments are generally referred to as the Federal Water Pollution Control Act Amendments and the 1987 legislation as the Water Quality Act of 1987.

The legislation utilizes technology-forcing standards to accomplish the two basic goals of improving the nation's municipal sewage-treatment plants and reducing industrial effluents to zero discharge. The 1972 legislation provided that there should be zero discharge by 1985 and that all the nation's surface waters should be both fishable and swimmable by 1983. Obviously, both dates have long since passed and the goals have not been realized. Industries were given until 1977 to install "best practicable control technology" to reduce discharge to zero. The 1987 amendments directed industry to install the "best available technology" no later than March 31, 1989, and failure to meet the deadline would expose the industry to enforcement action. The 1972 amendments provided substantial federal funding for the construction of municipal sewage-treatment plants.

The 1987 amendments provided for federal funding through 1994, and transition to full state and local funding responsibility after that date. These amendments contained several other significant provisions as well. One provision added a new dimension to the control of toxic pollutants. In addition to adhering to the standards established by the national legislation, states were required to identify "toxic hot spots" and implement strategies to eliminate them. These hot spots were surface waters that would remain polluted by toxic chemicals even after the implementation of best available control technology. In addition, states were required to establish designated uses for surface water (water supply, recreation, industrial, etc.) and set maximum concentrations for various pollutants for each use. These levels serve as a backup to technology-based levels set by the EPA.

A second significant provision of the 1987 amendments directed states to develop plans for nonpoint source pollution. States were encouraged to address problems of groundwater pollution as a part of their nonpoint source pollution plans. Federal assistance was authorized in the amount of up to 60 percent of the costs of developing these plans.

The chief enforcement tool of the Clean Water Act is the National Pollutant Discharge Elimination System (NPDES) permit. All existing and new industrial and municipal dischargers must obtain permits from the EPA, or from the states whose programs have been certified, before discharging effluents into the nation's streams. Municipalities are required to have in place secondary treatment processes for waste water. Both industry and municipalities are required to maintain a monitoring system for all discharges and to keep records of the results. The permit is issued for five years and must be renewed to allow continued discharge. The EPA may issue a compliance order or bring a civil suit in the U.S. district court against a violator. Individuals also are authorized to bring citizen's suits in the district courts against violators of effluent limits. Individuals may also bring suits against the administrator of the EPA if he or she fails to perform a nondiscretionary duty prescribed by the Act.

A second major piece of legislation aimed at ensuring a safe water supply is the Safe Drinking Water Act. The primary objective of this Act and its five amendments is to control contaminants in the nation's drinking water. The Act directs the administrator of the EPA to promulgate regulations establishing the maximum levels (MCLs) of various contaminants. Regulated contaminants include designated inorganic chemicals, organic chemicals, radionuclides, microbes, and turbidity. The EPA was required to contract with the National Academy of Sciences to study the maximum contaminant level for each of these. The Academy's report, entitled "Drinking Water and Health," is an important reference. The administrator was also to issue guidelines to the states relative to contaminants that affect the odor and appearance of drinking water. These standards are not enforceable at the national level but are dependent on state action.

The Safe Drinking Water Act requires the application of best available technology. However, it provides for variances from the standards under two circumstances. The first is when the nature of the raw water precludes reduction of the contaminants to the maximum allowable level through the best available technology. The second instance is when there are certain compelling reasons, such as cost, for not meeting the standard. In both cases, the application for exemption must include a plan for bringing the system into compliance.

In addition to setting regulations on contaminant levels, the Safe Drinking Water Act provides for protection of underground water. It required the administrator of the EPA to promulgate regulations for underground injection wells, in order to establish minimum standards for the injection of waste in underground wells. It established a permitting system to be implemented by states. No new underground injection would be allowed except those with permits. However, the states could not interfere with the underground injection of brine from oil and gas production, and there is a waiver of both the regulations and permitting requirements when national security interests are at stake. Amendments to the Act in 1986 provided for a significant national grant program to protect underground water sources.

How effective are the Clean Water Act and the Safe Drinking Water Act in ensuring a safe water supply? Obviously, both the interim goal (all waters fishable and swimmable by 1983) and the basic goal (zero discharge by 1985) of the Clean Water Act have not been realized. Several important factors need to be considered in evaluating the effectiveness of American water policy.

The first factor has important implications for technology-forced standards. The Clean Water Act and the Safe Drinking Water Act require the utilization of best practicable control technology or best available control technology, depending on the circumstances of each discharger. The essential issue, then, becomes the effectiveness of technology-based standards. Do current best available and best practicable technology provide adequate protection for water systems? How confident can policy makers and citizens be in technology? A look at municipal sewage-treatment technology will help provide some answers to these questions.

Municipal sewage-treatment technology is divided into two stages. Prior to the Clean Water Act most municipalities used only what is known as primary treatment. This consists of several processes. First the sewage is run through screens to remove large objects such as rats and grapefruit. The sewage is then run through grinders to reduce the remaining large objects to smaller particles necessary for settling. The third step involves settling chambers where the suspended (and ground) solids settle to the bottom. These solids that settle to the bottom are known as *sludge*. Finally, chlorine is pumped into the settling chambers to kill bacteria.

The Clean Water Act required municipalities to utilize secondary treatment also. Either of two methods may be used. In the first method, water from the settling chambers seeps through trickling filters, which consist of stones three to ten feet deep. Bacteria gather on these stones and consume up to 90 percent of the remaining solid matter in the water. The second method of secondary treatment is known as the *activated sludge process*. Waste water is pumped into an aeration tank, where it is mixed with air and bacteria-laden sludge. The bacteria consume solid matter and the air replenishes the oxygen content of the water. On completion of the secondary treatment process, the waste water is either released into a stream or utilized in some other fashion.

Waste water reclamation or reuse has received considerable attention in recent years. In point of fact, all municipal waste water is reused in one fashion or another. When the waste water is returned to the natural hydrologic system, indirect reuse occurs. Indirect reuse has the advantage of various natural processes, such as sunlight, natural biochemical interaction, and dilution, that improve the quality of the water. Direct reuse transmits the waste water directly to some planned use. There is a wide variety of planned uses, and the applications of direct reuse are increasing substantially.

Direct reuse applications can be for either potable (drinking) or non-potable uses. Applications for potable purposes have been limited. In the United States no municipality makes direct use of waste water for potable purposes. Several municipalities have experimented with pilot programs for emergency situations, most notably Chanute, Kansas, and Ottumwa, Iowa. The first application of treated waste water for potable purposes was in Windhoeck, Southwest Africa. Windhoeck developed a one million gallon daily reclamation plant which it brought on line in 1968. During favorable periods the reclaimed water was mixed with water from conventional sources; during unfavorable times the reclaimed water was not utilized. The plant operated until 1971, providing about 13 percent of the city's water needs (Kasperson and Kasperson 1977:41). Israel has a very cohesive and unified plan for water allocation. Its Water Law of 1959 provided for the integration of all aspects of waste use in the country. A National Plan for the reuse of waste water emphasizes use of the treated water in the region in which it was produced. Public acceptance of the plan was high at its inception and appears to remain strong (Feldman 1977:114).

An interesting aspect of the reuse question has to do with the relative risks associated with direct versus indirect use. There are some risks associated with both types. A breakdown in a municipal sewage treatment plant would contaminate water in both cases. Moreover, Windhoeck found that even with the plant functioning normally there were times when the condition of the treated water made reuse unfeasible. Additionally, neither primary nor secondary treatment removes all viruses from water. Special screening devices are required for some viruses. Finally, the wide range of chemical compounds in water are a special problem for reuse.

The most frequent direct reuse application of waste water for nonpotable purposes is for irrigation. Most commonly, treated water is sprayed on land surfaces. This is an important component in the agriculture of a number of arid regions, including Israel with interregional transfers of treated water.

Spray fields appear particularly suited also to tree production, sod farms, and grazing pastures. Lesser uses of waste water include irrigation of some golf courses, parks, and green belts.

A second form of reuse for nonpotable purposes is high-volume water use in industry. The cooling of boilers in the steel, petroleum, and chemical industries are the most common applications.

Recreation is the third nonpotable reuse of treated water. Santee, California, was the pioneer in this reuse. From treated waste water, Santee created four artificial lakes, open to a wide range of recreational activities, including boating and fishing. Swimming was restricted to a pool filled with both reclaimed and conventional water. Problems that developed with the project, including the presence of dissolved solids in the water, led to a cease and desist order from the Health Department.

The fourth and most controversial reuse application for nonpotable purposes is to replenish the groundwater. Groundwater is located in aquifers, or large underground layers of porous rock and sand. Some aquifers are so large they extend over several states. Groundwater levels are dropping and aquifers are being depleted in many areas. The artificial recharge of the groundwater supply is an important and technologically feasible process. Several methods are used. Holding ponds impound the reclaimed water and permit percolation into the groundwater table. Also, surface spreading, particularly at shallow depths so as not to interfere with vegetation, is an efficient way to facilitate percolation to the groundwater table. The third approach, injection wells, pumps the treated waste water directly into the depleted aquifer. The recharged aquifer can then be used as a source of water or as a buffer to prevent salt water incursion. Holding ponds and surface spreading have the advantage of permitting the biochemicals in the soil to remove pollutants from the water. With direct injection wells the waste water is merely diluted with existing water in the aquifer.

In addition to the efficiency of technology, a second factor in an evaluation of water policy has to do with the condition of certain highly endangered fresh water lakes. The case of the Great Lakes is particularly instructive. Described as the "freshwater seas" by the French Jesuits who explored them in the seventeenth century, the Great Lakes contain one-fifth of all the surface fresh water in the world and 95 percent of all surface fresh water in the United States.

Quality of the water in the Great Lakes is monitored by the International Joint Commission, which was created by the Boundary Waters Treaty between the United States and Canada in 1909 and consists of representatives of the two nations. In response to the widespread concern for pollution of the lakes, the United States and Canada signed the Great Lakes Water Quality Agreement in 1972. Under this agreement, significant action has been directed to two of the major sources of contamination: municipal sewage and industrial waste water. The two countries together have spent nearly $9 billion in building and upgrading municipal sewage-treatment facilities.

A 1966 assessment identified five major problems in the Great Lakes (Federal Water Pollution Control Administration 1966): overenrichment, buildup of dissolved solids, bacterial contamination, chemical contamination from industrial releases, and oxygen depletion. Overenrichment accelerates what is known as eutrophication, or "aging" of the lakes. It is simply the process of adding nutrients, primarily nitrogen and phosphorus, to the lakes. In the 1960s nearly all of Lake Erie was eutrophic, leading to the conclusion that it was a "dead lake." Lake Ontario exhibited accelerated eutrophication and the southwestern section of Lake Michigan showed symptoms. The dissolved solids and bacterial concentration problems were linked to inadequacies in municipal water-treatment systems. Chemical contamination can be persistent. The International Joint Commission identified nearly 300 chemical compounds in the Great Lakes, including dioxins, mirex, and PCBs. Moreover, in 1985 the International Joint Commission identified 42 toxic hot spots and designated them as areas of special concern. Hot spots are found on each of the lakes and on both the Canadian and American sides. In all, the 40 million people living in the Great Lakes area seem to be exposed to more toxic chemicals than those in any comparable region of the United States and Canada (Cobb 1987:24).

A third indicator of how well water quality policy is working is the data from the water quality monitoring network in the United States. Important components in that network are various monitoring stations, known as NASQUAN stations, administered by the National Academy of Sciences. Results from the analysis of these data are somewhat encouraging but not promising. The oxygen content of surface waters in the United States has improved; the primary reason seems to be the effort to reduce oxygen-demanding wastes through the construction of municipal and industrial waste facilities. The algae growth in American surface waters does not seem to have improved, however. Algae growth is stimulated by increased levels of nitrogen and phosphorus. In the United States over 80 percent of these pollutants are from nonpoint sources and are thus hard to control. Finally, the NASQUAN data indicate that there has been no increase in heavy metal concentrations in American surface waters. Lead has decreased in a number of surface waters. Taking all these factors into account, a valid conclusion seems to be that some progress has been made in the United States but the overall objectives of the Clean Water Act are far from being realized. Most progress has occurred in the control of point source pollution, particularly municipal oxygen-demanding wastes. Nonpoint source pollution and hot spots in the nation's waters remain serious problems.

The American record, modest as it is, compares favorably with those of other industrialized nations. The Organization for Economic Cooperation and Development (OECD), a multinational organization established by a 1960 treaty, monitors the state of the environment in member countries. Its most recent report was issued January 1991, and several features of that report are instructive.

In OECD countries the oxygen content of surface waters has

improved as measured by BOD. As in the United States, this improvement seems attributable primarily to the attention given to municipal waste facilities. In the Netherlands, for example, stream pollution from oxygen demanding waste was reduced from the equivalent of the sewage from 40 million people to that of 6 million during 1969–1988 (OECD 1991:60). However, algae growth in surface waters has become a major problem in member nations. The increase resulted from nonpoint sources, agriculture fertilizers, and animal manure. With the exception of lead, there was no progress in OECD countries in the reduction of heavy metals in surface waters. For example, France, Western Germany, Luxembourg, the Netherlands, and Switzerland in 1985 discharged 56 tons of chloronitrobezene, 24 tons of cadmium, 500 tons of copper, and 37 tons of chloroanilines into the Rhine River. Finally, the report expressed special concern for the deterioration in the ecosystems of lakes. Sweden reported that 16,000 lakes have been acidified to the extent that sensitive organisms have disappeared and expensive liming programs have had to be put in place. Clearly, as the report indicates, "much remains to be done" with regard to surface water quality (OECD 1991:60).

GROUNDWATER: THE NEW KID ON THE BLOCK

Groundwater is the fresh water beneath the earth's surface. It is located in great underground aquifers occurring in permeable rock, sand, and gravel. Globally, groundwater is ubiquitous but, like surface water, not evenly distributed around the world. Groundwater resources in the United States are enormous. The Water Resources Council has estimated that there are 65 quadrillion gallons or 200 billion acre-feet of groundwater within 2,000 feet of the surface that is recoverable through practical means (Water Resources Council, 1980). Withdrawals of approximately 83 billion gallons a day constitute only a fraction of the potential use. Other nations derive a much higher percentage of water from groundwater. For example, about 80 percent of the tap water supplied in the Netherlands is derived from groundwater (van Duizjvenbooden 1985:93).

Several physical factors are important to know for an understanding of groundwater contamination. The first is that there are two major types of aquifers—confined and unconfined. The unconfined aquifers are not overlain with impermeable material. These are subject to contamination by surface percolation. Confined aquifers are bounded by impermeable material. Some have recharge zones, or areas where water percolates from the surface to the aquifer, when the impermeable rock forms an outcropping at the surface; others have no recharge zone. Since confined aquifers are under great pressure, they are sometimes referred to as *artisian* aquifers. The second physical factor is that the natural quality of groundwater varies significantly depending upon the geological characteristics and climate conditions of the region. Leaching from the soil may affect the acidity of water in aquifiers. Naturally occurring radionuclides may penetrate the aquifer. A common occurrence that renders aquifer water unusable is the presence of high levels of salt from a variety of sources. The final physical factor of aquifiers that is important in regard to contamination is that the water in them has varying rates of movement. In nearly all instances, movement of the water is very slow. It is not uncommon for water in an aquifer to move only a few feet a year.

Considerable progress has been made in identifying the sources of groundwater contamination (National Academy of Sciences 1984). Contaminants generally travel in *plumes*. The migration rates of plumes vary substantially, depending again on a number of geological factors. In a significant number of instances the migration rates are relatively slow, and so the plume will reach an aquifer many years after a contaminant has been released on the land surface or through deep well injection. The amount of the contaminant in the plume that will reach the aquifer also varies according to geological and other considerations. For example, trees are capable of removing some heavy metals from the soil, and percolation over permeable rocks removes other types of contaminants. All of these factors combine to make prediction of the extent of groundwater contamination from any given source a very difficult task.

There are five major sources of groundwater pollution. The first is on-site storage of wastes. In industrialized nations in the past almost every major industrial and agricultural facility disposed of its waste on site. In some instances the practice remains an unavoidable temporary consequence of hazardous waste management as wastes accumulate until they reach the volume sufficient for transport to a disposal facility. On-site storage remains common in many Third World Countries.

Nonpoint and small point sources are a second and very intractable source of groundwater contamination. Nonpoint sources are extremely difficult to track, arising as they do from multiple fertilizer, herbicide, and pesticide applications. Small point sources are such things as septic tanks. When properly installed in soils with good drainage, septic tanks contribute little to groundwater pollution, although some seepage may eventually pollute groundwater. However, the EPA concluded that about one-third of all U.S. septic tanks are improperly installed or are not operating properly (EPA 1980).

A third source of groundwater contamination is found in municipal waste-disposal systems. Municipalities worldwide have disposed of both their solid and sewage wastes in the vicinity of the municipality—whatever the geological conditions. Municipal sewage-treatment facilities are the source of a variety of viruses in groundwater. Little analysis has been conducted on this problem, except on a local level when a health problem has occurred. For a solid waste landfill to be effective against groundwater contamination, it must be located over rocks or clay with low permeability. Even when properly situated, landfills pose a number of problems for groundwater.

The fourth source of groundwater contamination is evaporation ponds. These are used for the disposal of wastes, including a wide range of chemicals, dissolved in water. Linings are often placed in the ponds to prevent leakage, but no liner has been developed that can resist the corrosive effects of chemicals over a long period of time (twenty years).

The fifth source of groundwater contamination, deep well injection of toxic wastes, is considered by many to be a solution to the groundwater contamination problem rather than a source of pollution. For example, deep repositories are often presented as the most technologically feasible method of disposal of high-level nuclear waste. As we shall see later, understanding of this factor is limited and utilization of deep well injection and repositories is accompanied by substantial uncertainty.

Public policy response to groundwater contamination at both the national and multinational level has been late in developing. In the United States the Council on Environmental Quality did not mention groundwater in its reports until 1979. The evolution of groundwater policy in America has resulted in a situation that can only be described as "multiple sources of authority and diffusion of responsibility" (Kenski 1990:60). Thus there is no single statute with the objective of protecting groundwater supplies. Instead, authority for protection of groundwater by national action is found in sixteen different statutes. That authority is dispersed among at least eleven national agencies, and the situation is even more complicated at the state and local levels. Groundwater laws vary substantially between the states. Most states (41) rely on general environmental laws, such as state equivalents to the Clean Water Act, to protect groundwater. The remainder have specific laws designed to establish groundwater policy. As in the national government, 47 states have more than one major agency responsible for groundwater policy (Kenski 1990:87).

What is the effect of this fragmented policy situation? The multiple sources of authority and diffusion of responsibility have created substantial problems in the effort to protect groundwater quality. A report of the National Academy of Sciences concluded that, "one can question whether we have moved very far toward developing a rational strategy of waste disposal that provides long-term protection to society and the environment" (National Academy of Sciences 1984:60). An EPA task force on groundwater suggested that the situation may become worse, for several reasons. Among the most important of these are that both the federal and state laws lack consistency, inconsistent policies lead to confusion among state health and environmental agencies, and coordination and enforcement problems are common (EPA 1983:30). Concern has been voiced regarding the effectiveness of specific statutes. For example, a study of the Safe Drinking Water Act concluded that the Act had failed in its implementation (Feliciano 1987:4). Combining all these evaluations, the best and most balanced position is that groundwater pollution is a serious problem but has not reached a crisis level (Lehr 1985:24).

Both the utilization of and the quality of groundwater vary substantially among OECD countries. Some nations have increased the proportion of their drinking water that is drawn from surface sources. These include Canada, Japan, Norway, Spain, Sweden, and the United Kingdom. While groundwater supply is enormous, it nevertheless is limited, and overuse has caused aquifer depletion in some regions. In many nations, municipal water systems are small and serve essentially rural communities. These systems normally rely on groundwater supplies that require little treatment (OECD 1991:65).

At present there are no international conventions on groundwater, although some conventions do have direct implications for groundwater quality. The most important of these is the Basel Convention on the Control of Transboundary Movements of Hazardous Wastes, signed in 1989. This convention will be discussed in a later chapter.

THE OCEAN: THE WORLD'S ULTIMATE SEPTIC TANK

The ocean is an essential but complex part of the global ecosystem. Most people do not know that the ocean produces roughly the same plant life as do the continents. As a result, it is an important part of the carbon, oxygen, hydrogen, and nitrogen cycles. Additionally, the ocean is in constant interaction with the atmosphere. This interaction has significant, but not fully understood, effects on the earth's weather. The importance of the ocean is captured in the phrase "global regulator," a concept that refers to the capacity of the ocean to absorb carbon dioxide. This absorption is one of the more important elements in controlling earth temperatures.

The complexity of the ocean ecology has produced a fundamental disagreement among scientists about the ocean's capacity to absorb pollutants. On the one hand, there are those who argue that the ocean has an almost limitless capacity to cleanse itself (Isaac 1978:36). In this view, the ocean has been able to absorb and neutralize the wastes that flow into it, with a few exceptions such as PCBs. These analysts also have a strong faith in the capability of marine monitoring systems to identify problems in the ocean (Goldberg 1981:4). On the other hand, there are those who view the ocean as a complex interrelated system that would be put at risk by overloading with wastes. These analysts argue what is known as the "diversity and productivity theory." In their view the ocean is a high diversity system with many species of life bound together in complex interactions. One measure of the health of the system, then, is the number of species present—the higher the number of species, the more productive the system will be. Thus anything that threatens the number of species is a threat to the overall health of the system.

Most public policy on the ocean is based on the second view with its concern for the anticipated effects of contaminants that enter the ocean. This concern was certainly the basis for the marine environmental legislation in the United States in the 1970s (Spiller and Rieser 1986:390) and for the policy response in other countries such as Sweden (Lundqvist 1974:10). It is significant that this anticipatory public policy occurred in an area in which there is substantial disagreement and where environmental degradation has not progressed to a crisis point.

Waste input into the ocean comes from two sources. Most of the wastes are from land-based sources: sewage, industrial discharges, and runoff from agricultural applications. Some contaminants are discharged directly into the ocean by commercial ships and some are transported from distant sources by the atmosphere. Ocean-based sources contribute the remainder of contaminants; these are primarily oil spills, ocean dumping, and offshore energy production. Most of the land-based wastes concentrate in and affect most seriously the coastal zone. The open ocean receives fewer wastes and from more diffuse sources. This distinction is important. The coastal zone is much more sensitive to contaminants and presumptively less able to cleanse itself than the vast open ocean. The coastal zone is the source of much marine life, particularly of commercially important shellfish. It is also the center of most ocean based recreational activities. Public policy has not yet responded adequately to the important difference between contaminants in the coastal zone and contaminants in the open ocean.

The most visible and highly publicized form of ocean pollution is oil pollution. On an average, between 3 and 4 million tons of oil enter the ocean each year. Of this amount 25 percent comes from private use sources—automobile leaks, personal spills, and the like, that wash off the land in nonpoint source fashion and flow to the ocean. An additional 10 percent comes from oil rain. These are hydrocarbons that are released from auto and truck exhausts, reach the clouds, attach themselves to rain, and fall to the ocean. In total, oil rain accounts for approximately 600,000 tons of oil a year. Another 10 percent of the oil entering the ocean comes from natural leaks on the ocean floor. Offshore energy production accounts for another 6 percent.

The major cause of oil pollution of the oceans is marine transportation, accounting for 34 percent of the oil entering the ocean each year. Three types of activities produce most of this pollution. The first is *lightering*, the process of moving oil from large supertankers to smaller ones. The supertankers used to transport oil are too large for most ports, so the oil must be transferred to smaller tankers for unloading. In this process, spills occur routinely although marine monitoring systems do not record the volume of oil lost. "Cleaning out at sea" is a second activity that results in oil pollution. Some of the approximately 50,000 merchant ships and millions of pleasure craft on the ocean "wash out" their bilges at sea or dump their ballast water. Both contain oil. Third, in spite of public perceptions, oil spills account for approximately one-twentieth of ocean oil pollution from marine transportation. Oil spills, nevertheless, are routine—some 15,000 are reported each year. The fact that some spills are catastrophic in their dimensions has produced special public interest and specific public policy responses. The largest single spill involved the ship *Atlantic Express*, which released 276,000 tons of oil off the coast of Tobago. By comparison, the *Exxon Valdez*, familiar to most Americans, released 35,000 tons of oil off the coast of Alaska in 1989.

The United States and Canada have developed the most sophisticated response strategy to oil spills. Known as the National Oil and Hazardous Substances Contingency Plan, this is a multistage strategy. The first stage is containment designed to keep the oil from spreading. Booms or floating barriers are used to keep the oil in place or to act as "herders" to move the pollution from one area to another. The U.S. Coast Guard boom, called the "Open Water Oil Containment System," shoots out into the water like a jack-in-the-box. Exxon's boom is put together in sections.

The second stage in the process is pickup or removal. Unfortunately, there is no effective method for this stage. In one type of effort, skimming, the oil is sucked from the surface with a vacuum; the skimmers are best used in large, open areas. Another method is to pump the oil into the hold of a ship. The U.S. Coast Guard's pump is known as ADAPT (Air Deliverable AntiPollution Transfer System). Also, absorbents are used to soak up oil like a sponge. Different materials are used, including straw, foam, cotton, and shredded paper. Some chemical absorbents are available but disposal is a problem. Removal can occur through several devices. Burning can be used, but it is safe only on the open seas. Sinkage involves pouring powders, such as from brick dust or specially treated sand, on the oil. This too can be used only on the open seas and requires a special permit. Detergents break up the oil into tiny bubbles, which then oxidize and evaporate. The detergent is biodegradable and in time is ingested by bacteria. One of the most intriguing forms of removal is the use of microorganisms. These bacteria are genetically engineered new life forms specially bred to eat oil. In 1980 the U.S. Supreme Court approved a patent for a special bacteria that can digest four components of oil at the same time; previous bacteria could digest only one component of oil.

The final stage of the strategy for dealing with oil spills is the storage or disposal of the dispersants and absorbents used in the cleanup. Again there is simply no effective way to accomplish this task. The most widely used means, burying the material, is the worst possible way. Oil residues on the absorbents do not decompose. Burning is also discouraged but is utilized. Land spreading remains as the most feasible; the oil-soaked materials are spread on the ground and allowed to rot.

One of the major problems in marine transportation is associated with the practice known as the *flag of convenience*. Most tankers and merchant ships are registered in the most convenient country. The most convenient countries are those with lax ship construction standards, minimal safety standards, and the like. Panama and Liberia are the world's "most convenient" flags. The United States has passed regulations denying entrance to American ports to some of the most flagrant violators of construction and safety standards.

While oil spills are the most publicized form of ocean contamination, sewage constitutes the largest volume of pollution discharged into the ocean. The problem is global. The most polluted regions of the ocean are contiguous to India, Pakistan, Bangladesh, Thailand, Malaysia, Indonesia, and the Philippines (UN Environment Programme 1988). In OECD countries there has been a trend toward increased treatment of sewage but with important variations among the member countries (OECD 1991:73). Many OECD countries reported continued closures of shellfish harvest and swimming areas as a result of contamination by sewage wastes. In the United States the National Oceanic and Atmosphere Administration reported that treatment plants discharged 3.3 trillion gallons of sewage into the ocean in 1980 and estimated that the volume will rise to 5.4 trillion gallons by 2000 (Morganthan 1988:45). Since there are densely populated cities on the American coast, about 35 percent of all treated municipal sewage is discharged into ocean waters. Many of these cities are also located on some of the nation's best-known bays and harbors, which are, as a result, badly polluted. Boston Harbor received considerable political attention in 1988 as one of the most polluted areas in the nation. The New York City harbor receives the city's sewage, about 1.7 billion gallons a day, during periods of heavy rain. The city's sludge, 8 million tons a year, is deposited in the Atlantic Ocean about 106 miles offshore. Only the United States and Great Britain currently dump significant quantities of sewage sludge at sea (World Resources Institute 1987:131). Public health authorities in coastal states regularly close shellfish harvesting and swimming beaches that exceed acceptable levels of contamination (see the map in *Time*, August 1, 1988, p. 50).

Sewage, along with agricultural applications and industrial discharges, has contributed to increased levels of nitrogen and phosphorous in the ocean. These compounds serve as nutrients for algae that have proliferated in many areas. The "red tide" that periodically appears in Japan's ocean waters is a form of algae. These algae both reduce the level of oxygen in the water, literally suffocating fish, and produce a form of toxin which makes shellfish unsuitable for human consumption. "Dead zones" have begun to appear in many areas of the ocean. A massive fish kill of fluke and flounder (one million) occurred in the Raritan Bay in New Jersey as the fish were trapped in dead water. A 300-mile-long and 10-mile-wide dead zone drifted in the Gulf of Mexico in 1988 (Toufexis 1988:46).

Many analysts believe that the major long-term threat to the ocean is from land-based chemical discharges. Various chemical compounds have increased concentrations in the ocean. These include DDT, PCBs, chlordane, toxaphene, lindande, dieldrin, and tributyltin. These compounds enter the ocean through industrial discharges, agricultural applications, municipal waste water, and atmospheric deposition. Such pollutants from the Rhine River are affecting the seal population in the Wadden Sea of the Netherlands. In the United States, Commencement Bay, on which Tacoma, Washington, is situated, is so polluted that the EPA has designated the area a superfund site. Elliot Bay, on which Seattle sits, is polluted with copper, lead, arsenic, zinc, cadmium, and PCBs. Exacerbating such problems is the fact that the wind transports these chemical compounds and distributes them globally regardless of origin.

Radionuclides enter the ocean from human sources and a much higher level from natural sources. One of the most controversial uses of the ocean is for the depositing of radionuclides. The United States, Japan, and some Western European countries have engaged in ocean dumping of radioactive waste since 1940. In total, approximately 90,000 tons of nuclear wastes were deposited in the ocean in 1983 (OECD 1985:79). The London Dumping Convention of 1972 prohibited the depositing of high-level nuclear waste in the ocean. A moratorium on the dumping of intermediate- and low-level waste was declared in 1983 and extended indefinitely in 1985. Airborne radionuclides originate from a number of sources including atmospheric testing of nuclear weapons, industrial facilities, research laboratories, and the weapons industry. Additionally, there is naturally occurring radiation; some of it is similar to background radiation on the continents and the rest is from atmospheric deposition from a variety of sources.

Litter has become an increasing problem in the ocean all over the world. Convenience packaging items, fishing gear, and raw plastics are the most common forms of pollution. Commercial ships discharge an estimated 6 million metric tons of litter each year. Recreational use of beaches accounts for much more. A national beach cleanup in the United States in 1988 yielded over 907 tons of litter, 62 percent of which was plastic (OCED 1991:79). Plastic litter has washed up on beaches even in remote areas of the Arctic and South Pacific. Commercial and recreational fishing account for substantial fishing gear litter. While the real figure may be much higher, 5,000 animals are known to have been caught in fishing gear off the Norwegian Coast in 1987. In the North Pacific 3,000 northern fur seals are estimated to die each year as a result of being entangled in discarded or lost fishing gear. Public policy response to contamination of the oceans from all sources has been largely anticipatory in nature. There are various international conventions, regional conventions, and national laws establishing policy for the protection of the ocean.

International law has addressed the problem of ocean pollution. The UN Convention on the Law of the Seas, adopted in 1982, defines pollution of the oceans as "the introduction by man, directly or indirectly, of substances or energy into the marine environment, including estuaries, which results or is likely to result in such deleterious effects as harm to living resources and marine life, hazards to human health, hindrance to marine activities, including fishing and other legitimate uses of the sea, impairment of quality for use of sea water and reduction of amenities" (Kiss 1991). The first convention addressing the problem of marine pollution was the Convention for the Prevention of Pollution of the Sea by Oil, adopted in 1954. However, the reach of this convention was very narrow, limited to deliberate discharges in specified sensitive zones. The first attempt at a comprehensive convention was the United Nation's Conference on the Law of the Sea in 1973. Considerable support existed for declaring the seas the "common heritage of mankind" and making them manageable by an international body. However, the result of the conference was substantially more modest. The participating nations failed to agree on a comprehensive treaty. Instead, the 1982 Convention on the Law of the Sea declared only the deep seabeds a "common heritage" and specified that all nations should benefit from deep seabed resources. Participating nations were also split on the issue of how those resources would be exploited. The Convention provides for mining under the supervision of an International Seabed Authority, but several major seabed mining nations, including the United States, the United Kingdom, and West Germany, rejected the Authority proposal and have enacted legislation to provide for national control of seabed mining. Additionally, the treaty established Exclusive Economic Zones, giving a nation complete economic sovereignty over the ocean within 200 miles of its coast. This provision effectively eliminates the possibility of uniform regulation of fisheries. As if trying to compensate for this decision, the treaty provides that nations are responsible for protecting their ocean resources in the common good of humanity.

The most effective convention, the International Convention for the Prevention of Pollution from Ships, attempts to control vessel source pollution. Known as MARPOL, the Convention was adopted in 1973. It sets minimum distances from land for the dumping of sewage, garbage, and toxic waste from commercial ships. It establishes limits on the amount of oil discharged from ships. An annex to the Convention, adopted in 1989, prohibits the dumping of plastics in the ocean and sets limits on other types of wastes. However, military ships were exempt from the prohibition on plastics disposal. Some nations, including the United States, require their military to comply with the annex. Most analysts are in agreement that MARPOL has been a factor in reducing the levels of discharge into the ocean.

The discharge of other types of pollutants was addressed by the London Dumping Convention of 1973, which banned the discharge of heavy metals, petroleum products and carcinogens, including radionuclides, into the sea. The Convention put specific limits on lead, cyanide, and pesticides, and discharge of these substances is allowed on a permit basis only.

The largest body of international law on marine pollution is based on various conventions entered into by nations on a regional basis. Some of these conventions deal with only one type of pollution. Examples are the Bonn Agreement for Cooperation in Dealing with Pollution of the North Sea by Oil adopted in 1969, the 1972 Oslo Convention for the Prevention of Marine Pollution by Dumping from Ships and Aircraft, and the 1976 Paris Convention for the Prevention of Marine Pollution from Landbased Sources. Other regional conventions attempt a comprehensive control of marine pollutants. The best example is the 1974 Helsinki Convention on the Protection of the Marine Environment of the Baltic Sea Area. A third regional approach is referred to as the regional seas program. This program, begun in 1974 under the auspices of the United Nations Environment Programme, attempts to set general principles of pollution control and leave the detailed regulations of specific sources to separate protocols. The first such effort was the 1976 Convention for the Protection of the Mediterranean Sea against Pollution. Subsequent protocols established regulations with regard to ocean dumping, oil pollution, and other types of hazards. With the Mediterranean Plan as a model, other regional seas programs were adopted, including the 1978 Persian Gulf and the Gulf of Oman, the 1981 Gulf of Guinea, the 1981 Caribbean and Gulf of Mexico, 1982 Red Sea and the Gulf of Aden, and the 1986 South Pacific plans. More than 120 nations are participants in the plans.

A final element of international law on marine pollution is various bilateral conventions, agreements entered into by two nations. For example, much of the technology and process relating to oil spills are a part of a 1974 agreement between the United States and Canada. Most bilateral conventions have topics such as fisheries or aquaculture that are indirectly related to the environment.

In addition to the international effort to control the pollution of the seas, there have been significant national actions to prevent marine pollution. The United States has the most extensive network of such domestic regulations in effect, with thirteen pieces of legislation: the Coastal Zone Management Act (1972), the Deepwater Ports Act (1972), the Marine Mammal Protection Act (1972), the Marine Protection Research and Sanctuaries Act (1972), the Federal Water Pollution Control Act Amendments (1972), the Endangered Species Act (1973), the Deep Water

Port Act (1974), the Fisheries, Conservation, and Management Act (1976), the Outer Continental Shelf Lands Act (1978), the National Ocean Pollution Research and Monitoring Act (1978), the Deep Seabed Hard Mineral Resources Act (1980), the American Fisheries Promotion Act (1980), and the Ocean Thermal Energy Conversion Act (1980). Several common threads run through all these acts (King 1986: 302). The first is that these laws were anticipatory in nature. That means that they tried to prescribe in advance a policy for conditions determined by analysts to lead to depletion, destruction, or scarcity of marine resources. The legislative records of these acts reflect "a clear bias toward the future" (King 1986:308). The second common thread is a concern for the ocean as a resource. The intent of the legislation was to ensure a supply of energy and raw materials for the future. Thus the future orientation of policy makers was directed not so much toward environmental quality or the ecosystem as toward economic objectives.

In addition to national legislation, U.S. states have taken initiatives to conserve the marine environment. Eleven of the 23 coastal states have adopted laws to prohibit some uses of nonbiodegradable plastics. Chesapeake Bay states are a good example of other efforts; Maryland, Pennsylvania, Virginia, and the District of Columbia signed an agreement in 1987 to limit the amount of runoff and point source discharge into the Chesapeake Bay. Individual state programs are also important. The state of Washington has an ambitious program to clean up pollution along its shoreline. The state established the Puget Sound Water Quality Authority, which has developed plans for reducing commercial, urban, and agricultural discharge. A cigarette tax provides revenue for the program.

Subnational action has occurred in other countries as well. In Germany, Schleswig Molstein adopted a plan for the protection of the Baltic Sea. The plan required that municipal sewage and point source effluents be free of phosphates by 1991. Sewage facilities must eliminate nitrates from their waste water by 1996 (*The German Tribune*, Sept. 18, 1992, p. 9).

Given this policy response, is there an overall threat to the ocean? This question brings us back full circle: The ocean is a complex biotic system with adaptation capacities that are little known by scientists. Additionally, monitoring of the marine environment is of recent origin (National Research Council 1990). Responsibility for marine monitoring in the United States is fragmented among several agencies, including the EPA, the National Oceanic and Atmospheric Administration, the Army Corps of Engineers, and the Minerals Management Service of the Department of Interior. Authority for marine monitoring is scattered through 25 legislative acts. This fragmentation has produced substantial problems. The National Research Council concluded that "the lack of communication and coordination among the entities sponsoring or conducting monitoring and making environmental management decisions inhibits the proper design of monitoring programs and limits the usefulness of monitoring results" (1990:15). This fact, along with other inadequacies in the monitoring program, makes it very difficult to arrive at conclusions relative to the overall health of the marine environment.

As with most other environmental problems, then, there is considerable uncertainty relative to the situation. There are indicators that substantial problems exist. The ocean is seriously polluted in some specific locations, as the dramatic map of ocean pollution with closed beaches and fisheries attests. Additionally, there are some sporadic general problems, such as the "red tide" in the Pacific. On the other hand, there are grounds for optimism. One of the most important of these has to do with the anticipatory nature of marine policy. This is one of the few environmental areas in which instruments of policy at all levels are based in a concern for the intergenerational effects of environmental degradation. It may be the only area in which American environmental policy reflects a conscious choice of future quality over present value. The environmental policy area needs more such actions.

Chapter 5

Chemical Dependency and Environmental Degradation

Modern urban industrial societies are characterized by chemical dependency. The numbers are staggering. This is true in part because the number of distinct chemical compounds that can be formulated is limited only by the imagination of inventors. And the data suggest that the imagination of chemists is active. The American Chemical Society's list of new chemical compounds is growing at a rate of more than 5,000 weekly. Of this number, about 1,500 new chemicals are introduced commercially each year. There are now over 4 million chemicals registered in the United States, and approximately 70,000 of them in regular use. They are produced by over 120,000 firms whose output represents about 8 percent of the gross national product. The 70,000 chemicals in regular use are found in every sector of American society. Most households, for example, are not conscious of the extraordinary range of chemicals that are involved in the normal routines of the home.

   This extraordinary use of chemicals results in substantial waste. Combining all sources of chemical wastes, one ton of chemical hazardous waste is created every year for each American. In total, the United States produces over 260 million metric tons of chemical hazardous waste each year. However, this is not distributed evenly over the country. Louisiana (3.2), West Virginia (2.8), Tennessee (2.6), and Texas (2.2) are the leaders in tons per person. South Dakota (.5), Arizona (.4), Hawaii (.4), and Alaska (.2) produce the smallest amount of hazardous waste per person.

Unfortunately, there are no reliable data on how much chemical hazardous waste is produced worldwide. Some estimates place the world figure at 375 million metric tons a year. Another estimate, however, projects nearly 500 million tons for only nineteen countries (Sadik 1988:12). Whatever the volume, the utilization of chemicals and the accompanying waste are a pervasive part of the global environment.

CHEMICAL RESIDUALS AND THE TIME HORIZON

Chemical hazardous waste policy is characterized by a high cultural discount rate. In nearly all societies, present consumption is valued more highly than future environmental quality.

One of the most important effects of a high cultural discount rate is upon risk assessment. It results in a limited effort to assess risk and a willingness to accept high levels of risk. Thus in the chemical hazardous waste area a very limited effort has been made to determine risk. To put the matter as succinctly as possible, data are not available on the toxic effects of many chemicals. The National Research Council estimates that the toxic effects of 80 percent of chemicals in use are not known (National Research Council 1984). As few as 2 percent of all chemicals have been rigorously tested for their toxicity. This neglect is due in part to the almost compulsive drive to increase the number of chemicals in use. In addition, the problem has a snowballing effect—the large number of chemicals in use poses a special problem relative to the assessment of risk. Testing of many chemicals is complicated and expensive. Toxicity tests often require extended time, particularly those to determine the effect of prolonged exposure. The high cultural discount rate means that societies will commit neither the resources nor the time necessary to assess risk. Therefore, humans are exposed to a pervasive and personal hazard from chemical substances with little guidance as to the risks associated with that exposure.

An extraordinary range of potential health risks are associated with exposure to toxic wastes. These are summarized in Table 5.1. The effects are divided into short term, intermediate term, and long term. The table demonstrates one of the paradoxical aspects of chemical hazardous waste policy—the fact that the effects are often simultaneously immediate and long term.

A second result of a high cultural discount rate is to create substantial uncertainty relative to the objectives of policy. In other words, a high cultural discount rate produces substantial uncertainty in the production function. Viewed on a multinational basis, there are two broad objectives or production functions in the hazardous waste management area. The first involves the reduction of the amount of waste that is produced. Waste reduction is the primary strategy utilized in Europe. The second broad management objective involves the reduction of the hazard associated with waste, whatever level is generated. Hazard reduction is the primary strategy in the United States. Cross-nationally, then, major differences exist in policy approach.

Table 5.1   Notations Used to Specify the Health Effects of Exposure to Toxic Chemicals

Short-Term Effects

ALR	Allergenic—systemic reaction such as might be experienced by individuals sensitized to penicillin.
BPR	Blood pressure effects—any effect that changes any aspect of blood pressure away from normal—increased or decreased.
CNS	Central nervous system—includes effects such as headaches, tremor, drowsiness, convulsions, hypnosis, anesthesia.
GIT	Gastrointestinal tract effects—diarrhea, constipation, ulceration.
IRR	Irritant effect—any effect on the skin, eye, or mucous membrane.
MMI	Mucous membrane effects—irritation, hyperplasia, ciliary activity changed.
SKN	Skin effects—such as erythema, rash, sensitization of skin, petechial hemorrhage.

Intermediate-Term Effects

BCM	Blood-clotting mechanism—any effect that increases or decreases clotting time.
COR	Corrosive effects—burns, desquamation.
CVS	Cardiovascular effects—such as increased or decreased heart activity from an effect on ventricle or auricle; fibrillation; or dilated or constricted arterial or venous system.
TFX	Toxic effects—used to introduce the principal organ system affected as reported or the pathology.

Long-Term Effects

BLD	Blood effects—effect on all blood elements, electrolytes, pH, protein, oxygen-carrying or oxygen-releasing capacity.
CAR	Carcinogenic—producing cancer—a cellular tumor, the nature of which is fatal or is associated with the formation of secondary tumors (metastasis).
CUM	Cumulative effect—substance is retained by the body in greater quantities than it is excreted, or the toxic effect is increased in severity by repeated bodily insult.
DDP	Drug dependence—any indication of addiction or dependence.
EYE	Eye effects—irritation, diplopia, cataracts, eye ground, blindness by effects on the eye or the optic nerve.
GLN	Glandular effects—any effect on the endocrine glandular system.
MSK	Musculo-skeletal effects—such as osteoporosis, muscular degeneration.
MUT	Mutation or mutagenic—transmissible changes produced in the offspring.
NEO	Neoplastic effect—the production of tumors.
PNS	Peripheral nervous system effects.
PUL	Pulmonary system effects—effects on respiration and respiratory pathology.

RBC   Red blood cell effects—includes the several anemias.

SYS   Systemic effects—effects on the metabolic and excretory function of the liver or kidneys.

TER   Teratogenic effects—nontransmissible changes produced in the offspring.

WBC   White blood cell effects—effects on any of the cellular units other than erythrocytes, including any change in number or form.

Unspecified Effects

UNS   Unspecified effects—the toxic effects were unspecified in source.

A CROSS-NATIONAL VIEW: CHEMICAL WASTE POLICY IN THE UNITED STATES AND EUROPE

Public policy response to chemical residuals varies widely between the United States and Europe. We will examine this response, beginning with the experience in the United States.

The United States: Fragmented and Contradictory Waste Policy

American public policy attempts to control the total hazardous waste stream. The objective is to ensure an environmentally benign production, utilization, and disposal of chemical residuals. However, American chemical residual policy is fragmented among several important statutes, and responsibility for policy is dispersed among several agencies and levels of government. This fragmentation results in important contradictions in American policy and considerable doubt about policy effectiveness.

The first effort at controlling toxic wastes was the Federal Insecticide, Fungicide, and Rodenticide Act of 1947. The objective of this Act was to control the use of pesticides in agricultural applications by requiring the registration of labels. Before a pesticide could be marketed, it had to be "registered," that is, a decision had to be made as to what uses were safe and at what levels of application. Pesticides that were highly toxic, that were persistent in the environment, or that posed risks to nontarget organisms were denied registration. The standard to be used in the registration decision was the finding of "no unreasonable adverse effects" from use of the pesticide. The Act was completely rewritten in 1972, to update both standards and implementation procedures.

Two important components of American policy were legislated in 1976. These are the Toxic Substances Control Act and the Resource Conservation and Recovery Act. TSCA's primary thrust is toward the identification and control of toxic substances, and RCRA establishes a hazardous waste management program.

Since most chemicals, including many in widespread use, have not been tested for their toxicity effects, the Toxic Substances Control Act established a process for testing chemicals. It created an Interagency Testing Committee to assist the EPA in determining which chemicals should be tested. Additionally, EPA was given rather general regulatory authority over chemical hazards, including the prohibition of the manufacture of chemicals, restrictions on their use, limitation on the volume of production or concentration of use, the requirement of proper notification to consumers (such as labeling), and certain controls over disposal methods. The standard guiding this regulatory activity is the prevention of "an unreasonable risk of injury to health or the environment."

The Resource Conservation and Recovery Act of 1976 is actually an amendment to the Solid Waste Disposal Act of 1965. The Act is so comprehensive, however, that it is generally considered separate legislation from the SWDA. The RCRA attempts to regulate the entire "waste stream." Producers of hazardous waste must comply with regulations regarding record keeping, reporting, the labeling of wastes, the use of appropriate containers, the provision of information on the waste chemical composition, and the use of a manifest system. The manifest system, which is also required of transporters of hazardous waste, provides a tracking system for the waste from point of origin to the disposal facility. EPA's regulatory authority over treatment, storage, and disposal facilities is exercised through a permitting system. The operating procedures, accident response plans, and closure techniques of such facilities are regulated.

Following the partial preemption strategy of implementation, the RCRA authorizes states to carry out their own programs. States must meet three criteria. First, they must develop a regulatory program equivalent to the national program. The assumption of equivalency means "equal to" or "greater than," so a state program may contain more stringent regulations than those of the EPA but not less stringent. Second, a state's program must be consistent with the federal and state programs applicable in other states. Presumably, the EPA administrator would exercise discretion against a state only when the conflict posed substantive problems in program administration. Finally, a state program must reflect adequacy of enforcement. Most states have received authorization to operate the elements of the program contained in the RCRA.

The next statute that is an important component of U.S. hazardous waste policy is the Comprehensive Environmental Response, Compensation, and Liability Act of 1980 (CERCLA), commonly referred to as the Superfund. It authorizes the national government to respond to releases of hazardous substances. Such substances are given the broadest of definitions as any threat to the health of "any organism." However, EPA is to give priority to those substances that threaten public health or drinking water.

The National Contingency Plan, developed by the EPA to implement response to hazardous sites, established a response strategy that consists of two types of actions. The first is the short-term removal of hazardous substances. This strategy is designed for emergency situations where the release poses a health or safety risk or threatens to contaminate a water supply. The second strategy involves long-term cleanup efforts, at sites that the EPA finds to be the most serious hazards. These sites are placed on the National Priority List, which the EPA constructs utilizing such standards as the quantity and nature of the hazardous materials, the likelihood of their contaminating a water source, and the proximity of the release to population centers or sensitive natural environments. The National Priority List contains about 1,200 sites.

The arrangements for payment of cleanup efforts and the role of state governments are important features of the Plan. To pay for the cleanup, CERCLA established the Superfund. Money for the Fund is raised primarily by taxes on crude oil and on 42 selected chemicals. The corporate environmental income tax is a new approach to funding environmental programs; the rate is 0.12 percent of taxable income in excess of $2 million.

In addition to the tax, the income derived from recoveries from parties responsible for the hazard is an important but highly controversial aspect of the Fund.

CERCLA defines the liability of responsible parties and makes provisions for financial compensation. The general rule is that any owner, operator, generator, or transporter of hazardous waste is liable for cleanup costs and environmental damage for the release of hazardous substances. Owners and operators of vessels and facilities are required by the Act to show evidence of financial responsibility, either in the form of insurance or by participation in "risk retention groups" for self-insurance. Both cleanup costs and EPA's enforcement costs are collectable.

Several features of the liability provisions have sparked intense controversy. The most controversial is the assignment of liability on the basis of status rather than conduct. In other words, owners, operators, generators, or transporters of hazardous waste can be liable even though their action contributed nothing to the release. In additional, such individuals or firms may be liable retroactively. As a result, a purchaser of a contaminated site incurs cleanup liability. The claim, then, is that placing a site on the Superfund list effectively freezes the sale of that property. While the Superfund list currently contains about 1,200 sites, about 30,000 have been identified as potential Superfund sites. It is common practice now for the sale of commercial property to include sale contract and deed provisions relative to the presence of hazardous waste on the site. The third controversial feature of the liability provisions is the assignment of "joint and several liability." This means that all parties involved in the handling of hazardous waste are liable jointly and individually for damages from releases. The claim is that the EPA has manipulated this provision by negotiating a settlement with one party as a means of forcing another party to settle; it is true that EPA may release a party from future liability as a part of a settlement agreement. Finally, it is claimed that the assignment of liability is enormously complex, expensive, and time consuming. Potentially responsible parties challenge the EPA at every step in the process. As a result, the process is characterized by substantial litigation.

There are both general and specific standards that cleanup efforts must meet. The general standards require that the cleanup must protect the public health and the environment and be cost effective in both the long and short term. The specific standards are the recommended maximum contaminant levels in the Safe Drinking Water Act and the Clean Water Act's water quality standards. It is generally agreed that the specific standards become the operative ones when a cleanup is actually undertaken.

Two other acts round out the American experience with hazardous waste management policy. The first is the Hazardous Materials Transportation Act of 1975, which gives the Department of Transportation broad authority to regulate the transportation of hazardous materials. The materials subjected to regulation are those defined in the RCRA. The primary enforcement tool is the classification of waste and the establishment of procedures for safely transporting each category. Since most hazardous waste is disposed of in commercial waste management facilities, most generators will be subject to the HMTA.

The final act is the Medical Waste Tracking Act of 1988, which was partially a response to medical waste washing up on the shores of the eastern United States in the late 1980s. The Act established a pilot tracking program for the identification, transportation, and management of medical waste, including cultures and stocks of infectious agents, human pathological wastes, human blood and blood products, sharps that were used in animal or patient care, contaminated animal wastes, wastes from humans who are in isolation, and unused sharps. The two-year pilot program was conducted in Connecticut, New Jersey, New York and the states bordering the Great Lakes. The presumption was that final regulations applicable to all medical providers would be issued at the conclusion of the pilot project.

The experience of EPA with these statutes demonstrates the highly contradictory nature of U.S. policy toward hazardous waste. One source of this contradiction is found in the problem of defining chemical hazardous waste. Particularly in the RCRA, Congress established a statutory definition that was extremely broad and qualitative:

The term *hazardous waste* means a solid waste, or combination of solid wastes, which because of its quantity, concentration, or physical, chemical, or infectious characteristics may: (A) cause, or significantly contribute to, an increase in mortality or an increase in serious, irreversible, or incapacitating reversible, illness; or (B) pose a substantial present or potential hazard to human health or the environment when improperly treated, stored, transported, or disposed of, or otherwise managed. (RCRA, Sect. 1004)

Because of the broad scope of this definition, important decisions have to be made before a given material is defined as hazardous waste.

The first phase in the definition of hazardous waste is to decide whether or not the waste is solid waste. Hazardous waste in U.S. policy is only solid waste; if a material is not a solid waste, it is not hazardous whatever its characteristics might be. While the definition of solid waste is very broad, there are important exceptions to this definition, as we will see below. The second phase in the definition process is to determine if the material is a *waste*. This is not an easy determination to make (Wagner 1990:11). The decision hinges on actions taken to discard the material. A material is waste if actions have been taken to dispose of, burn, accumulate, store, treat, or recycle it. The third phase in defining hazardous waste is to determine whether or not the material is a *listed hazardous waste*. Listed wastes are defined as hazardous on the basis of certain criteria established by the EPA. It must be determined whether the material (1) is ignitable, corrosive, reactive, or toxic, (2) is fatal to humans in low doses, is acutely toxic to animals, or causes irreversible health problems, or (3) contains any constituent material listed in the EPA regulations. A listed waste always remains hazardous whatever its subsequent treatment unless it is delisted. Further, listed wastes are deemed hazardous whatever the level of hazardous constituents found in them. The final phase of definition is the determination of *characteristic waste*. A material that is not in the listed waste category may nevertheless be hazardous if tests show that it exhibits certain characteristics. Thus characteristic wastes require testing of the specific material. In summary, this complex process for defining hazardous waste is the source of considerable contradiction in U.S. hazardous waste policy.

One of the most important contradictions resulting from the definition process is the large number of materials exempted from the definition of hazardous waste. Wagner (1990) has identified three sets of exemptions. First are those materials excluded from the definition of solid waste. Some important materials are in this group. Materials classified as "domestic sewage" are excluded both by the RCRA and EPA regulations; the RCRA specifically excludes solid or dissolved material in domestic sewage and EPA regulations exclude untreated sanitary waste. The EPA estimates that approximately 300 million metric tons of waste are discharged annually under the untreated sanitary waste exclusion. Other materials not defined as solid waste include industrial point source discharges regulated under the Federal Water Pollution Control Act, irrigation return flows, radioactive wastes regulated under the Atomic Energy Act, mining wastes that are not removed from the site, certain chemicals used in the pulpmaking process in the paper industry, spent sulfuric acid, and secondary materials that are returned to the original process.

The second set of materials exempt from regulation are wastes that are not defined as hazardous. Wastes generated by a household are excluded regardless of quantity or characteristics. Furthermore, "household" is taken to mean not only private residences but hotels, motels, and recreational areas. This exclusion, then, covers hundreds of commercial products used regularly that can cause serious environmental problems. Other wastes not defined as hazardous include agricultural wastes that are returned to the soil as fertilizers, mining waste that is returned to the mine site, and discarded wood materials that fail toxicity tests.

The third category of exclusions is wastes that are managed in accordance with specific requirements. The major examples here involve small-quantity generators and farmers. Small quantity generators are those who produce less than 100kg of nonacutely hazardous waste a month. Such a generator is excluded if the materials are handled in the specified manner. Farmers are excluded if they dispose of the pesticide on their own farm in accordance with labeling instructions. The sum of all three categories of exceptions is a significant amount of hazardous material.

Relative to implementation, hazard reduction strategies concentrate on reducing the level of risk, whatever the volume of waste generated. Table 5.2 summarizes the most important factors associated with the two methods of hazard reduction: treatment and disposal. Several factors relative to each method need comment.

The United States places major reliance on land disposal of hazardous waste, either in injection wells or landfills. The Office of Technology Assessment estimates that up to 80 percent of hazardous waste generated in the United States is land disposed (1983:80). About 25 percent of the U.S. total is disposed of through deep well injection, that is, the injection of liquid waste into subsurface rock formations. The liquid waste is pumped into the well under sufficient pressure to displace the natural liquids and gases present in the porous rock. Some injection zones are at a depth below underground sources of drinking water (Class I wells) while some are above underground sources of drinking water (Class IV wells). The majority of wells are those that were used for oil and gas production (Class II wells) or for mining (Class III wells). When the well has reached capacity or injection operations have stopped, the well is sealed. This plugging usually involves pouring cement into various sections of the well. The number and location of the plugs differ from state to state. Considerable disagreement exists on the optimum technology.

Table 5.2   Alternative Hazard Reduction Strategies

	Disposal	
	Landfills and impoundments	Injection wells
Effectiveness: How well it contains or destroys hazardous characteristics[a]	Low for volatiles, questionable for liquids; based on lab and field tests	High based on theory, but limited field data available
Reliability issues	Siting, construction, and operation Uncertainties: long-term integrity of cells and cover, liner life less than life of toxic waste	Site history and geology; well depth, construction and operation
Environmental media most affected	Surface and groundwater	Surface and groundwater
Least compatible waste[b]	Liner reactive; highly toxic, mobile, persistent, and bioaccumulative	Reactive; corrosive; highly toxic, mobile, and persistent
Costs: Low, moderate, high	L–M	L
Resource recovery potential	None	None

	Treatment		
	Incineration and other thermal destruction	Emerging high-temperature decomposition	Chemical stabilization
Effectiveness: How well it contains or destroys hazardous characteristics	High; based on field tests, except little data on specific constituents	Very high; commercial-scale tests	High for many metals, based on lab tests
Reliability issues	Long experience with design	Limited experience; mobile units; onsite treatment avoids hauling risks; operational simplicity	Some inorganics still soluble; uncertain leachate test; surrogate for weathering
Environmental media most affected	Air	Air	None likely
Least compatible waste[b]	Highly toxic and refractory organics, high heavy metals concentration	Possibly none	Organics
Costs: Low, moderate, high	M–H (Coincin. = L)	M–H	M
Resource recovery Potential	Energy and some acids	Energy and some metals	Possible building material

[a]Molten salt, high temperature fluid wall, and plasma are treatments.
[b]Waste for which this method may be less effective for reducing exposure, relative to other technologies. Waste listed do not necessarily denote common usage.
Source: Office of Technology Assessment 1983:157.

There are important questions in regard to the effectiveness of deep well injection. The possibility of contamination depends a great deal on the characteristics of the site. The confining bed can fracture for several reasons, including some unanticipated event. For example, the waste is pumped into the well under pressure, and fracturing can occur if that pressure is too high. In addition to fracturing, the waste can migrate upward outside of the well casing or through an improperly plugged well. Finally, waste can migrate horizontally if there is damage to the walls of the well. Such damage can occur as a result of corrosion from corrosive chemicals injected into the well, from subsurface pressure exerted on its walls, or from corrosive agents occurring naturally (some wells are bored through sandstone bearing saltwater). As a result of these sources of potential contamination, the ability of injection wells to contain the waste depends on a large number of factors, most of which are site specific. Thus there is considerable uncertainty about the effectiveness of injection wells.

The disposal of waste in landfills involves the burying of waste in excavated trenches or cells. Usually a series of cells are constructed in the landfill site. Each cell normally contains about 150,000 square feet, depending on ground and base slopes, and each cell is doubly lined. The first liner consists of a five-foot wall of specially mixed clay, and the second liner consists of synthetic membrane polyethylene. Estimates of the life of the polyethylene liner vary but such liners are temporary. The clay liner, then, is the most important long run factor in isolating the cell from moisture and leakage. Lateral drains are laid at the bottom of each cell to form a leachate collection system. The drains slope toward a pump, which removes any leachate accumulated through the drains. Such liquid is sent to a treatment plant. Two monitoring wells, usually within 50 feet of the cell, permit testing for potential leakage into the soil and subsequently into the groundwater table. As a cell is being filled, a cover layer of soil is placed on top of the material at the end of each working day. In this way, cell subareas are constructed, separating potentially incompatible wastes which might react if they came into contact. These buffer materials may constitute up to a half of all the material in a cell. When a cell is full, it is capped with another polyethylene liner and a three-foot layer of clay.

As with deep well injection, a number of problems exist with landfills. It is generally recognized that all liners are subject to breaches in their physical integrity (Office of Technology Assessment 1983:178). Also liners may fail as a result of improper installation. For example, there can be creeping of the liner on sloping walls of the cell. Liners may fail after proper installation. Liners are subject to tears and punctures. There may be incompatibility between the liner and chemicals that are placed in the cell or from microbes that invade the cell. Once a liner has been installed, it is impossible to inspect it during the filling process. Furthermore, the leachate collection and recovery drains are subject to failure. The pipes can be crushed, they can be clogged by plant roots or other sources, and the pumps can fail. Finally, the cover or cap can be the source of contamination. It can be harmed by roots from plants and by burrowing animals. The freeze and thaw cycles during the winter can also cause cracking in the cap. Erosion and differential settling of the cover can cause cracking or depression in the cover. After a study of the performance of landfills, the Office of Technology Assessment concluded that considerable uncertainty exists about the capabilities of each of the control features of landfills (1983:184). As a result, the 1984 Amendments to the Resource Conservation and Recovery Act attempt to discourage the use of landfills for the disposal of hazardous waste.

Both landfills and injection wells, then, are characterized by high levels of uncertainty relative to the effectiveness of the technology. A second set of methods for hazard reduction utilizes various treatment methods.

Treatment technology is designed to decompose or break down the waste into nonhazardous constituents. The most widely used technique is exposure to high temperatures. Both liquid and solid waste can be incinerated, although liquid waste is more amenable to the process. To protect against air pollution, the incinerator cannot emit more than 180 milligrams of particulate matter per cubic meter of stack gas. Incinerators generally are equipped with scrubbers to remove particulate matter from the exhaust gas. Incinerators that operate at sea, however, are not subject to this requirement. Such incinerators are governed by the Marine Protection, Research, and Sanctuaries Act of 1972, which does not require scrubbers.

The destruction efficiency of all incinerators depends on a number of factors. The most important is the nature of the waste to be destroyed. Some chemicals tend to extinguish combustion and are thus difficult to destroy. Operating factors also affect the efficiency of the incinerator. It is especially critical to maintain adequate temperature within the kiln, to sustain adequate mixing of the waste to ensure even combustion, and to allow adequate time for decomposition.

There is substantial disagreement on the effectiveness of incineration. The sharpest disagreement has to do with *incinerability*, the concept used in the regulatory process as a measure of the efficiency of the incineration. The idea is that by the time the waste that is the most difficult to burn is destroyed, all other wastes have been destroyed also. Thus the most difficult to burn waste is selected to determine the efficiency of the burn. Since incinerability is not a physical attribute of any material, disagreement exists over what measures of incinerability should be used to determine which material is most difficult to burn. A second problem is that regulations do not apply to facilities that burn waste primarily for its fuel value. These co-generation facilities will be discussed in a later chapter. A third problem is inadequate monitoring systems. The EPA standard requires the removal of 99.99 percent of the hazardous constituent. However, there are no existing tests that accurately measure the efficiency of the burn in all instances. On an industry-wide basis, adequate monitoring systems are not in place. Even if they were in place, the OTA concluded that the measurements currently used in daily monitoring of incinerators cannot reliably represent destruction efficiency at the 99.99 percent level. Finally, waste is often transported from the site to the incinerator, increasing the probability of a spill. The risk of a spill during transportation to incineration at sea is particularly problematic.

In summary, the fragmented hazard control policy in effect in the United States presents a number of basic problems. As a result of the contradictory definition process, American policy is limited and restricted even given the commitment to regulate "the entire waste stream." The patchwork of laws governing hazardous waste makes for serious problems of coordination. The hazard control strategy tends to isolate chemical waste policy from policies relative to clean air and clean water. The partial preemption strategy of RCRA has resulted in state assumption of responsibility, and states vary widely in the quality of their programs and in levels of enforcement. Perhaps most important is the serious doubt as to the effectiveness of land disposal technology in reducing risks. All of these elements suggest that American policy is defective and should be reexamined. A useful part of that reexamination would be a comparison of American and European policy.

Clean Technology and an Integrated Approach: The European Experience

The European approach to environmental policy is built on the twin pillars of clean technology and an integrated management approach. This approach is linked to important elements in the political culture of the region, including a scarcity of vacant land, high reliance on groundwater sources, a conservation ethic resulting from post-World War II shortages, and a tradition of cooperation between government and industry in a number of policy areas (Davis, Huisingh, and Piasecki 1987). Most of these factors are not present in the American political culture, and at least one of them, the fourth, may conflict with important elements in the political culture of the United States. However, the European experience with waste reduction, recycling, and waste treatment are practices which should inform hazardous waste management in all countries and are adaptable to the American experience (Piasecki 1984).

The core of the European strategy is the reduction of waste. Strategy is referred to in terms of *low-waste technology* and *clean technology*. Low-waste technology is defined as "the practical application of knowledge, methods and means, so as—within the needs of man—to provide the most rational use of natural resources and energy, and to protect the environment" (Economic Commission for Europe 1984). The economic assumptions underlying this definition include the idea that waste is an indication of inefficiencies. Thus when the environment is protected by the reduction of waste, the economics of production are also improved. Further, the European approach assumes that it is better to reduce the generation of waste than to incur the financial costs and the health and environmental risks associated with hazard reduction. Given all these things, low-waste technologies may have environmental, economic, and production advantages.

In the European experience, low-waste technology involves four basic strategies (Davis, Huisingh, and Piasecki 1987:202): source segregation or separation, process modifications, end product substitution, and recovery and recycling. A brief explanation of each strategy is helpful.

Source segregation and separation is the least costly method of waste reduction. It involves removal of the hazardous constituents from other solid waste to prevent the contamination of larger volumes of waste. For example, toxic metals can be removed from water to render the water non-hazardous, and then can be easily disposed of through municipal sewage systems.

Process modifications involve changes in a firm's operational methods. These can be either small modifications in operations such as the raw materials used or larger changes in equipment for production processes. The primary goals of such changes are increased efficiency of the production process and improvements in the product. Waste reduction, then, is a secondary goal. However, Europe has made waste reduction through process modification an important goal.

End product substitution is the replacement of a hazardous waste product by a product that would eliminate or reduce the hazard. For example, silicone oils can replace PCBs as electrical insulation fluids, significantly reducing the hazard both to the environment and to workers who manufacture the product. Generally, end product substitution will occur only if there are advantages to either the manufacturer or the user, or if government provides incentives for end product substitutions. It is not common for manufacturers to utilize end product substitution when the only advantage is the reduction of risk to health or the environment.

Recovery and recycling are technically different but are often a part of the same process. *Recovery* is the separation of hazardous constituents from the total waste material; *recycling* is the use of the material recovered from the waste. The reuse can be either directly in the production process or in the form of selling recovered material on the market. Most of the material that is reused in the production process is the result of in-plant recovery. In this situation, the waste generator recovers and recycles the material. The material that is recycled on the market is usually the result of commercial or off-site recovery. Generally, these commercial recovery facilities are owned by independent companies serving several generators.

These strategies for waste reduction are pursued through a policy of extensive cooperation between government and industry. One element in this cooperation is a high level of government support for low-waste technology strategies. European governments have relied heavily on education, with regard to both general benefits and specific technologies, in encouraging the application of low-waste technologies. European nations, individually and collectively through the European Council of Ministers, have reflected a willingness to invest heavily in waste reduction research. Many countries have utilized various economic incentives to encourage waste reduction technologies, such as tax incentives for capital investments in waste reduction, grants and low-interest loans for retrofitting equipment, and taxes on waste generation. While some European nations have implemented command-and-control strategies, mandatory regulations are not vigorously enforced. Somewhat ironically, when control intervention occurs, government action tends to be "sustained and blatant" and "more easily tolerated by European industries" (Piasecki and Davis 1990:12). The main thrust of the programs remains the encouragement of industrial efficiency through the conscious choice of technology.

Along with the commitment to clean technology, European policy includes the important feature of integrated hazardous waste facilities. These facilities include all or most of the processes and technologies needed to manage hazardous materials. Five processes are normally involved. First, waste transfer processes analyze the chemicals and separate them into various groups for further processing. Second, liquid organic recovery processes analyze and recover valuable constituents in solvents, waste oils, and other liquid organic materials. Third are solidification and stabilization processes. Solidification processes convert liquid wastes and sludges into solids by special additives; stabilization adds other agents to inorganic solids and waste water sludges to render them harmless. Fourth, there are various processes for treating waste water. Water contaminated with certain inorganic liquids can be treated chemically so that all harmful materials are removed to the point that the water meets most national specifications for drinking. Some dissolved toxic organic substances can be removed to the extent that they are not detectable except with sensitive instruments. Finally, the incineration process exposes organic liquids and organic solids to high temperatures that destroy the hazardous compounds by breaking them down into their basic chemical elements. Harmful by-products to the burning process are removed by scrubbers so that the vapor released from the stack is clean. The integrated facility contains each of these processes in one building. These facilities more closely resemble chemical plants than they do the land-based dumpsites that are the core of American hazardous waste management.

An excellent study of the European integrated facilities identified several advantages and disadvantages of the approach (Davis 1990). There are three advantages. The first is the economic advantage of having all administrative and support services for the waste stream in a single place. For example, the integrated facility requires only one laboratory, whereas separate facilities for each process would require several laboratories. Second, facility engineers can choose the most appropriate technology from among the full range of technologies available at the time the waste is received. Without an integrated facility, the choice of technology would be made either by the generator of the waste or by its transporter. Costs, availability, or sheer convenience rather than engineering considerations might be the basis for such "up front" decisions. Third, the integrated facility makes it easier for regulatory agencies to inspect and control operations.

Two disadvantages are present in the integrated facility. Most important is the difficulty in siting such facilities. Most of the facilities in Europe were built before the rise of widespread public concern for hazardous waste management. More recent attempts to site facilities have met with intense opposition from a number of points (Davis 1990:44). Waste management companies in the United States have had virtually no success in siting large integrated facilities. American experiences suggest that Europeans will face similar problems with new facilities. A second problem is that a large integrated facility increases the distances hazardous materials have to be transported before processing. Therefore both the risks and costs of transportation are increased. Both disadvantages can be mitigated somewhat by public ownership and financing of integrated facilities. This is the practice in Denmark, Sweden, Finland, and several states in Germany.

What conclusions can be drawn from the European experience? The most important is that clean technology presents the possibility of waste reduction to the point where land disposal is unnecessary. Consequently, solution to the land disposal problem does not depend on the development of new technologies. Rather, as the authors of the study of European policies concluded, the transition from land disposal methods depends on "fully committed government policies that facilitate the use of these technologies" (Piasecki and Davis 1990:12).

The second conclusion to be drawn from the European experience is that government must assume a proactive position in hazardous waste management. A part of the strength of the European approach is that government has assumed the ownership of risks. Two observers of the European practice describe the system succinctly:

> The most striking feature of the (European) examples ... especially in comparison to the United States, is the extent of public ownership of the waste disposal facilities. By financing capital investments and taking responsibility for operations, the governments ... have, in effect, assumed responsibility for

the risks of hazardous wastes. The liability and responsibility of the generator ... ends once [the waste] is ceded to the public authorities. This contrasts with the principle of generator responsibility in other countries, including the United States. (Piasecki and Davis 1990:114).

It certainly contrasts with the specific liability features of the American Superfund legislation.

European experience contrasts, then, in several important ways with American hazardous waste policy. European strategy is a waste reduction strategy; American strategy is a hazard reduction strategy. European strategy involves integrated management; American strategy is fragmented and contradictory. Governments in Europe assume most of the liability risks associated with those facilities; liability in the United States falls upon the generator and transporter.

TOXICITY AND WHERE WE LIVE: CHEMICAL ADDITIVES IN FOOD

Chemical hazardous wastes illustrate in dramatic form another of the paradoxical elements of pollution—the associated risks are both global and individual. We have examined the macroscale aspects of chemical hazardous waste. Equally important are the microscale aspects of chemical residuals. A good example of the microscale dimension is the food we eat. The eating of prepared or packaged food is universal in economically advanced nations and widespread in economically less-developed nations. The use of chemicals in the production of food may be a more serious problem in the less-developed nations simply because regulations on use are not as effective. Public policy in most countries has had to deal with the problem of toxicity in food. The risks, as with indoor air pollution, are magnified by the pervasiveness of exposure.

As with the general environment, toxicity in food occurs both naturally and as a result of human activities. Toxicity occurs naturally in a wide variety of foods. The risk associated with eating mushrooms that have been gathered from the woods is well-known. It is not as well-known that all parts of the potato except the tubor are toxic. Some naturally occurring materials and bacteria are highly toxic; it has been estimated that seven pounds of botulin could destroy the entire population of the world from botulism.

Human-based toxicity results from the additives that are induced into the food chain. These can be induced either directly or indirectly. There are over 2,000 different materials that constitute the direct additives used in foods. Some, such as vitamins, minerals, and trace elements, are added to enhance or conserve nutrient value. Others may serve to maintain or improve the physical properties of the food—various flavorings, coloring agents, texture agents, or materials to achieve consistency in prepared foods. Indirect additives are induced in the food chain in either the production or processing phases. Pesticides, fertilizers, and growth hormones are added in the production phase. Chemical changes resulting from processing the food or from chemically processed packaging materials are examples of indirect additives in the processing phase. Public policy response to additives in food varies among nations, from extensive regulation to virtually no regulatory response. The American experience is one of the oldest and most extensive policy responses.

This American response includes several important pieces of legislation. The first was the Federal Food and Drug Act of 1906. Among other things, this Act prevented the sale in interstate commerce of food to which any ingredient had been added that made it injurious to health. The Food, Drug, and Cosmetic Act of 1938 expanded the scope of regulation to include any poisonous or deleterious substance. Provisions relative to misbranding were also strengthened. However, chemicals could still be introduced into food without prior tests to determine whether they were safe.

The 1938 Act was subject to two important amendments. The first was the Food Additive Amendment of 1958, which attempts to control the level of risk associated with food additives, including food colorings, and with additives in animal feed. Its most important principle is referred to as the Delaney principle, so named for Congressman James J. Delaney, who introduced it. The Delaney principle stipulates that "no additive shall be deemed to be safe if it is found … after tests which are appropriate for the evaluation of the safety of food additives to induce cancer in man or animal." The Delaney principle is sometimes associated with a "zero risk" requirement, but such an association is not altogether accurate. Rather, it requires "appropriate tests" to determine whether the additive "induces cancer." Problems arise from disagreements as to what constitute "appropriate tests" and what "induces cancer." While the Food and Drug Administration has used the Delaney principle sparingly, it is generally agreed that its existence has proven to be a strong deterrent to risky actions by food processors (Lowrance 1976:82).

The second important amendment to the Food, Drug, and Cosmetic Act is the Color Additive Amendment of 1960. This requires that toxicity tests be conducted on any substance added to food. The additive is administered to some animals (the experimental group) and not to others (the control group) in order to determine the highest dietary level with no detectable adverse effect on the animal. This level is then divided by 100 and the result is presumed to be the "safe" level for the human diet.

The most important legislation to control indirect additives to food is the Federal Insecticide, Fungicide, and Rodenticide Act, passed in 1947 and amended in 1972, 1975, 1978, and 1988. We discussed this act earlier in the chapter, in the section on U.S. policy. In summary, it requires that all pesticides marketed in the United States undergo a premarket review of potential health and environmental effects. The standard that EPA is to apply in the determination of whether or not to register the pesticide is that of "unreasonable adverse effects." The tests required to make such a determination often are complex and costly.

Several comments need to be made on the impacts and outcomes of these statutes. First, in the United States chemical additives to food have been more studied, regulated, and controlled than any other area of the environment. A strong case can be made that this regulation occurred before any significant damage was done to human health. If this is the case, and we believe that it is, then the regulation of additives to food is one of the few success stories in anticipatory environmental policy. Second, on the other hand, the great number and variety of additives, particularly when indirect additives are included, is itself a basis for concern. The human organism does seem to be able to tolerate small amounts of many different toxic chemicals simultaneously. However, the carrying capacity of the human body is not known. Additionally, some chemicals accumulate in the body, and the effect of the buildup may be quite different from the effect of each incremental small dose. Third, chemicals in the body do have antagonistic interactions. In this sense, chemicals function much like drugs that pose little or no risk when taken separately but pose a danger in combination. Generally, there is more evidence of antagonism among chemicals in the body than there is of reinforcement or of a neutral effect. Finally, there appear to be significantly higher risks associated with poor eating habits than from chemical additives in food. Poor eating habits may be the major problem associated with food intake among Americans.

When food additives are examined from a multinational perspective, there are serious problems. Some countries, among them nations from which the United States imports significant amounts of food, have few or ineffective regulations on food additives. This is true particularly of indirect additives. The results of lack of regulation are monumental. The World Health Organization estimates that up to 1 million pesticide poisonings occur worldwide each year with approximately 20,000 resulting in death (World Health Organization 1990:86). Most such poisonings occur among farmers in less-developed countries who are exposed to pesticides without training in their use and who thus fail to take proper safety precautions. Furthermore, legal loopholes in the United States allow manufacturers to sell pesticides overseas that are banned in this country. For example, DDT and benzene hexachloride are banned from use in the United States but account for 75 percent of all pesticide use in India. A General Accounting Office report concluded that about 25 percent of all pesticides sold overseas are banned, restricted, or unregistered for use in the United States (General Accounting Office 1989). This situation poses a serious problem for consumers in the food-producing country, and the problem is compounded when some of the produce is sold to the industrial nations. In the United States less than 1 percent of imported produce is inspected for pesticide residues. As a result of this fact plus increased pesticide use in the United States, a report prepared under the auspices of the National Academy of Sciences concluded that approximately a million cancer deaths will occur in the United States during the lifetime of the present generation as a result of pesticides in food (Mott and Snyder 1987:6).

To resolve the additive problem and accomplish other desirable outcomes, irradiation has been proposed as a technology. This involves exposing the product to low levels of radiation, in most cases gamma rays emitted by radioactive Cobalt 60. One important requirement is that the energy level of the radiation be kept below the level that causes induced radiation in the food. For that reason, proponents of the process argue that irradiation does not result in radioactivity in food and does not constitute an additive subject to the various regulations on food additives. Foods most likely to be irradiated are chickens, potatoes, strawberries, wheat, milk, cod, redfish, onions, rice, dates, cocoa beans, spices, and pork. The process has generated ardent proponents and strong opponents.

The proponents claim a number of beneficial outcomes of the technology. One of the most important is the effect on spoilage. In essence, irradiation kills the bacteria and fungi responsible for spoilage. Thus it would reduce or eliminate the need for preservatives such as nitrates in various processed foods as well as the application of chemicals to preserve the shelf life of fruits and vegetables. Control of spoilage would ease the problem of world hunger, since some countries lose 30 percent or more of their food production to spoilage or insects. Second, irradiation would reduce the cost of food by lowering the need for freezing or continued refrigeration. Irradiated milk, for example, has a shelf life of several months without refrigeration. Further, items processed in specialized areas of the world could be shipped chilled rather than frozen, including fish, meats, fruits, and vegetables. Finally, proponents argue that irradiation does not significantly alter either the nutritional value or the taste of the food. Some claim that the nutritional value may be improved with irradiation, since most foods would not have to be cooked as long.

Opponents have serious reservations about irradiation. The major concern focuses on what happens during the irradiation process. Gamma rays break down every chemical bond in the food, and the free molecules can then recombine into any number of chemical elements. It is the recombination of molecules and its unpredictability that is a concern. Recombined chemicals that have been identified in irradiated food include formaldehyde, benzene, peroxide, and formic acid. Formaldehyde is a carcinogenic and peroxide is a mutagenic. Most of the compounds formed by irradiation have not been identified and thus have not been tested for their toxicity. Current American policy requires labeling of irradiated whole foods, but there is no requirement of notice for packaged foods that contain irradiated ingredients or for food sold in restaurants or schools.

The extent of irradiation of food varies substantially among the countries of the world. In the United States its use is restricted basically to individuals with critical immunity problems who cannot tolerate any disease-causing organism, and to astronauts. Japan and India employ the technology more extensively with the primary purpose of preventing spoilage. European applications are significant but in a midrange between the limited U.S. use and the more extensive use in Japan and India. Even if the technological questions could be resolved, consumer understanding and acceptance of irradiation would be an important element in increasing use of the technology in industrial nations (U.S. Department of Energy 1984).

WHITHER CHEMICAL HAZARDOUS WASTE POLICY IN A CHEMICALLY DEPENDENT WORLD?

The modern world is on a chemical fix of staggering proportions. And the use of chemicals is far from stagnant. Of the approximately 5,000 new chemicals appearing on the American Chemical Society's list each week, approximately 1,500 are introduced commercially each year. Over 4 million chemicals are registered for use in the United States, and approximately 70,000 are in regular use. Such extensive and pervasive use of chemicals generates substantial amounts of waste. The United States produces over 260 million metric tons a year, or over one ton per person in the country. Data on the worldwide production of chemical waste are not as reliable, but estimates range from 375 to over 500 million metric tons for only nineteen countries. The use of chemicals and the accompanying waste are a pervasive part of the global environment. Major problems exist within public policy on both a national and multinational basis.

One of the most important problems for public policy on chemical waste is the high cultural discount rate present in all societies: In all nations, present consumption is valued more highly than future environmental quality. The discount rate does vary somewhat among nations. For example, Sweden, while reflecting a high cultural discount rate, places more value on future environmental quality than does the United States with its very high cultural discount rate (Lundqvist 1974:10). The global high cultural discount rate has resulted in a very limited effort in all countries to assess the risks associated with the use of chemicals. Only about 2 percent of all chemicals have been rigorously tested for their toxicity. An inescapable conclusion to such data is that the world's population is subject to a pervasive and personal hazard in the use of chemicals with little guidance as to the associated risks.

A second global problem in chemical waste policy is that there is substantial uncertainty relative to the objectives to be accomplished in such a policy. In other words, there is considerable uncertainty with regard to the production function. In the United States the objective is hazard reduction, so the strategy is to reduce the hazard associated with chemical waste, whatever the level of generation. European nations aim for the objective of waste reduction, so the strategy seeks to reduce the amount of waste that is generated.

The United States places major reliance on land-based disposal. Given the high levels of uncertainty surrounding this technology, it is hard to avoid the conclusion that the United States is content to rely on an "easy fix" technology rather than committing resources to determine the most effective technology. This "out of sight, out of mind" position seems to be a product of the high cultural discount rate that is characteristic of chemical waste policy.

On a comparative level, the basic question is which approach, the American or European, results in a reduction of pollution from chemical hazardous waste. Unfortunately, this question is impossible to answer given the current state of cross-national studies in environmental policy. This situation places in stark relief the importance of the perspective emphasized in this book—namely, that environmental policies in all nations must be informed by the practice and experience in other countries. Significant differences exist in the approaches of the United States and European countries. What features of each serve well the purposes of environmental quality? What institutional arrangements facilitate the implementation of strategies adopted by policy makers? What should be the basic objectives of a particular environmental policy subset? Who should be responsible, including legal liability, and for what? At this juncture in the cross-national study of chemical hazardous waste policy, the best that can be done is to utilize existing knowledge to raise the right questions and to attempt to make informed judgments on the basis of the information available.

Chapter 6

Nuclear Waste

In many ways, nuclear waste policy may be described as the "new kid on the block" of environmental policy. In the early stages of nuclear development, most wastes were the product of weapons research. Scientists and policy makers alike assumed that such waste could be easily managed through deep geological disposal. Additionally, most individuals involved in the American nuclear program were more interested in the development of new technology than in the dull and seemingly unproductive question of waste disposal (Walker, Gould, and Woodhouse 1983:2). However, with the spread of nuclear technology to commercial and industrial applications, the level of nuclear waste began to grow exponentially. Nuclear waste management became an important item on the public policy agenda of those nations utilizing the technology. Somewhat ironically, then, serious public policy concern for nuclear waste management is less than two decades old. Thus the policy process in most countries, including the United States, is still in the developmental stage.

TYPES AND SOURCES OF NUCLEAR WASTE

Radioactivity is a pervasive and ubiquitous component of the environment. Radiation occurring through natural processes is called *background radiation.* Natural materials contain both stable and unstable isotopes. The unstable isotopes, called *radionuclides*, spontaneously transform to other nuclides by giving off radiation. This transformation process is called *radioactive decay.* The concept of *half life* refers to the time required for the atoms of a radionuclide to decrease by 50 percent as a result of radioactive decay. Some isotopes have a short half life of 0.2 seconds and others a very long half life of 2 million years. Since radionuclides are present in all natural materials, all rocks, soils, plants, and animals contribute to background radiation through the process of radioactive decay. Different types of rocks and soils vary in the release of radioactivity. Some geographical areas have high concentrations of unstable rocks and soils and therefore high levels of background radiation. Other geographical areas have fewer unstable rocks and soils and a low level of background radiation. In Switzerland, for example, the average exposure to background radiation is 2.4 mSv, with ranges from 2 to 5 mSv in different areas of the country (Chapman and McKinley 1987:7). Globally, the average annual exposure to background radiation is 2 mSv, making background radiation the highest effective dose equivalent from any source. The next highest is medical exposure at 0.4 mSv, then fallout exposure at 0.02 mSv, and nuclear power exposure at 0.001 mSv (UN Environment Programme 1985). The amount of risk associated with exposure to each type of radiation and the results of cumulative exposure are difficult to determine.

Radioactive wastes also result from many human activities. Defining and classifying the sources of this waste is a difficult task. The International Atomic Energy Agency (IAEA) uses a definition that emphasizes the two primary hazards associated with nuclear waste: the degree of radioactivity and the level of heat. Such an emphasis is important in determining the degree of containment necessary to reduce the risks and the time frame required for that containment.

The International Atomic Energy Agency suggests classifying radioactive wastes into five types. Class I waste is high level and long lived. It is characterized by high radiotoxicity and high heat output over a long period of time. Class II waste is intermediate level and long lived. This waste is characterized by intermediate radiotoxicity, low heat output, and a long half life. Class III waste is low level and long lived, characterized by low radiotoxicity and insignificant heat output but long half life. Class IV waste is intermediate level and short lived. It has intermediate radiotoxicity, low heat output, and short half life. Class V waste is low level and short lived, with low radiotoxicity, insignificant heat output, and a short half life. Public policy in most countries, the United States included, has shortened the list of classes to high-level nuclear wastes (HLW) and low level nuclear wastes (LLW).

ें   *A Note on Notations*

We have attempted to avoid the use of technical language to keep the discussion intelligible to the lay reader. However, there are occasions when some scientific language is useful for the general reader. In thinking about radiation, the two key factors are the strength or level of radiation emitted and how much radiation is absorbed by the matter exposed to it. Thus, it is important to develop a standard that can measure the absorption rate of matter that is exposed to radiation.

The traditional way to express radiation dose was in units of *roentgen*. A roentgen is the amount of X-rays or gamma rays that produces ionization equivalent to one electrostatic unit. The human dose measurement based on the roentgen is the *rem*, which is short for *roentgen equivalent man*. The rem takes into account the biology of the human organism and the type of radiation involved. Alpha radiation, for example, is twenty times more damaging to human tissue than Beta radiation. The absorption rate of human tissue is different from the absorption rate of other forms of matter.

Recently a change occurred in the way of expressing the level of exposure to and absorption of radiation. The more recent notation is based in the *Bequerel*, which measures the radioactivity of any material by the number of nuclei that decay each second. A Bequerel, noted as Bq, is a decay rate of one nucleus per second. The measure of the absorption rate is referred to as the *Gray* and noted as Gy. A Gray is the radiation required to cause one kilogram of material to absorb one joule of energy. As with the roentgen standard, if the material absorbing the radiation is human tissue, a large number of biological and radiation factors affect the transaction. Thus the attempt to relate the Gray to human tissue produced the *Sievert*, which measures the radiation dose equivalent to the Gray when the absorbing material is human tissue. The individual human dose equivalent is expressed as Sieverts, noted as Sv, and the dose equivalents to populations as *man Sieverts*, noted as mSv.

For the lay reader, an understanding of the strength of exposure and the absorption rate is more important than understanding the scientific notation. Without that understanding, radiation tends to be a mysterious unknown whose effects are catastrophic regardless of the strength of exposure or rates of absorption.

The two-category classification simplifies the identification of the sources of nuclear wastes. High-level nuclear wastes (Class I and II wastes) result from the nuclear fuel process. Fuel production, usually referred to as fuel fabrication, is the source of significant high-level waste. These wastes are in the form of the hulls or containers for the fuel elements and also storage pond residues. The largest volume of high level waste is produced in the reprocessing of spent fuel. In this process, the spent fuel rod is exposed to a solvent, usually tribtyl phosphate, to recover uranium and plutonium. The large volume of liquid waste resulting from this reprocessing is highly radioactive and has a high heat output. Some spent fuel rods are unreprocessed and are referred to by the delightful acronym SURF. These unreprocessed spent fuel rods are highly radioactive and generate high levels of heat.

Low-level nuclear waste in most countries consists of those wastes in Classes III, IV, and V. The level of radioactivity may vary from low to intermediate and the half life from short to long. This mixture of classes in this definition thus fails to distinguish between levels of radioactivity or the time required for radioactive decay. American policy did not recognize these differences until 1983. Regulations issued by the Nuclear Regulatory Commission established three categories of low level waste, dubbed Class A, B, and C. Classes A and B waste must decay within 100 years to a point that is nonhazardous to an individual experiencing inadvertent exposure. The difference between the two classes is that Class B waste requires stricter packaging than Class A waste. Class C waste is material that will remain hazardous for 500 years or more. In addition to these three classes, there are substantial amounts of material that have low levels of radioactivity and can be handled on site, either by incineration, dilution, or storage, until the radioactivity has decayed. A number of hospitals manage such low-level waste on site.

The primary source of low-level waste is the commercial use of nuclear materials. There has been increasing utilization of nuclear materials in the production of electricity, in industrial processes, in academic research, and in medicine and radiopharmaceuticals. In the United States 1.1 million cubic feet of low-level wastes were disposed of in commercial sites in 1990. Of this amount, nuclear power plants accounted for 56 percent by volume and 79 percent by radioactivity, radiopharmaceuticals and nuclear fabrication plants accounted for 31 percent by volume and 19 percent by radioactivity, government accounted for 6 percent by volume and 2 percent by radioactivity, and academic and medical institutions accounted for 6 percent by volume and 0.2 percent by radioactivity (English 1992:3–4). The waste is in any number of physical forms, including some very ordinary products. General contaminated trash consists of such things as paper, gloves, and construction debris. Discarded contaminated equipment takes the form of tools, sealed carriers, and pipes. Wet waste consists of cleanup solutions and filter aids. Organic compounds such as oils, greases, and resins are often contaminated. Finally, there are various radioactive gases, such as Kr-85, that are classified as low-level waste. Gaseous waste, unlike solid low-level waste, is not buried.

Considerable low-level waste is produced in the mining cycle for uranium-bearing ore. *Mill tailings*, which are various soils and rocks left over from the mining process, are usually simply left in piles on the mining site. Abandoned mine buildings and equipment may also be contaminated. The United States in particular has had to address the problems associated with mining operations.

The significant volume of wastes resulting from human activities and the hazards posed by them have forced nations with nuclear capacity to address the problem of radioactive wastes. Among the most difficult aspects of setting a policy have been the determination of risks and the identification of standards of acceptable exposure.

RISK, TIME, AND THE CULTURAL DISCOUNT RATE

The early years of nuclear research and development were characterized by a high cultural discount rate. The history of nuclear research reveals an emphasis on technological development during the formative years with considerable complacency toward the long term effects of nuclear waste. Additionally, involvement in nuclear development was limited to a narrow range of scientists, research institutions, and firms. This emphasis on technological development and limited participation in that development were powerful factors in leading scientists and policy makers to recognize few if any technical problems in waste disposal if criteria were reasonable. The problems in nuclear waste disposal, in their view, were nontechnical, involving political, sociological, and philosophic issues.

Several developments combined to produce a change in the time horizon for nuclear policy. The first was the spread of nuclear technology to multiple industrial, commercial, and medical-pharmaceutical applications. The volume of waste accompanying this spread of technology increased exponentially, thereby expanding the concern for the associated risks from a narrow range of scientists onto the public agenda. A second factor was various dramatic instances of near catastrophe in the nuclear power industry. The accidents at Chernobyl in the Soviet Union and Three Mile Island in the United States focused the issue of hazards in new ways. Most important, these events convinced the public that nuclear technology posed hazards that are unique. The long half life of some waste forced scientists to establish with a degree of certainty what would happen with the waste 10,000 years into the future. Science had not been expected to predict the performance of one of its by-products over such a long period of time and with such certainty. As a result, the nuclear waste issue became a scientific, social, and political issue.

These developments had important consequences for nuclear waste policy. The first result was a radical shift in the time horizon from a high to a low cultural discount rate. With the possible exception of some Third World nations, emphasis began to be placed on future safety rather than on present consumption in the form of technological development and the nuclear generation of electricity. Plans for the construction of new nuclear electric power facilities were cancelled or postponed in nearly all nuclear countries. The second consequence was that the scientific community had to face the serious technical issues associated with nuclear waste disposal. The most important of those technical issues was the development of appropriate standards of exposure and the identification of environmentally safe means of disposal of waste.

The development of appropriate standards on radiation dose limits is a bifurcated process. At the international level, it involves several important agencies of the United Nations and a nongovernmental organization. The UN agencies are the International Atomic Energy Agency (IAEA) and the United Nation's Scientific Committee on the Effects of Atomic Radiation (UNSCEAR). The IAEA's primary function is the dissemination of information on all aspects of nuclear safety. UNSCEAR is a standing committee of the General Assembly with the primary purpose of assessing the radiological effect of all radiation sources, including background radiation. The nongovernmental body is the International Commission on Radiological Protection (ICRP). This group issues recommendations on radiation protection which are generally regarded as the most authoritative on the subject of radiation risk. The ICRP works very closely with UNSCEAR to develop an international consensus on the basic principles of radiation risk management.

Radiation risk management is based on the concept of dose limitation (ICRP 1977). This concept embraces exposure to radiation from all sources, including background radiation, medical applications, and the nuclear power industry. Three principles form the basics of the system. First, no practice should be adopted unless it has a positive net benefit. When there is a probability of the release of radionuclides into the environment and resulting harmful effects, benefits must be larger than the harm. Second, all doses should be kept as low as reasonably achievable. This principle assumes that the reduction of risk to zero is both impractical and unnecessary (Chapman and McKinley 1987:8). Rather, risk management is to seek "optimization," or the dose that is reasonably achievable, taking economic and social factors into account. Third, doses to individuals shall not be greater than the limits promulgated by the ICRP; the recommended criterion is a risk of 10^{-5} a year. Application of this criterion to various radionuclides produces varying levels of exposure. In other words, acceptable levels of exposure to Cesium 137 are different from acceptable levels of exposure to Strontium 90. It is generally agreed that the acceptable levels of exposure recommended by the ICRP are low (Roxburgh 1987:20).

The second level in the bifurcated process of standard development is that of national governments. The ICRP recommendations serve as a

baseline for most national standards. And so there is substantial commonality in the standards of most countries. However, radiological exposure standards differ in detail from country to country. In some countries
they are more stringent than those recommended by ICRP. Switzerland
and Sweden have adopted radiation dose standards for nuclear waste
management that for all practical purposes would make radiation from
waste indistinguishable from background radiation. The dose limits
adopted in the United Kingdom are essentially equivalent to the recommended levels of ICRP. The British standard is defined as "a risk to an
individual in a year equivalent to that associated with a dose of 0.1 mSv:
about 1 chance in a million" for any single nuclear waste depository
(Roxburgh 1987:25).

How do these standards convert to health risks that are meaningful to
individuals? The short-term effects of exposure are related to the levels of
radiation. For the individual, exposure to 200 to 600 rems will produce serious health effects, including internal bleeding and infection. Whole body
exposure to 600–1000 rems results in a mortality rate of between 80 and 100
percent. Exposure to radiation above 1,000 rems results in death within
fourteen days. The effects vary somewhat depending on treatment, particularly in the low-level exposure range. For example, exposure to up to 600
rems can result in death, but the mortality rate varies between 0 and 80
percent depending on the therapy available (Stolwijk 1983:80). Average
annual exposure to background radiation is 0.108 rems and from total man-
made radiation 0.190 rems. Assuming a life span of 70 years, total lifetime
exposure on the average is 13 rems.

Identifying the long-term effects of exposure to radiation is a more
difficult matter. Table 6.1 outlines the three major categories of long-term
effects of radiation and their specific health risks. Determining the relationships between level of exposure and these long-term effects is a complex
problem. However, there are some generally accepted baselines with
regard to each category. The baseline concept for mutation is known as the
doubling dose. This is the total dose exposure over the reproductive lifetime
that would result in a doubling of spontaneous mutations. This number is
probably somewhat over 100 rems (UNSCEAR 1977:22). In regard to
human development, studies of individuals exposed to radiation from
Hiroshima, Nagasaki, and the Marshall Islands found that exposure to 25
rems resulted in some mental defects and exposure to 50 rems resulted in
profound retardation (Stolwijk 1983:85). In the area of somatic effects, the
most frequently occurring form of cancer resulting from exposure is
leukemia. UNSCEAR estimates a total of 20–50 excess deaths from
leukemia per million people per rem exposure. Increases in thyroid, breast,
lung, and gastro-intestinal cancer also occur. The exact relationship
between level of exposure and increased risk of cancer is difficult to establish and varies with the type of cancer.

Table 6.1   Long Term Health Effects of Radiation Exposure

Category	Specific health risks
Genetic effects	
Dominant mutation	anemia, dwarfism, extra fingers and toes, Huntington's chorea
Recessive mutation	sickle cell anemia, cystic fibrosis, Tay-Sachs disease
Human development	reduced growth rates, mental retardation, microcephaly
Somatic effects	cataract formation, reduced fertility, cancer induction

Whatever the difficulty of establishing the complex relationship between level of exposure and unwanted effect, the potential risks posed by radioactive waste and the time frames associated with those risks underline the importance of an effective nuclear waste management program. Clearly there is a need that mandates a policy. Unfortunately, policy in all countries has been slow in developing.

NUCLEAR WASTE MANAGEMENT: A PROBLEM IN SEARCH OF A SOLUTION

Considerable commonality exists among nations on the standards for exposure to radiation. For nuclear waste management, the problem becomes that of finding the appropriate policy to ensure that exposure from all sources is below acceptable limits. There is substantial disagreement among nations and diversity in nuclear waste management approaches.

There are two basic elements in nuclear waste management policy: reprocessing and containment. *Reprocessing* is a variant on recycling. It involves several types of chemical and mechanical processes to recover fissionable uranium, plutonium, thorium, and other valuable material from nuclear waste. The liquid residue from reprocessing is highly radioactive. Vitrification of that residue involves exposing it to very high heat to solidify it. The resulting product is a glassy type of substance. The second element, *containment*, involves confining the waste in a disposal facility for the period of time that it poses a hazard. Depending on the half life of the material, this time frame could be relatively short or very long. The mix of the two elements, reprocessing and containment, determines the nature of a specific nation's nuclear waste policy.

Basically, there are four options available for containment. The first is geological containment. Deep geological disposal involves placing the waste at depths of 2,000 to 3,000 feet. The medium within which the repository is located is either salt, granite, shale, or basalt. Intermediate-level geological disposal involves placing the waste at a depth between the surface and 2,000 feet. Shallow geological disposal involves placing the waste in surface or near-surface facilities. The containment structures themselves are specially constructed trenches. The second option is ocean disposal. Subseabed disposal calls for the waste to be placed in repositories beneath the ocean floor, either beneath the sediment or in various rock formations. Another strategy of ocean disposal, tried on an experimental basis by the United States, is to place the waste in special packaging on the ocean floor. A final strategy of ocean disposal is to disperse the waste in the ocean. The third option is dispersal of the waste above ground. This option is considered viable only for those wastes with a very short half life and low levels of radioactivity. Such waste is held on site, usually that of the generator, until normal decay processes render the waste harmless. The final option is to contain the waste in outer space. Discussions relative to the dismantling of nuclear weapons by the United States and the former Soviet Union included consideration of projecting the highly radioactive wastes into the sun. These four options present complex problems of choice for policy makers.

Giving a clear picture of the cross-national situation with regard to nuclear waste policy is difficult because of the wide variation among nations. Some nations have made strong commitments to reprocessing (Japan, for example) while others give reprocessing a low priority (Canada, for example). The situation is further obscured by the fact that most national programs are still at the research stage. At present, no nation has made the choice of the proper mix between reprocessing and containment, and only one nation has chosen a specific containment option. The United States has adopted a policy that provides for one specific repository at Yucca Mountain, Nevada. Table 6.2 summarizes the current state of nuclear waste policy. It should be emphasized that the data on containment are reflective only of the research emphasis each nation has adopted. For example, Argentina has chosen deep geological disposal in granite rock as its research emphasis, but that does not mean that it has or for that matter will ever site such a facility. What it means is that Argentina is putting most of its research effort into exploring the effectiveness of deep geological disposal in granite rock. The table reflects clearly the diversity in approaches among nations.

The experience of the United States with nuclear waste policy is the most instructive relative to understanding the problems and prospects for nuclear waste management. This is not to say that the American approach is necessarily superior or will lead to more risk reduction than other approaches. But, just as the experience of the European community can instruct other nations in the problems and prospects for hazardous chemical waste, a great deal can be learned about nuclear waste from examining the American experience.

Table 6.2   Cross-National View of High-Level Nuclear Waste Policy

Country	Reprocessing and vitrification	Containment Research Emphasis	
		Disposal method	Medium
Argentina	Yes	Deep geological disposal	granite rock
Belgium	Yes	Geological disposal	clay
Canada	No	Deep geological disposal	crystalline rock
Denmark	No	Deep geological disposal	salt
Germany	Yes	Deep geological disposal	salt
Finland	No	Deep geological disposal	crystalline rock
France	Yes	Mixed: Deep geological disposal	granite rock
		Subseabed disposal	deep ocean
Italy	No	Deep geological disposal	clay
Japan	Yes	Mixed: Geological disposal	granite
		Subseabed disposal	deep ocean
Netherlands	No	Mixed: Geological disposal	salt
		Subseabed disposal	deep ocean
Sweden	Yes	Geological disposal: mixed depths	crystalline rock
Switzerland	No	Deep geological disposal	crystalline rock
Russia	Yes	Geological disposal near surface	unknown
United Kingdom	Yes	Mixed: Deep geological disposal	Not determined
		Subseabed disposal	deep ocean
United States	Yes	Deep geological disposal	Tuff (Yucca Mountain)

Source: Information reported in Neil A. Chapman and Ian G. McKinley (1987). *The Geological Disposal of Nuclear Waste*. Chichester: John Wiley and Sons, pp. 232–242.

U.S. NUCLEAR WASTE MANAGEMENT: FROM COMPLACENCY, TO BELATED RESPONSE, TO POLICY PARALYSIS

The early years of nuclear development in the United States were marked by considerable complacency toward the nuclear waste problem. As a result, policy response was late in developing. For a number of reasons, implementation of that policy has been marked by considerable problems, both technical and political. As a result of these factors, the best descriptive phrase for nuclear waste management policy in the United States at the present time is "policy paralysis".

American policy is based on several important distinctions relative to the kinds of nuclear waste. The first distinction is between nuclear waste resulting from military versus commercial operations. The second distinction is between high-level waste, low-level waste, and uranium mill tailings. The first distinction is relatively straightforward; the second is complex and somewhat contradictory.

Military nuclear waste, referred to as *transuranic waste* (TRU) in the United States, is handled separately from commercial waste. It is stored at several places, principally at the Savannah River Plant in South Carolina and the Hanford Reservation in Washington state. In addition to transuranic waste, the military also produces substantial volumes of low level waste. This too is located in a number of land burial sites across the country, the most important being the Savannah River Plant, Hanford Reservation, Idaho National Engineering Laboratory, and the Oak Ridge National Laboratory. Military handling of nuclear waste is not subject to the same public scrutiny as the management of commercial waste, but there is substantial evidence that most military sites, for both TRU and low-level waste, have experienced considerable problems with containment.

Civilian nuclear waste is subject to policy defined in several acts passed around 1980. Civilian high-level waste is subject to the Nuclear Waste Policy Act of 1982, passed only after considerable debate and gridlock in Congress. Civilian low level waste is subject to the Low Level Radioactive Waste Policy Act of 1980. Policy relative to uranium mill tailings is defined in the Uranium Mill Tailings Radiation Control Act of 1978. These acts form the core of American policy toward the management of commercially produced nuclear waste.

The Nuclear Waste Policy Act (NWPA) attempted to define a comprehensive policy on the management of high-level nuclear waste. General authority for regulating high-level waste was vested in the Nuclear Regulatory Commission, and specific authority to implement the provisions of the Act was vested in the Department of Energy (DOE). The Act provided for the establishment of an Office of Civilian Radioactive Waste Management in the Department of Energy to implement the management program. The DOE was required to apply to the Nuclear Regulatory Commission for authority to construct a repository.

Several provisions of the NWPA need emphasis. The first required the development of permanent underground repositories. The 1982 Act required the DOE to recommend three sites to the President by January 1, 1985, for the first repository and five additional sites by July 1, 1989, for a second repository. However, amendments to the Act in 1987 (the Nuclear Waste Policy Act Amendments) specified characteristics of the first site which limited the choice to Yucca Mountain, Nevada, and permanently deferred selection of a site for the second repository. The repository was authorized to receive either spent fuel (unreprocessed) or the vitrified waste from reprocessing. The Act provides that the United States will take title to the waste deposited in a repository.

A second provision of the Act authorized temporary federal storage of some waste. The spent fuel rods from nuclear power plants had been stored either at the reactor site or at a few commercial storage sites, but these sites were being strained to capacity. The nuclear power industry strongly supported the NWPA, in part because of the urgent need for additional capacity. The Act provided that spent fuel rods could be stored at an existing federally owned site or at new storage facilities built by the government at the reactor site. However, spent fuel rods could be stored away from the reactor site only if the utility had filled all existing space at that site and could not reasonably provide additional storage there. As with the waste deposited at the permanent repository, the national government would take title to all waste designated for temporary storage. It would take possession of the waste at the reactor site and be responsible for transporting it to the storage facility.

The third major provision of the Act established a mandatory consultative process on site selection between the Department of Energy and states and Indian tribes that might be affected by the decision. It further allowed a state or Indian tribe to veto a DOE decision to locate a repository within its borders. However, the veto could be overridden by a vote of both houses of Congress within 90 days of the state or tribal action. A subsequent study clearly demonstrated that states were not satisfied with these attempts to provide for state concerns (Herzik and Mushkatel 1992:139). Considerable tension developed between the states and the Department of Energy regarding site location of the first repository. This tension essentially resulted in a stalemate that was ended only when Congress passed the Nuclear Waste Policy Act Amendments of 1987, which pointed to the Yucca Mountain site.

As if these state–federal tensions were not enough, the policy prescribed by the Act made no provisions for the role of local governments. Since a nuclear waste repository concentrates the risks and disperses the benefits, it is reasonable to assume that the NIMBY syndrome will be a factor in stimulating local obstructionist tactics. Such tactics may be reduced by the choice of the Yucca Mountain site by the fact that 80 percent of the land in the county (Nye County) is owned by the national government. In any event, relations between the national and state governments in nuclear waste management have been fraught by tensions and conflict. The NWPA does not seem to have provided adequately for intergovernmental factors involved in siting nuclear waste repositories.

A fourth provision of the NWPA required the Department of Energy to determine the need for monitored, retrievable storage facilities (MRS). The MRS would be an above ground storage of the spent fuel until it could be retrieved for reprocessing. In 1985 the DOE announced the selection of three potential sites in Tennessee: the Clinch River Breeder Reactor site, the Oak Ridge National Laboratory Reservation, and the TVA's Hartsville Nuclear Power Plant, all on land owned by the national government. Reaction by state officials in Tennessee was quick and clear—they adamantly opposed the location of an MRS in the state (McCabe and Fitzgerald 1992:168). Public reaction was also highly negative. In spite of this intense opposition, DOE requested Congress to approve the construction of an MRS facility in Tennessee. The governor and state legislature filed notices of disapproval with Congress. The intense political struggle was the occasion for the passage of the Nuclear Waste Policy Act Amendments of 1987 wherein the DOE proposal to build an MRS in Tennessee was specifically annulled and revoked.

In an attempt to alleviate some of the basic sources of conflict, the Amendments created two conciliatory institutions: the MRS Commission and the High Level Waste Negotiator. The primary responsibility of the Commission was to review the need to create an MRS and to evaluate the technical problems associated with such a facility. The Commission made its report to Congress in 1989. On the issue of technical merit the Commission straddled the fence, concluding that both the MRS and No-MRS proposals were environmentally safe. Relative to need, the Commission recommended the construction of two temporary facilities with specific capacity limits, with a review of the need for additional facilities in the year 2000. In a sense, the Commission simply sidestepped the need issue. The High Level Waste Negotiator was to be located in the Executive Branch but independent of the Department of Energy. The primary responsibility of the Negotiator was to identify a state or Indian tribe willing to host a repository or an MRS. The Amendments prohibited negotiations with local governments. The Negotiator has announced his support for a variety of incentives, such as co-location of other federal projects and monetary benefits, to stimulate state interest and reduce local opposition. To date, no state or Indian tribe has expressed a willingness to host an MRS facility.

The final provision of the NWPA dealt with the issue of funding.

There were various estimates on the costs of the waste management program established in the Act, all in the billions of dollars. This cost was to be met by a tax on nuclear-generated electricity. Fees levied against the nuclear power industry would be paid into a Nuclear Waste Fund. The initial fee was set at one mill per kilowatt hour of electricity generated. Additional funds would be generated by a one time fee on utilities sending spent fuel rods to a storage facility. Monies in the Nuclear Waste Fund were targeted primarily to the construction and operation of a permanent repository.

The NWPA exempted the waste produced by defense activities from its provisions. However, if military waste was placed in a repository constructed under terms of the Act, the national government would have to pay its pro-rata share of the cost of the facility.

American policy on low-level nuclear waste was stated in the Low Level Radioactive Waste Act of 1980 (LLRWA). As with high-level waste, primary responsibility for establishing the standards and criteria for low-level waste management was vested in the Nuclear Regulatory Commission. Beyond this, the Act established two important policy principles. First, the Act specified that low-level waste management is a state and not a national responsibility. Congress provided a number of incentives to stimulate state assumption of that responsibility. However, as with many other features of environmental policy, a number of states simply failed to act. As a result of state recalcitrance, Congress amended the law in 1985 to force states into action by requiring them to take possession of low-level waste by 1996. The Amendments further provided that states were liable for any harm resulting from their failure to take possession of the waste. This effort to force action met with considerable opposition, including a challenge to the constitutionality of the Amendments. In 1992 the U.S. Supreme Court, in its decision on *New York vs. United States*, upheld the financial incentives of the Low Level Radioactive Waste Act of 1980 as being well-established principles of federal practice. However, in a decision with great significance for national regulatory authority, the Court struck down the mandatory provisions of the 1985 Amendments. The Court argued that when states refuse federal benefits rather than participate in the national program, Congress may not simply order them to participate. Such an order, the Court argued, violated the Tenth Amendment, which reserves to the states all powers not specifically granted to the national government. The case was obviously a major setback to the exercise of national power. Some states have been extremely reluctant to participate in nationally established policy, even when offered a wide range of incentives. Since *New York* v. *United States* prohibits the use of coercive powers when incentives fail, the American policy system will have to find noncoercive means of coping with the intergovernmental complexity of environmental policy generally and of nuclear waste policy specifically.

The second principle of the LLRWA encouraged states to form regional compacts for low-level waste disposal. However, there were basic problems in the formation of compacts, and as a result, the only compact region that functioned was the Southeast Regional Compact. The major factor contributing to the successful formation of this compact was the existence of a low-level commercial facility at Barnwell, South Carolina. That facility is reaching capacity, however, and South Carolina has announced that another state will have to host the next facility. The tensions created by the attempt to identify a second host state have put severe strains on the compact to the point where there is a high probability that it will disintegrate.

The Low Level Radioactive Waste Act prescribes shallow-land burial, that is, near-surface disposal of the waste in excavated trenches. The typical trench size is 40 feet wide at the top, 25 feet wide at the bottom, 20 feet deep, and 600 feet long. However, the Nuclear Regulatory Commission regulations permit a depth of up to 100 feet (10CFR61). The wall and bottom of the trench are of concrete. The clay naturally present in the site reduces the migratory rate of radionuclides. A typical facility has a number of trenches spaced about 20 feet apart.

There is considerable uncertainty surrounding trench technology. Successful shallow land burial depends on several factors, including proper site selection, proper trench design and construction, good waste-acceptance criteria, and good operating practices. However, even when these factors are at their optimum, problems still occur with trench technology. The most important of these is the bathtub effect. When the trench is filled, it is covered with 2 to 10 feet of fill dirt. As a result of factors such as weather patterns and the nature of the fill material, the capping material may be compromised, allowing the infiltration of water. This water settles into the trench, filling it as water fills a bathtub. The water, carrying radionuclides, then seeps out into the ground surrounding the trench. A similar problem occurred at several facilities where the trenches were located below the groundwater table. At the Oak Ridge National Laboratory, for example, radionuclides that have leached from trenches installed below groundwater tables have been detected as far south as Knoxville. A third problem results from the variety of wastes that are defined as low level. As was indicated earlier, the definition of low-level waste is based on exclusion, not level of radioactivity, heat generation, or hazard. In other words, all waste not defined as high-level or transuranic waste is low-level waste for policy purposes in the United States. This means that a wide variety of waste is placed in low-level facilities, even given good waste-acceptance criteria and management. The complex chemistry of both the materials placed in the trenches and groundwater presents enormous problems for low-level waste management.

As a result of these problems, shallow-land burial resembles a junkyard dumping system. At the very best, the conclusion must be reached that shallow-land burial will not retain the waste indefinitely. As a consequence, decisions have to be made regarding acceptable migration rates of the radionuclides. Certainly each facility should have monitoring programs to ensure that migration is detected at the site. At the worst, there is a real question as to whether shallow-land burial is safe. Surveys indicate that any migration of radionuclides from such facilities is unacceptable to the public. Thus if safety is defined as acceptable levels of perceived risk, shallow land burial of low-level nuclear waste does not present a safe disposal alternative.

The mining of uranium ore in the United States has left 24 sites with the problems of uranium mine tailings. All but one of the sites are located in the west; the eastern site is in Canonsburg, Pennsylvania, in the town's industrial park. The tailings, residual dirt, and ore left over from the mining process, amount to about 25 million tons of material contaminated with radionuclides. The tailings create a three dimensional hazard. First is the possibility of erosion of the pile onto adjacent property. Second, the tailings emit radon gas and gamma radiation into the air. Third, groundwater contamination is possible if radionuclides leach from the pile into the groundwater system.

American policy response to uranium mine tailings is contained in the Uranium Mine Tailings Radiation Control Act of 1978. The Act places overall authority over nuclear mine tailings in the Nuclear Regulatory Commission. Specific authority to implement the provisions of the Act is vested in the Department of Energy, which in turn must meet the standards adopted by the Environmental Protection Agency and must obtain a Nuclear Regulatory Commission license for its program at each site. The Act further provides that the DOE enter into cooperative agreements with affected states and Indian tribes to accomplish remedial action. The nature of those cooperative agreements is left unspecified except with regard to cost sharing. The national government is to assume 90 percent and the states 10 percent of the costs. When the site is on Indian lands, the national government is required to assume 100% of the costs. The DOE was to adopt standards by March 1983 and complete the stabilization program by March 1990. These schedules, like those of most in the environmental policy area, simply were not met.

Several provisions of the Act deal with specifics of waste management. One requires the DOE to seek expressions of interest for the reprocessing of the tailings. Efforts in this regard have been unsuccessful. The DOE is also required to take title to repository sites. As a result, it is made the responsible agency for long term monitoring and maintenance of tailings sites.

The Department of Energy has defined a mine tailings management program on the basis of the three-dimensional nature of the hazard.

Relative to radon gas and gamma radiation emission, the DOE has decided to use either earthen covers or asphalt emulsion, depending on the specific geology of the site. Relative to leaching into the groundwater, the DOE will use impermeable covers, construct slurry walls, or move the pile to a low-level waste facility. Relative to erosion onto adjacent property, the DOE has chosen earthen covers, the erection of protective berms, the construction of diversion channels, the contouring of the tailing site, and physical removal of the tailings to a low level depository. In addition to dealing with the piles themselves, the DOE has to make choices relative to cleanup of the buildings on the site and of land adjacent to the pilings. For building cleanup, there is a choice between excavation and removal of the building and the use of sealants and mechanical systems to control the hazards. The only alternative that appears viable for cleanup of adjacent land is excavation and removal to a low-level waste depository.

A review of the provisions of the Uranium Mine Tailings Radiation Control Act and of the DOE's experience with it leads to several important conclusions. First, efforts to prescribe completion dates for standard development or program implementation are virtually meaningless. The major reasons for failure to meet target dates appear to be political factors, intergovernmental complexity, technical uncertainty, and bureaucratic intransigence. Second, the technical uncertainties in the alternative remedial actions are significant. For example, there is a distinct possibility of cover rupture and groundwater contamination regardless of the remedial action taken if the pile is stabilized in place. Given all these uncertainties, it is hard to avoid the conclusion that the Department of Energy simply cannot meet the EPA's longevity standard of 200 to 1,000 years. The third conclusion is that in uranium mine tailings we see most clearly a problem in search of a policy. American policy response has been slow developing, limited in scope, locked in policy paralysis, and marked by technical uncertainty.

What lessons can be learned from the American experience with nuclear waste management? Certainly one of the most important is that the confidence in an easy fix through deep geological disposal was misplaced. Several international agencies and a number of countries have conducted extensive research on the problems involved, but they are of such magnitude in terms of both technology and time that it is not possible to develop a repository that will contain the risks. A second and related lesson has to do with low-level waste. Trench technology, which is at the heart of shallow-land burial, does not contain the risk. The best characterization that can be made of the American system is that it resembles a junkyard dumping system. Given these problems, the American experience demonstrates that neither technology nor policy have developed to a point where we can be confident that the risks associated with nuclear waste are at acceptable levels.

Another set of lessons from the American experience has to do with political and institutional arrangements. At the political level, it is clear that waiting until the volume of nuclear waste reaches a critical point before taking action is a mistake. The monitored retrievable sites proposed by the Nuclear Regulatory Commission were a response to an immediate need for disposal facilities by the nuclear power industry. The extent of the problem was such that the NRC had little alternative but to adopt a "decide, announce, and build" approach. The formidable political backlash to that strategy resulted in the failure to site a facility. While hindsight is cheap, it is also instructive. Hindsight suggests that an anticipatory policy leading to action before a pressing problem developed would have provided the possibility of policy success. At the institutional level, the American experience suggests that central governments cannot force state and regional bodies to act. A wide range of tactics were designed to obtain the cooperation and support of states and of Indian tribes—ranging from information through incentives to coercion—but none of them has proven effective in solving the complex intergovernmental problems associated with nuclear waste management. While the American federal system is unique in a sense, it is doubtful that central governments can implement an effective nuclear waste policy through the exercise of central authority alone.

The final lesson to be learned from the American experience is the need to develop policy-making processes that can accommodate an uncertain science. Public policy literature generally speaks of the collision of science and policy, pointing to the need to accommodate the findings of science with the realities of politics. But something more is at work in nuclear waste policy, something traceable in large part to the role of time. Nuclear waste policy demands a time scale that is beyond the realm of science. In fact, nuclear waste policy demands a time scale that is beyond common understanding. How are we to conceptualize conditions 500,000 years from now?

There are two perspectives on the appropriate approach to the long half life of some radionuclides. The first approach, touted as the pragmatic view, argues that long time scales are not meaningful for public policy and urges that the time scale for policy purposes be limited to one that is understandable. A period of about 500 years is the preferred one in this view. The other perspective argues for the adoption of a cut-off time beyond which exposure levels would not be calculated. A figure of 10,000 years has been suggested for the cut-off date (Chapman and McKinley 1987). However, this figure is either too long or too short, depending on the kind of science one is doing. For the social scientist, 10,000 years is too long for rational predictions of social and political conditions. For the geologist, accustomed to long time frames, 10,000 years is probably too short. Thus it is difficult to obtain agreement on the appropriate time frame for nuclear waste policy.

DECOMMISSIONING NUCLEAR POWER PLANTS: THE OPPORTUNITY FOR ANTICIPATORY POLICY

General nuclear waste policy worldwide has been slow in developing. Recognition of a need for a policy response, even to a problem with the ramifications of nuclear waste, does not necessarily translate into viable policy. Thus the world faces a serious problem of nuclear waste without an adequate waste management policy. One area of nuclear waste, however, presents the possibility of anticipating the problem and developing a policy response in advance of a crisis. That area is the decommissioning of nuclear power plants.

There are approximately 250 nuclear power plants in operation around the world, plus a number of other reactors, largely in research facilities. Since 1960 more than 65 reactors in various locations have been decommissioned. With regard to nuclear power plants, the best estimates suggest a life of about 30 years. Using this estimate, over 100 of the 250 nuclear power plant reactors will have to be decommissioned during the early 2000s. Decommissioning will become a regular industrial activity for which there must be a public policy response in several countries.

Decommissioning involves the management of three types of radioactive waste. The first is the irradiated fuel and water coolant in the reactor itself. The irradiated fuel would be either reprocessed or placed in temporary facilities for spent fuel rods. The water coolant would have to be managed as high level nuclear waste. The second type of waste is the contamination that occurs on the surface of the reactor. During operations, a thin layer of radioactivity, referred to as *crud*, forms on the inner surface of the reactor. It can be removed only by special cleaning devices including water jets and brushes. The resultant fluid must be disposed of as high-level nuclear waste. The third type of radioactive waste is induced radioactivity in the structural steel and concrete skin of the reactor. Management of this type of waste depends on the type of decommissioning that occurs.

There are three types of decommissioning. Stage 3 decommissioning is the most comprehensive. It involves the removal of all radioactive materials. Once this occurs, the remaining plant is demolished and reused as fill material. It is possible to do so because the major part of a nuclear power plant—80 percent of all materials—is never contaminated. Stage 2 decommissioning involves sealing off the highly radioactive parts of the plant, namely the reactor and its immediate environs; radioactive materials in that area are allowed to decay naturally. The less radioactive materials are decontaminated by various processes and then, along with noncontaminated materials, are removed from the plant site. Stage 1 decommissioning leaves the plant virtually intact. All easily removable radioactive materials, such as the irradiated fuel rods and spent fuel rods, are removed from the site and all else is left. The assumption is that a maintenance and monitoring staff will be left in place. Since this action commits substantial monies without producing a return, Stage 1 decommissioning is generally viewed as only an interim measure.

Decommissioning of the average power plant results in significant amounts of nuclear waste. A Stage 3 decommissioning, favored by most policy makers, produces 300+ cubic meters of highly radioactive waste, 2000+ cubic meters of material with induced radioactivity, and 50,000+ cubic meters of nonradioactive waste. Clearly, national policy systems need to anticipate the production of such volumes of waste and develop adequate policy for its management.

CAN WE LEARN FROM POLICY STALEMATE?

Nuclear waste is a serious environmental problem in search of a policy solution. The early years of nuclear research were marked by considerable complacency relative to the management of the by-products of nuclear fission. This complacency was accompanied by the accumulation of substantial volumes of nuclear waste in some countries, including the United States. Policy response to the problem has been slow in developing. Primary reliance is still on storage. One objective of storage is the retrieval of energy left in the fuel rod after it has been used in the reactor. However, it is more likely that the most important reason for storage is the inability to develop acceptable options for the permanent disposal of the material. The most difficult problem in developing long term storage technology is the extremely long period of time over which containment of some radioactive material is required. The complex nature of the interaction of radionuclides with other materials, including groundwater, further exacerbates the problem of developing policy solutions.

One of the most important policy issues is the development of acceptable procedures for obtaining collective consent on policy alternatives. Unfortunately, the absence of such procedures has led to substantial mistrust of the nuclear waste policy process, particularly in the United States. As a study of nuclear waste policy observed: "…opposition to the nuclear waste repository program goes beyond a simple 'not-in-my-backyard' syndrome. Instead, the credibility and equity of the entire waste repository program" is found lacking (Pijawaka and Mushkatel 1992:89). Thus the most significant problems for nuclear waste management may be the lack of public confidence in the policy process coupled with the scientific complexity of the problem.

The starting point for learning from previous policy stalemate seems to be acceptance of two important facts. The first is that it is difficult if not impossible to prove that the risks associated with any policy alternative on nuclear waste are acceptable. The second unavoidable fact is that nations with substantial defense and commercial applications of nuclear energy cannot continue with policy stalemate. Temporary storage and junkyard dumping systems do not add up to permanent solutions. In fact, continued use of such systems will make the problem even more difficult to solve. On the other hand, barring an unanticipated breakthrough in technology, nuclear waste management will require acceptance of a technology that puts future generations, for long time periods that are meaningful only in computer models, at greater risk than we have been willing to accept in other policy areas. Past policy failure has not necessarily harmed future generations, although it may have done so. But past policy failure has placed future generations at greater risks than we would be willing to accept for ourselves.

Chapter 7

Solid Waste

If nuclear waste policy is the new kid on the block, solid waste is the great granddaddy of all environmental problems. Martin Melosi, the self-styled "garbage historian," has produced an excellent historical account of human experience with solid waste. Melosi summarized that experience in this way:

> Since human beings have inhabited the earth, they have generated, produced, manufactured, excreted, secreted, discarded and otherwise disposed of all manner of waste. Among the myriad kinds of rejectamenta, refuse—solid waste—has been one of the most abundant, most cumbersome, and potentially the most harmful. (Melosi 1981:3)

Melosi describes interesting first approaches to the problem of solid waste. One of the earliest known examples of central planning for solid waste was the city of Mahenjo-Daro in the Indus Valley. That plan included the construction of homes with built-in rubbish chutes and trash bins, a drainage system, and a scavenger service. The first solid waste landfill was probably that of Athens in ancient Greece. In response to a crucial problem with solid waste, the city council passed an ordinance in about 500 B.C. establishing a municipal dump outside the city. The action included a prohibition against littering, which was defined as throwing garbage into the street. Rome in the period of the Caesars depended on open dumping, which resulted in a significantly dirty and unhealthy environment. Out of these early practices, two features of public policy emerged: the principle of local responsibility for solid waste and the utilization of landfills as the technology for solid waste disposal.

One of the problems in thinking about solid waste is definition. As with so many other areas of environmental policy, there is no universally accepted definition of solid waste. Therefore the data on a transnational basis is not comparable. What one country reports as solid waste is often different from what is reported by another country. More important, public policy response varies with the different definitions. For example, if solid waste is defined to include all industrial solid waste, then some highly toxic hazardous waste is included in the definition and shallow land burial would be an inappropriate policy.

In general, three categories of waste are included in the definition of solid waste. The first is municipal waste. This includes household waste, waste similar to household waste generated by small commercial and industrial firms, and waste from lawns and gardens. Biodegradable organic waste is the largest proportion of municipal waste in all countries. Plastic has steadily increased as a component of municipal waste in all countries. Recycling efforts have reduced the quantities of glass, metals, and paper. The second category of solid waste is industrial waste. The amount of this waste is continuing to increase significantly. In OECD countries, for example, the volume of industrial waste produced rose from 1,000 million tons in 1980 to 1,500 million tons in 1990. The OECD reports include hazardous waste as industrial solid waste, but fortunately, they do provide a separate accounting for the hazardous constituents of industrial waste. Thus we know that of the 1,500 million tons of industrial waste generated in 1990, 299 million tons were hazardous waste. The third type of solid waste is referred to by the acronym SQHW (small-quantity hazardous waste). Data from other regions of the world, particularly South America and Asia, do not account separately for the hazardous constituents of industrial waste.

The mix of these three categories of waste form the definition of solid waste for policy purposes in all countries.

Differences in the mix are seen clearly in the definitions adopted by the OECD and the United States. The OECD defines solid waste as "all substances undiluted in water or in the air which a holder wishes to or must dispose of, with the exception of radioactive wastes from nuclear activities" (OECD 1991:145). This definition encompasses all three categories of solid waste. In the United States, solid waste is defined as "garbage, refuse, and other discarded solid materials, including solid-waste materials resulting from industrial, commercial, and agricultural operations, and from community activities, but does not include solids or dissolved material in domestic sewage or other significant pollutants in water resources, such as silt, dissolved or suspended solids in industrial waste water effluents, dissolved materials in irrigation return flows, or other common water pollutants" (The Solid Waste Disposal Act: P.L. 89–272). This definition excludes most hazardous waste, both chemical and nuclear.

The American policy definition, however, is not as sharp as it appears on the surface. The Resource Conservation and Recovery Act initially exempted commercial and industrial firms that produced less than 1,000 kilograms of hazardous waste per month. Amendments in 1984 lowered that monthly exemption to 100 kilograms, but small-quantity hazardous waste is excluded from policy on hazardous waste and presumptively remains solid waste. Additionally, there has been very little effort to segregate household waste in the United States. Collectively, households produce all types of small quantity hazardous waste. The situation is made even more complex because U.S. municipalities vary significantly in their solid waste practices: Some collect and dispose of virtually all forms of solid waste; others require industrial and commercial generators to provide for their own waste. Even within categories, practices differ. Some municipalities collect yard waste while others refuse to do so. Thus what actually "shows up" in the municipal waste stream in the United States might be significantly different from typical household waste and might vary from locality to locality. The best that can be said is that solid waste policy in the United States places primary emphasis on municipal waste, loosely defined.

In spite of the differences in the materials constituting the solid waste stream, public policy in most countries has been remarkably similar. The common features of solid waste policy—landfill technology and local government responsibility—were established as early as 500 B.C. Because of the almost universal application of these features, most policy analysts believed that the basic questions of solid waste policy had been settled. Several developments occurred, however, that resulted in the unsettling of this well-established policy area.

THE UNGLUING OF A SETTLED POLICY AREA

The most important single factor in the reemergence of solid waste as an environmental problem is the increase in the volume of waste generated. Reliable data on solid waste have been available only since the early 1970s in industrialized nations and are still unavailable in less-developed countries. Thus time series analysis is not possible, except over short time frames. Table 7.1 presents the situation with regard to OECD countries, where there are reliable data. In total volume, municipal waste increased from 3 million to 4 million tons in slightly over ten years in these countries. Per capita waste generated also increased dramatically, from 407 to 513 kilograms in the same period. The reasons behind this increase are complex.

Table 7.1   **Municipal Waste Generated Annually**

	Total (1000 tons)				Per capita (kg/cap.)			
	Mid 1970s	1980	Mid 1980s	Late 1980s	Mid 1970s	1980	Mid 1980s	Late 1980s
North America	151,000	173,000	194,000	225,000	633	687	734	826
Japan	38,000	42,000	42,000	45,000	341	355	344	394
OECD Europe	104,000	110,000	120,000	136,000	277	323	346	336
OECD	302,000	337,000	370,000	420,000	407	436	493	513

Source: OECD 1991:14.

Popular thinking on the increase in the volume of municipal waste has tended to concentrate on the phenomenon of the "throwaway society." In this view, the problem is a result of an increase in the nonconsumable disposable goods people acquire that they cannot or will not recycle. There are substantial data to support this view. A large volume of nonconsumable, disposable products is in the form of packaging material, usually either paper, glass, metal, or plastics. These materials constitute a large proportion of the total municipal solid waste stream. In the United States the best estimates of the composition of the municipal solid waste stream are as follows: paper and cardboard 34.7 percent, plastics 6.7 percent, glass 9.0 percent, metals 8.8 percent, and other inorganics 40.8 percent (World Resources Institute 1992: 319). Not all of these materials, then, are packaging materials, and determining the relative contribution of packaging to the total volume of material is difficult, although some attempts have been made to do so. One of the better attempts found that packaging accounts for approximately 13 to 15 percent of the solid waste stream in Australia (Honeysett 1975:163).

While packaging has been made the fall guy of solid waste, packaging, ironically, can result in efficiencies in the management of solid waste. For example, the preparation of vegetables results in the generation of solid waste; handling that waste at the point of manufacture (packaging) is more efficient than handling it at the individual household level. Packaging, then, is a mixed bag so far as its contribution to the municipal waste stream is concerned (see the box entitled "The Demon Packaging May Not Have Such Long Horns"). An important factor in the negative connotation is litter. Litter is a highly visible result of packaging, is esthetically unattractive, and can be dangerous to human health and safety. Estimates on how much packaging ends up as litter are sketchy and unreliable. Honeysett estimated that approximately 1 percent of the solid waste stream in Australia consisted of litter. So, while the throwaway society is a part of the explanation for the increase in the municipal waste stream, it falls short of providing a full explanation.

ෂ *The Demon Packaging May Not Have Such Long Horns*

As a result of the outcry over the throwaway society, packaging has come under widespread condemnation. At best it is seen as an unnecessary evil—unnecessary because the motive behind it is sheer selfish convenience of both the producer and consumer, and evil because it adds to the volume of garbage in the environment. However, packaging is not exclusively an evil. Nor is it merely a convenience or a device for exploitation. Packaging serves important and sometimes necessary purposes.

Packaging serves at least four socially useful purposes. The first is protection of the public health. Food spoilage results from the growth of bacteria, fungi, and other agents injurious to human health. The tin can, for example, preserves food against this spoilage for long periods of time. Without it, the mass distribution of food would be very difficult. Second, packaging can contribute to public safety. Some materials have to be isolated from the environment—pharmaceutical products, pesticides, detergents, and others. Packages contain those materials and protect the environment from them. In addition, widespread concern for product tampering in the United States resulted in regulations to make packages more tamper proof. It would be nearly impossible to market tamper-free products in bulk. Third, packaging can contribute to better nutrition. Seasonal products can be eaten throughout the year as a result of packaging. Additionally, packaging allows the manufacture of seasonal foodstuffs when they are cheapest, thus increasing their availability to a wider range of the population. Finally, packaging can increase efficiency. The solid waste from vegetables prepared in bulk can be managed more efficiently than the waste from individual households. Further, the cooking involved in the packaging of some food reduces the cooking—and thus the amount of fuel—that must take place, decreasing what is required in the individual household.

So, while modern consumers may demand packaged products for convenience and producers may prefer them for certain market reasons, packaged products do serve useful purposes, including environmental purposes.

A broader explanation for the increased volume of waste is found in the lifestyle of an ever increasing urban/industrial society. The industrialized nations lead all other countries in pounds of municipal waste created per person per day, followed by the oil-rich nations of the Middle East. Table 7.2 presents data on the population, per capita GNP, and solid waste generated in selected countries. The important factor in that data is per capita GNP. The higher the per capita GNP, the more solid waste the country generates. Again, while time series data are unavailable, a corollary proposition that deserves attention is the effect of growth in per capita GNP on generation of solid waste. As a country's per capita GNP increases, does that country's production of solid waste increase? The strong relationship between these two factors suggests that the answer to that question is yes. Population, on the other hand, seems weakly associated with the generation of solid waste. The United States, with a population of 249 million, produces 230 million tons of solid waste per year; the former Soviet Union, with a population of 288 million, produces only 45 million tons; and Indonesia, with a population of 184 million, produces only 12.9 million tons (World Resources Institute 1993:463, 567, 603). Similar comparisons could be found among nations with smaller populations. The most important factor associated with the production of solid waste, then, is per capita GNP. Nations with high per capita GNP have the luxury of wasting materials; nations with low per capita GNP do not have that luxury.

**Table 7.2   Population, Per Capita GNP, and Solid Waste
Generated, Selected Countries**

Country	Population	GNP per capita	Solid Waste, millions of tons per year
Algeria	24,960,000	$1,947	2.6
Ethiopia	49,240,000	124	1.3
Nigeria	108,542,000	262	7.7
South Africa	35,282,000	2,514	4.2
Bangladesh	115,593,000	181	3.8
China	1,139,060,000	374	76.6
Iraq	18,920,000	1,915	6.0
Israel	4,600,000	9,922	1.9
Japan	123,460,000	23,072	53.2
Saudi Arabia	14,134,000	6,319	4.8
Belgium	9,845,000	15,730	3.8
France	56,138,000	17,052	30.2
Germany	77,573,000	19,633	21.0
Netherlands	14,951,000	14,878	7.6
United Kingdom	57,237,000	14,669	22.0
Canada	26,521,000	20,224	18.1
United States	249,224,000	21,039	230.1

Australia	16,873,000	16,192	11.0
New Zealand	3,392,000	11,798	2.1
Argentina	32,322,000	1,671	5.6
Brazil	150,368,000	2,952	22.7
Chile	13,173,000	1,808	2.3
Peru	21,550,000	1,543	3.0

Source: Data contained in World Resources Institute, *Environmental Almanac, 1993*. Boston: Houghton Mifflin, pp. 347–640.

Experience within the United States lends support to these conclusions. Total population of a given state is weakly associated with volume of solid waste produced, while per capita average income is strongly associated with it. Table 7.3 presents the data on the top and bottom five states in the production of solid waste. Indications also suggest that recycling programs can reduce the amount of solid waste generated. Connecticut, for example, has the highest per capita average income of any state in the nation at $16,094, but it ranks 32 in the per capita production of solid waste at 0.88 tons per year. The state has 150 curbside recycling programs which serve a population of 3,287,000. New Jersey has the second highest per capita average income at $15,028 and ranks 29 in solid waste generation. It has 525 curbside recycling programs serving a population of 8,846,000. Per capita income, modified by the effects of active recycling programs, is the most important determinant in the volume of solid waste generated within American states.

Table 7.3   Top and Bottom Five States in the Generation of Solid Waste

State	Population	Per capita average income	Total solid waste 1,000 tons	Per capita solid waste tons
California	29,760,000	$13,197	45,000	1.51
Missouri	5,117,000	11,203	7,500	1.47
Virginia	6,187,000	13,658	9,000	1.45
Ohio	10,847,000	11,323	15,700	1.45
Florida	12,938,000	12,456	18,700	1.45
Wisconsin	4,892,000	11,417	3,400	0.70
Vermont	563,000	11,234	390	0.69
Georgia	6,478,000	11,406	4,400	0.68
North Dakota	639,000	9,641	400	0.63
Mississippi	2,573,000	8,088	1,400	0.54

Source: Data contained in World Resources Institute, *Environmental Almanac, 1993*. Boston: Houghton Mifflin, pp. 231–281.

Several factors have combined with the consumption patterns of advanced nations to produce the solid waste problem. Among the most important of these developments is the pattern of landfill use. A good example is the United States, which has experienced a significant decline of landfill capacity for several reasons. There has been a dramatic trend toward closing existing landfills. Approximately 14,000 municipal landfills have been closed since 1978, and the EPA projects that as many as three-fourths of existing landfills will be closed by the year 2000 (EPA 1988). At the same time, new landfills are being built at a much slower rate than previously. The combination of landfill closing and a slower rate of new sitings produces an estimate of a 30 percent decline in landfill capacity in the five years between 1988 and 1993 (Denison and Ruston 1990:4). Moreover, the decline in capacity is not uniformly distributed across the country. Some areas have lost more capacity than others—and the loss of capacity seems to be concentrated in areas that produce the most waste. Thus the problem has reached crisis dimensions in some regions.

The increase in municipal waste generated and the decline in landfill capacity was accompanied by a growing concern for the effectiveness of solid waste management technology. This concern was centered on both the traditional technology associated with landfills and alternate technologies such as incineration. Landfill technology has not been environmentally benign. Landfills pollute through a variety of ways, including the release of liquids into both surface and groundwater, runoff of contaminated water into surface water systems, and the release of toxic gases into the air. The situation has been described this way:

> Even the best-designed landfills suffer inherent deficiencies. All of the structures built into the landfill to contain the waste—liners, leachate collection systems, and final cover materials—have finite lifetimes, whereas the wastes and their toxic emissions will continue to exist for decades longer. (Denison and Ruston 1990:6)

An EPA inventory of landfill performance confirms this observation. The EPA found that only about 25 percent of landfills have the capacity to monitor groundwater and, of these, 25 percent are contaminating the groundwater. Relative to surface water, only 12 percent of landfills have the capacity to monitor surface water systems, and of these, 60 percent are contaminating the systems (EPA 1986). These percentages are disturbing. Perhaps most disturbing is the fact that more than 20 percent (249 out of 1,177) of the sites on the Superfund National Priority List are municipal landfills. Of the twenty worst sites, eight are municipal landfills (Denison and Ruston 1990:6). Most of these sites, however, were in existence prior to the passage of the Resource Conservation and Recovery Act. Corrective action has been taken under the RCRA to prevent future dumping of highly toxic substances into municipal landfills.

The major alternatives to landfills are incineration, waste reduction, and recycling. While each of these strategies offers advantages, each also carries problems. The combination of landfill inadequacy and problems associated with alternate technologies has contributed substantially to the municipal waste management problem.

MUNICIPAL WASTE MANAGEMENT STRATEGIES: SOLUTIONS ARE NO LONGER AS ATTRACTIVE

Like the definition of solid waste, the terminology relative to solid waste management strategies varies considerably. A four-category scheme gives the clearest picture of the options available: disposal, waste reduction, recycling, and conversion. We will examine each of these strategies briefly.

Disposal

Disposal is the traditional strategy of managing municipal solid waste. The methods, ranked by frequency of use, are landfills, incineration, and ocean disposal.

Burying in landfills continues to be the primary means of disposal. In OECD countries about 70 percent of municipal waste is sent to landfills. Individual countries vary significantly in their practices, however. In Japan about 38 percent of municipal solid waste is sent to landfills, compared with 60 to 80 percent in the United States, depending on the definition of waste that is used (OECD 1991:15). Virtually all countries have adopted policies designed to decrease the volume of waste disposed of in landfills. One means of accomplishing that objective is to increase the technical requirements for landfill operations.

Until 50 years ago, landfills were essentially unregulated. There was no segregation of materials, a situation that resulted in the emplacement of very toxic materials in some municipal landfills. Most sites were vermin infested, potentially spreading disease over large areas. Odors were uncontrolled and often detectable for miles. Air emissions contained carcinogenic compounds such as benzene, chloroform, and carbon tetrachloride. Monitoring systems were inadequate, and leachate into both groundwater and surface water systems was common. Remedial action took the form of regulations to improve landfill siting requirements, operations processes, and closure precautions.

The landfills sited and operated under the new requirements are referred to as *controlled landfills*. Site selection is now subject to strict engineering requirements, relating to such factors as climate characteristics, topography, surface and groundwater systems, solid composition, and general land use plans for the locality and region. Site design plans have to include both the technical requirements and various environmental factors such as leachate systems and the control of gas emissions. Some countries are imposing esthetic requirements as well, such as control of odors and noise. Operating procedures are important components of the new regulations. For example, it is common practice to require that each day's deposit of waste be covered with a six-inch layer of soil. Controlled landfills must comply with the monitoring requirements established by the jurisdiction, relating particularly to leachate and gas and including the maintenance of a record system. Finally, a controlled landfill must be closed in the prescribed manner consistent with the final land use plans for the site.

The United States offers a typical example of these new requirements. From almost unregulated local control of solid waste, the United States now has regulations governing all facets of municipal solid waste management. The latest of these, which went into effect in October 1993, require the installation of plastic and clay liners similar to those required for chemical disposal sites. They also require the careful monitoring of the leaching of liquid and the escape of methane gas. Since many existing facilities cannot be upgraded to meet the new requirements, the regulations will force the closing of some landfills. This effect is so significant that the regulations may be viewed as serving the dual purpose of improving landfill technology and discouraging landfill use. In so doing, the regulations will also increase the cost of constructing and operating new landfills. This increase in cost will be accompanied by higher tipping fees (the charge for placing materials in a facility), a cost that increased 17 percent between 1988 and 1990 (World Resources Institute 1993:63). In spite of new regulations designed to improve landfill technology, however, landfills involve inherent deficiencies.

Deficiencies in landfill technology resulted in renewed interest in another traditional means of disposal, incineration. Technically, incineration disposes of waste by high temperature oxidation. In common parlance, the waste is burned. Like landfills, incineration is a long-standing practice. In ancient times it was quite common to increase the lifetime of a municipal dump by setting fire to it. Such a practice had undesirable side effects, including odors and toxic gases which spread for miles. England conducted the first systematic testing of incineration in 1874 (Melosi 1981:48), and European nations were quick to institute the practice. When it spread to the United States in the late 1880s, it was hailed as the perfect disposal method. In the words of a West Virginia health official in 1888, most American engineers believed that incineration provided "a means of entirely destroying these substances and their power to do evil" (Melosi 1981:47). American cities adopted the practice on a widespread basis, referring to incinerators as "cremators" or "garbage furnaces."

Utilization of incinerators has become a significant component of municipal solid waste management in a number of countries. Japan,

Sweden, and Switzerland burn over 50 percent of their municipal solid waste. In nearly all OECD countries the proportion of municipal waste incinerated increased during the 1980s (OECD 1991:150). In 1988 there were 525 incinerators in Europe and 160 in the United States.

Modern incinerators are furnaces that permit controlled burning of waste at very high temperatures, usually from 1,650 to 1,800 degrees Fahrenheit. Their design characteristics are much like those used in hazardous chemical waste management. Thus while there are several designs for incinerators, each basically involves an intake system and a combustion chamber. The efficiency of the burn depends on a number of factors, including control of the air supply in the combustion chamber and the nature of the material to be burned. In most nations there are less stringent requirements on incinerators designed to burn municipal solid waste than on those for hazardous chemical waste. The important policy question, then, is whether or not incinerators destroy solid waste's "power to do evil."

The bright promise of incineration has been dimmed somewhat by the finding of potentially significant environmental impacts. The two most important are emissions into the air and the ash that is generated by the process.

Several important issues surround the emissions from incinerators. First, incinerators emit criteria pollutants into the air. These include sulfur dioxide, nitrogen dioxide, carbon monoxide, and hydrocarbons. An interesting comparison was made between the projected emissions from the Brooklyn Navy Yard incinerator, the Hudson Avenue electric steam generation plant, and an industrial coal boiler, all operating in the New York City area. The incinerator was projected to emit 1,177 tons of sulfur dioxide per year, compared with 1,435 for the electric generating plant and 1,847 for the industrial boiler. Comparable figures for nitrogen dioxide were 2,973 tons for the incinerator, 1,300 tons for the electric generating plant, and 3,403 for the industrial boiler. Carbon monoxide emissions were 366 for the incinerator, 132 for the electric generating plant, and 187 for the industrial boiler (Neal and Schubel 1987:94). The industrial boiler would produce the same amount of electricity as the incinerator, and it is unlikely that incinerators would emit significantly lower levels of criteria pollutants into the air. An additional concern is the emission of metals from incinerators, including lead, cadmium, zinc, copper, manganese, silver, mercury, and tin. The Brooklyn Navy Yard incinerator is projected to emit 14.5 tons of lead annually, compared with a coal fired industrial boiler producing the same amount of electricity and emitting 3 tons per year (Neal and Schubel 1987:95). Metals are emitted into the air when they attach to fly ash particles. Emission levels can be reduced by various pollution control devices on the smokestacks of incinerators.

Beyond criteria pollutants and metals are certain emissions that are especially complex. These include PCBs and dioxins. Such chemical compounds may be formed in the combustion process by either the chemical breakup of materials or the interaction of chemical elements in the high-temperature process. PCBs are released when materials containing the compound are incinerated. Dioxins are formed by low-temperature burning of plastics, bleached paper, pesticides, and wood preservatives. The best evidence suggests that temperatures in excess of 1,300 degrees Fahrenheit are necessary to break the chemical bond of dioxins. Thus if incinerator temperatures are kept high enough, the risk of dioxin emission is low (Richard and Junk 1981:1099).

A second major concern with incineration is the management of the ash that is produced. There are two kinds of ash—fly ash and bottom ash. *Fly ash* is fine particulate matter that is emitted through the stack and is particularly troublesome because heavy metals, such as lead, attach to the ash. *Bottom ash* is the residue that is left in the incinerator. Approximately 20 to 25 percent of the material burned in an incinerator is left as ash, depending on the type of material and the efficiency of the burn. Disposal of bottom ash has become a divisive issue.

The hazardous materials present in bottom ash depend on the type of materials burned. Thus each burn will produce a different combination of hazardous materials. To meet the problem created by the uniqueness of each batch of ash, the EPA requires that bottom ash be tested for its hazardous content. However, little testing is actually done. A positive element is that most hazardous materials in bottom ash consist of metallic elements, and these can be removed by magnets or immobilized by lime or other additives. However, recovery has not proven to be economically feasible because of the low quality of the recovered product. Experiments are being conducted to determine the feasibility of using solidified bottom ash in such products as concrete blocks, road paving materials, and materials for the construction of fishing reefs. The results are still indeterminate. For example, concrete blocks containing bottom ash do not usually exhibit construction strength. A complex interaction between the aluminum in the ash and the alkaline materials in the cement reduces the strength of the block. As a result, most bottom ash is disposed of in regular municipal landfills, where it increases the problems of leaching into surface and groundwater systems.

The problems associated with emissions and disposal of ash have dampened the enthusiasm for incineration. Most technical analysis and conferences on the subject have concluded that these problems are manageable with current technology (Neal and Schubel 1987:105). The economic factors, however, are formidable. An incinerator with a capacity of 2,000 tons per day costs approximately $150 million to construct and has operating costs of about $15 million annually. Fees for using such facilities have to be set very high and encourage potential users to look to landfill. Additionally, the public does not seem to share the confidence of engineers in incineration technology, particularly when specific siting efforts are made. The political problems resulting from the NIMBY syndrome make siting efforts difficult if not impossible tasks.

The Uncertain State of Ocean Dumping

The ocean is the world's ultimate disposal site—the ultimate repository of virtually all pollutants. Historically, the ocean was viewed as an appropriate method of municipal waste disposal. Neal and Schubel (1987:66) report that the 1902 *Encyclopedia Britannica* hailed the advantages of ocean disposal. It was asserted that ocean dumping was a "clean method" of disposing of municipal garbage, that it did not adversely affect humans, that it added to the level of nutrients available to fish and aquatic life, and that it was easy, convenient, and economical. The siren song of ocean dumping was appealing indeed.

The adverse effects of pollution on the ocean were discussed in the chapter on water pollution. The United States moved to prevent ocean dumping in the Ocean Dumping Act of 1974, which banned the dumping of most materials found in municipal garbage. At present no city in the United States disposes of its garbage through ocean dumping.

However, there is no system in effect to monitor the practice of cities worldwide. Beyond doubt, many cities still dump their waste directly into the ocean or into estuaries that lead into the ocean. Additionally, commercial vessels release nearly all their waste into the ocean. These practices could produce the astonishing volume of 7 million tons a year. As if these two sources of trash in the ocean were not enough, individuals contribute through littering.

The ocean has a finite capacity for absorption of waste and renewal of itself. Humankind cannot continue to use it indiscriminately as the ultimate septic tank.

The problems associated with disposal methods have forced consideration of other strategies for the management of solid waste. Waste reduction, recycling, and conversion are designed to "make molehills out of mountains," as one commentator expressed their intent (Neal and Schubel 1987:127).

Waste Reduction

Waste reduction strategies are aimed at reducing the amount of materials entering the waste stream. There are two directions these strategies can take. The first is *source reduction*, that is, the reduction of waste at the point of manufacture. The second is *recycling*, which is discussed in the next section.

Waste reduction is an important component of chemical waste policy in Europe. The strategy is based on the assumption that any waste in the production or commercial process is an inefficiency that is costly to the firm. Waste can be reduced either in the production process itself or by producing products that are more durable. The later strategy would end the practice of building obsolescence into product lines. Unfortunately, there has been no public policy effort at source reduction of nonhazardous materials. Even in Europe the emphasis is on source reduction of hazardous materials, with recycling the preferred strategy for nonhazardous materials.

Recycling

Recycling refers to an effort to encourage consumer choice of products that reduce waste or to retrieve materials from the waste stream. Consumer action can take many forms. Consumers can make a conscious effort to buy high quality products with long product life. They can choose between products that are repairable and those that are not. Considerable emphasis has been placed on the need to choose products that minimize packaging requirements. An interesting variant on recycling is "yard sales" and consignment shops that are prevalent in many parts of the United States. These resales extend the useful life of the product. While consumer education programs have rightly emphasized the need to recycle, more attention needs to be given to the possibilities for waste reduction through informed consumer choice. Unfortunately, public policy has tended to neglect this important environmental strategy.

Recycling also involves all actions that retrieve materials from the waste stream for reuse. Materials that are most amenable to recycling are paper, glass, plastics, aluminum, and tin cans. However, recycling some of these products is not as easy as most people think. For example, there are about 40 regular grades and 30 special grades of paper in regular use in the United States. Of these, newspapers, corrugated boxes, and high-grade office paper have the greatest potential for recycling, while computer paper is difficult to recycle. Additionally, the supply of newspapers has outstripped the capacity of the system. Newspapers have to be "de-inked" and current de-inking capacity allows for the recycling of about 35 percent of all newspapers. Tin cans are also problematic. They can be either steel with a thin coating of tin or bi-metal made of tin-coated steel and aluminum ends. When the cans are melted, it is very difficult to separate the tin from the steel. Another complicating factor is that some tin cans are soldered with lead, which presents serious problems of furnace deterioration and release of lead into the air. Also, the resins in plastics must be separated.

Since some resins are amenable to that separation and others are not, the plastics industry has developed a coding system for stamping plastic containers to identify those which are recyclable. Aluminum cans and glass are the most easily recycled materials. The aluminum industry already recycles about 55 percent of all aluminum cans and believes that a 75 percent recycling rate is achievable. One reason is that aluminum is very energy intensive to produce; it takes 95 percent less energy to produce it from recycled material than from ore. Glass recycling is also practical and economical. Crushed used glass, called *cullet*, constitutes 30 percent of the material used to produce new glass products. The Glass Packaging Institute believes that a 50 percent reuse rate is achievable. The potential for recycling, then, varies significantly with the materials.

Despite this variation in potential, recycling does offer an important strategy for waste reduction. The experience of Japan is instructive in this regard. Japan recycled 50 percent of its waste paper, 55 percent of its glass, and 66 percent of its cans in 1988 (Corson 1990:270). Some of the remaining waste was converted into fertilizers and fuel gas. Thus only 27 percent of the waste stream was left to be disposed of through landfills. In contrast, the United States recycled 23 percent of its paper, 9 percent of its glass, and 25 percent of its aluminum in 1986. About 80 percent of all waste generated in the United States was destined for landfills.

The experience with recycling programs suggests two important conclusions. Japan's experience suggests that recycling is much more effective when efforts are made to deal with the mass of solid waste rather than concentrating on specific materials. Mass solid waste can be used to produce methane gas, fertilizers, and animal feed. Yard waste in particular can be composted to provide an important source of nutrients for a wide variety of applications. Several U.S. cities have successful composting programs, either distributing the compost to individuals or selling it to landscaping companies or in the "green thumb" market.

The second lesson to be learned from past recycling programs is the necessity of giving attention to developing markets for recycled products. The market for some recyclables is saturated and becoming so for others. Newsprint is a good example. Stockpiles of recyclable newspapers became so large that some recycling firms had to pay up to $20 a ton to have the paper hauled to a landfill. There are a number of ways that markets for recyclables can be stimulated. One is an education effort targeted at both manufacturers and consumers. Manufacturers have shied away from recycled materials under the assumption that they are inferior in quality to the virgin material. This is true in some instances. For example, de-inking reduces the quality of the recycled paper. Other recycled materials, however, are of as high grade as the virgin materials. In either instance, manufacturers need to be encouraged to look for applications of recycled materials. Consumers can make an important contribution to increasing the use of recycled materials, especially institutional consumers. In the United States several state governments direct their purchasing departments to buy recycled products when possible and economical. Many educational institutions have followed suit. Another way to develop markets for recyclables is to standardize specifications for certain products. For example, paper varies widely in quality, and the paper industry complains that a lack of standardization means that it cannot determine what kind of recycled paper to manufacture. Markets for recyclables can be increased also if equipment is designed to be compatible with recycled products. If it is technologically feasible to design complex computer equipment, it should be technologically feasible to design printers that can accommodate recycled paper. Finally, steps should be taken to encourage composting of yard waste. Fees could be established that encourage homeowners to compost, or regulations passed that require them to do so. Municipalities could establish composting systems on a commercial basis. There is no doubt that recycling without attention to markets reduces the effectiveness of the program.

Conversion

The final strategy in solid waste management is conversion. This tactic is often discussed with incineration because it involves burning of the waste, but there is an important distinction between the two. Incineration burns waste in order to destroy it; conversion burns waste in order to produce energy. Conversion systems, then, are often referred to as *waste-to-energy systems*.

Waste-to-energy plants must separate the waste in order to use it. Most plants use magnetic means to separate large metal items from the mass of waste. Various shredding and screening processes then remove other metals and glass. Materials isolated through these two means are either recycled or incinerated. The remaining material has a high energy content and is an efficient source of heat. It is sometimes mixed with coal or oil to augment the heat output. There were 27 waste-to-energy plants in the United States in 1992. They produced an annual equivalent of 16.4 million megawatts of electric power. Production of that amount of electricity would require approximately 30 million gallons of oil. In the process, the waste-to-energy plants consume over 80,000 tons of solid waste per day, about 6 percent of the total solid waste stream in the United States. In comparison, Japan burns about 23 percent and Germany 30 percent of their solid waste stream in waste-to-energy facilities (Corson 1990:270). Waste-to-energy plants in the European community burned 17 million tons of waste and produced energy equivalent to 17 million barrels of oil in 1988 (OECD 1991:150). All these factors mean that the conversion strategy should be considered separately from general incineration strategies as an approach to solid waste management.

MOUNTAINS OR MOLEHILLS: WHITHER
SOLID WASTE MANAGEMENT?

The twin pillars of solid waste policy have collapsed. The policies of local responsibility and disposal by landfilling are no longer sufficient to manage the increasing volume of solid waste in all nations. As a result, the policy system for the great granddaddy of all environmental problems is under severe stress.

The mountains of waste have made it necessary to seek new approaches. The most promising of these are waste reduction, recycling, and conversion. With the exception of chemical hazardous waste in Europe, no policy system is placing enough emphasis on waste reduction. In short, the volume of materials entering the waste stream must be reduced. Recycling is an effective way to reduce the waste stream and to recapture materials for reuse. Some nations, most notably Japan, have experienced considerable success with recycling programs. Conversion offers promise for benefits in both the environment and energy. With careful separation of materials, solid waste is an efficient energy fuel, particularly when augmented with other fuels such as coal and oil. These strategies have become a necessity in the management of the growing mountains of solid waste.

The new approaches, however, are not self-executing. Their success seems to depend on several important factors. First, attention must be paid to markets for products made from recycled materials. As a result of efforts to stimulate such markets, the markets have improved and the future is fairly bright for recyclable materials. Second, the success of new approaches depends upon careful planning for the design and implementation of the new technologies. The U.S. experience with waste-to-energy plants is instructive. The Environmental Protection Agency adopted a policy of research and development projects for alternative technologies, the most important being incineration. Two assumptions lay behind the EPA plan. The first was that the new technology should incorporate the most up-to-date state-of-the-art systems. The second was that European systems were essentially irrelevant to the U.S. program because they were designed several years earlier and were considered to be obsolete. Grants to local jurisdictions to conduct demonstration projects totaled millions of dollars. Neal and Schubel describe the results this way:

> These systems were essentially failures, although the nature of their design flaws became known only after large sums in construction and operation had been spent. Because of lack of ongoing, solid research...the pressures to identify quick solutions...led some municipalities to adopt technologies that were far from proven, and far inferior to the European systems which had evolved over the decades before. (Neal and Schubel 1987:92)

This experience not only suggests the need for careful planning before a crisis occurs, but also confirms one of the basic perspectives of this book. Nations can and must learn from other nations.

Alternate strategies for solid waste management, then, are in the initial stages of development. Considerably more research and planning are needed. What is clear is that historic strategies are no longer effective. New directions in policy must emphasize waste reduction, recycling, and conversion.

Chapter 8

Energy Policy

Energy policy illustrates one of the basic problems in understanding environmental issues—the complex interrelationships between the environment as a policy concern and other societal problems as policy concerns. Developments in energy production and use have important consequences for the environment. In the past these relationships were approached almost solely from the standpoint of the impact of energy production and use on environmental pollution, in what some analysts referred to as the "pollution-based approach" (OECD 1991:230). In this view, energy is seen as a policy field in its own right (Davis 1982). Now the approach is a more global one that attempts to identify the interrelationships between the economy, energy production and use, and the environment. This perspective is partly a result of the current interest in sustainable economic development. The two perspectives raise important questions. Should the focus be on energy and its effects on the environment? Or should the focus be on the environment with its effects on energy production and use? The perspective that is chosen makes a basic difference in problem description and policy prescription. How one looks at a problem determines to a great extent what one sees.

In this chapter the focus is on the environment and the effects environmental objectives should have on energy production and use. Such an approach is the more comprehensive one. It allows us to see both environmental problems and energy needs in the larger ecological context within which they occur. A focus on the environment with its effects on energy is more unifying. As those who are concerned with sustainable economic development have argued, environmental problems, economic activities, and energy activities are all parts of a complex whole. At the utilitarian level, a focus on the environment places the emphasis on the most important of the factors. While advanced nations are energy dependent just as they are chemically dependent, a world awash in energy is of little value if we have destroyed the ecological basis of life. The nuclear nightmare scenarios are correct in their assessment of priorities, whatever the accuracy of their calculations of probability. Thus the question is asked, how does the need for preserving the ecological basis of life affect the provision of an adequate and dependable supply of energy?

When the environment is the lens through which energy policy is analyzed, two concerns stand out. First, what are the environmental consequences of the present patterns of energy production and consumption? Second, are there alternatives to present patterns? The information essential to an answer to the first question has already been presented in preceding chapters. Answering the second question requires examining the environmental consequences of alternative sources of energy and the potential for energy conservation. The interest in alternative sources is based in the assumption that they would be more environmentally benign than traditional sources. The interest in energy conservation is based in the assumption that reduction in the use of traditional energy will reduce the levels of pollutants emitted into the environment. These two concerns are the twin pillars in an emerging environmental policy on energy. Before these two concerns can be addressed, however, energy needs to be placed in the larger perspective of environmental policy.

ENERGY CONSUMPTION, PARABOLAS, AND A SKY-HIGH CULTURAL DISCOUNT RATE

Modern advanced societies are energy dependent. Substantial amounts of production activities are energy intensive—that is, the most important factor in production is energy. Individual consumers in advanced societies have also become energy dependent. The range of household appliances, personal grooming aids, and recreational gadgets that are energy based is very wide. Governments in advanced nations are concerned with energy security as a part of overall defense policy. Energy use is a pervasive part of the way modern people live and modern societies function.

Several problems are associated with this pervasive use of energy. One of the most important is the parabolic increase in levels of energy consumption beginning with the Industrial Revolution. The evolution of energy use is instructive. Man without fire used approximately 2,000 kilocalories (kcal) a day. By the first century this number had increased to 12,000 kcal daily. By the 1860s, with the Industrial Revolution well underway, consumption rose to 70,000 kcal daily. In the late 1970s Americans consumed an average of 230,000 kcal daily. The consumption of 230,000 kcal daily is difficult to conceptualize. It is equivalent to the energy needed to heat 10,000 gallons of water 11 degrees Fahrenheit or to lift 710 million pounds a height of one foot. Furthermore, the increase in energy use has been significant since the 1970s. In OECD countries total energy use has increased by approximately 30 percent in the period between 1970 and 1988 (OECD 1991:222). Total energy use rose from 788.6 million tons of oil equivalent (MTOE) in 1970 to 4,002.9 MTOE in 1988 in OECD countries. Worldwide total energy consumption more than doubled, rising from 3,068.9 to 7,956.5 MTOE. Both advanced nations and the world generally are on the upward slope of the parabolic energy use curve.

✑ A Note on Energy Notations: Why Few of Us Can Understand Our Electric and Gas Bills

The measurement of energy, as the measurement of radioactivity, is expressed in terms that are sometimes confusing. A part of this confusion is traceable to "gobbledygook," that is, invented terms whose meanings are known only to insiders. The confusion is compounded by the fact that some of the invented terms lack precision. The most basic term for measuring the level of energy, the *Btu*, is illustrative of both problems.

The British thermal unit (Btu) is the standard measure for the amount of heat produced from any given source. It initially referred to the amount of heat produced by the burning of one wooden match tip, but has since been refined to refer to the amount of heat required to raise the temperature of one pound of water one degree Fahrenheit at a beginning temperature of 39 degrees. Thus the Btu does not touch the experience of most people in a meaningful way.

Certainly the *quad* is extraordinarily difficult for most of us to conceptualize. The quad is one quadrillion Btu of energy, expressed numerically as 1,000,000,000,000,000 Btu. The quad is necessary because of the enormous amounts of energy consumed in industrial societies.

The *barrel* is the basic notation for the energy available in oil. A barrel is 42 gallons. A gallon of oil produces 12,500 Btu.

The basic notation for the energy in electricity is the *kilowatt*. A kilowatt is 1,000 watts. In the United States the watt is defined as the rate of work represented by a current of one ampere under a pressure of one volt. A kilowatt hour, expressed as kWH, is the equivalent of 3,411 Btu.

Natural gas is normally expressed in *cubic feet* (cu. ft.). A cubic foot of natural gas produces approximately 1,031 Btu of energy. A *therm* is equivalent to 97 cu. ft. of natural gas and is equal to 100,000 Btu.

Now, is it any wonder that few of us understand our utility bills? Are we being deliberately confused or what?

The increase in energy consumption is a result of the fact that advanced societies have a sky-high cultural discount rate relative to energy. Immediate consumption is valued much more than future outcomes such as environmental quality. Advanced nations are on an energy consumption binge with little regard at the policy level for the environmental consequences. When faltering steps *are* taken in policy systems, those steps are rendered ineffective by inadequate implementation, postponement of deadlines and target dates, and a vast array of other stalling tactics. The possible exception is in the nuclear power industry in the United States. However, one of the important factors in the slowdown in nuclear power development was the ready availability of an acceptable substitute in petroleum. As with the production of solid waste, the most important factors associated with energy consumption are per capita GNP and domestic energy sources. Table 8.1 presents data on per capita GNP, energy requirements, and greenhouse gas emissions for selected countries worldwide. In regard to per capita GNP, the general proposition is that the more economic wealth a nation generates, the more energy it consumes. It is significant that the population of the country is weakly associated with per capita consumption. The second factor is the presence of domestic energy sources. When ranked by per capita energy use, the highest three nations are Middle East oil rich nations (Qatar, United Arab Emirates, and Bahrain). Of the top ten nations in per capita energy use, seven either are major producers of oil or have major oil and coal reserves. A valid conclusion is that the nations that have either economic wealth or energy resources are the nations that use energy. Those nations with low economic production or energy resources consume little energy.

Table 8.1   **Per Capita GNP, Energy Requirements, and Greenhouse Gas Emission, Selected Countries, 1990**

Country	Per Capita GNP	Energy Requirements			Greenhouse Gases	
		Total (Trillion Btu)	Per Capita (Million Btu)	Global Rank	% Global Share	Global Rank
Algeria	$1,947	650	27	8	0.21	110
Ethiopia	124	392	8	129	0.17	146
Nigeria	262	1,506	14	103	1.14	103
South Africa	2,514	N/A	N/A	N/A	1.08	38
Bangladesh	181	475	4	142	0.46	141
China	374	27,302	24	78	9.12	111

Iraq	1,915	543	30	69	0.26	84
Israel	9,922	379	84	39	0.14	37
Japan	23,072	15,707	128	29	4.66	29
Saudi Arabia	6,319	2,403	177	16	0.59	26
Belgium	15,730	1,861	189	14	0.37	32
France	17,052	8,355	149	23	1.53	49
Germany	19,633	13,881	179	18	3.44	21
Netherlands	14,878	2,803	189	15	0.52	36
United Kingdom	14,669	8,575	150	22	2.20	27
Canada	20,224	10,509	400	5	1.68	8
United States	21,039	76,355	309	7	17.81	6
Australia	16,192	3,573	215	12	1.13	7
New Zealand	11,798	631	188	16	0.15	19
Argentina	1,671	1,962	61	44	0.59	73
Brazil	2,953	6,967	47	55	3.93	54
Chile	1,808	567	44	59	0.11	108
Peru	1,543	459	22	84	0.47	65

Source: Data contained in World Resources Institute, *Environmental Almanac*. Boston: Houghton Mifflin, pp. 347–640.

An analysis of American experience results in some interesting conclusions. Table 8.2 presents data on per capita income, per capita consumption of energy, and greenhouse gas emissions of the top and bottom five states in the United States. These data are consistent with one finding from cross-national analysis. Energy use is higher in energy-producing states than in non-energy-producing states. The presence of energy resources in the jurisdiction seems to be linked to a higher propensity to use energy. An additional and somewhat surprising conclusion is that there is higher per capita energy use in rural states than in urban states. Some of this can be explained on the basis of regional location. Alaska, Wyoming, and North Dakota, three of the top five states in per capita requirements, are in a climate that requires high use of energy for heating. The other two, Louisiana and Texas, are oil-producing states. Therefore, there are factors other than the rural character of the state, but the rural nature does have a strong association with energy use. The popular notion that energy use per capita is much higher in the urban states is simply not true. New York, for example, is fiftieth among the American states in per capita energy use and forty-seventh in emission of greenhouse gases.

Table 8.2   Top and Bottom Five States in Annual Per Capita Energy Requirements

State	Per Capita Income	Per Capita Energy Used (million Btu)	Total (million tons)	Greenhouse Gases Per Capita (tons)	Per Capita Rank
Alaska	9,615	991	n.a.	n.a.	n.a.
Wyoming	9,826	786	54.8	114.4	1
Louisiana	8,961	783	172.9	39.23	4
Texas	10,645	569	459.0	27.26	12
North Dakota	9,641	467	43.5	65.22	2
Vermont	11,234	232	8.4	15.17	41
Massachusetts	14,389	229	89.9	15.27	40
New Hampshire	13,529	224	15.9	14.62	43
Rhode Island	12,351	218	11.7	11.76	48
New York	13,167	200	219.0	12.23	47

Source: Data contained in World Resources Institute, Environmental Almanac. Boston: Houghton Mifflin Co., pp. 231-281.

The tables reveal the strong association between levels of energy used and greenhouse gas emissions. This association is the factor that links environmental policy to energy policy in an intrinsic way. As the World Resources Institute observed, the production, destruction, and consumption of energy in combustion are the most important sources of environmental stress. Environmental policy must address the question as to whether energy use patterns can be altered in ways that result in more environmentally benign consumption of energy. This concern involves the twin factors of energy use reduction, often referred to in policy systems as energy conservation, and alternative energy supplies.

ALTERNATIVE ENERGY SOURCES
IN AN ENVIRONMENTAL PERSPECTIVE

Alternative energy sources may take many forms. While there is no general agreement on what constitutes alternative energy sources, the term is used to refer to energy sources other than the fossil fuels—coal, oil, and gas. In this book we will also include nuclear fuel and hydroelectric sources as traditional energy sources. The alternative fuels are solar energy, biomass energy, wind energy, geothermal energy, and various energy sources still in the experimental stage. Two questions relative to alternative sources are important. First, what is the energy potential in each source? Second, what are the environmental consequences of each?

Solar Energy

Solar energy technology attempts to capture energy directly from the ultimate source of all energy, the sun. Two types of collectors are currently in use. The first is a flat-plate fixed collector. These are used to heat space and water for residential use. Such systems need a standard heating unit for auxiliary heat when there are extended periods without sunshine. The second type of collector is the photovoltaic cell, which converts solar energy into electricity. Usually the cells are mounted on the ground, but NASA has experimented with mounting the cells on satellites. Photovoltaic cells were the source of energy for the Skylab space station for 171 days, even with the cell on one wing nonfunctional. There has been limited experimentation with mounting photovoltaic cells on satellites and transmitting the electricity back to earth on microwave beams.

Projections regarding solar energy are mixed. The most optimistic projections are that it can provide 10 percent of total energy requirements in the United States by the year 2000 and 25 percent by the year 2025. However, this optimism was dimmed considerably with the near abandonment of solar research funding by the government in the 1980s. In addition, there are two important problems to be solved before solar energy can become an important energy source. The first is that both types of collectors have very low conversion ratios. This means that high levels of energy from the sun are required to heat water or produce electricity. That is, neither type of collector is efficient. The second problem is cost. Both heat and electricity can be produced more cheaply by other means. Substantial developmental work needs to be done before solar energy can be an economic and efficient alternative energy source.

At first glance, solar energy would seem to be a perfect source of energy in terms of its environmental effects. However, whether or not solar systems are environmentally benign depends on how such systems are implemented. For example, there are 800 million square miles of hot desert area in the world. It would take only 0.4 percent of that area, covered with solar collectors operating at only 10 percent efficiency, to supply the present energy needs of the world. However, the land area required, even though it is small a percentage of the total desert area, is still a very large land mass. An additional technical problem is that the longest economical transmission of electric power is about 400 miles, so any large-scale reliance on solar energy would have to locate solar collector fields in numerous areas rather than in one.

In addition to the land area required, there is considerable uncertainty relative to the environmental effects of widespread use of solar energy. The ecosystem is complex, and the rays of the sun are its most important element. What happens if the quantity and quality of the sun's rays are altered? Would climate patterns be affected? Would the delicate ecosystems of desert areas be changed? These questions remain unanswered and may be unanswerable given the current state of the art for dealing with such complex issues.

Biomass Energy

Biomass energy may be derived in two ways. The first is to burn wood or solid materials collected in the municipal and industrial waste stream. The second is to convert biological materials in the solid waste stream into fuels such as ethanol and methanol. At present biomass sources produce approximately 2.8 quads of energy or 3.3 percent of total U.S. energy consumption. Of this amount, 98 percent is generated from burning either wood or municipal waste. The remainder is derived from ethanol. One of the promising developments in biomass energy is a generator fueled by wood from fast-growing trees. The increased application of this technique along with the traditional solid waste strategies make biomass an important potential source of energy. Some estimates, including those of the Department of Energy, place the potential at approximately 55 quads by the year 2000. The United States in 1990 utilized a total of 85 quads of energy from all energy sources.

The environmental consequences of biomass energy are the same as those associated with the incineration of solid waste. The most pressing problem is convincing households and businesses to separate the organic and inorganic waste materials. Beyond this, the state of the art in such technology as burning fast-growing trees is such that important questions still remain about environmental consequences. How effective are the scrubbers? What is the content and how is the ash to be treated? How are the tree farms to be managed so that the planting and harvesting cycle is environmentally benign? Biomass, then, is a significant source of energy but the environmental consequences of tapping that source are not fully known.

Wind Energy

The third alternative source of energy is wind energy. Along with wood for fire, winds have been a source of energy since antiquity. Actually, wind energy is an indirect application of solar energy, since wind is the by-product of the atmospheric absorption of solar energy. The total potential energy in wind is large, but capturing it is very difficult and large-scale generation of energy from wind is not technologically feasible at present. Small-scale applications in the one-to-five kilowatt range are the most feasible.

At present, there are 16,000 wind generators in the United States, most of them on "wind farms" in California. These generators supply approximately 2 billion kilowatts of electricity each year. The Department of Energy estimates that wind energy may contribute as high as 3.3 quads, or 4 percent of the energy consumed in the United States, by the year 2000. The Energy Minister of Great Britain estimated that wind energy could generate up to 30 billion kilowatt hours, or about 10 percent of Britain's needs, by the year 2025. A Finnish government estimate placed the figure at about 10 percent of that country's needs. One of the problems with these estimates is that the cost of wind-generated electricity is relatively high, averaging about 8 cents per kilowatt compared with 4 cents from conventional sources. However, if fossil fuel prices continue to rise and technology in wind generation improves, the cost of wind-generated electricity may come down to about the same as that from conventional sources.

At first glance, wind generation of electricity seems to be environmentally benign. The Department of Energy concluded that the most significant environmental impact of wind is that there is virtually no impact (DOE 1990). There are, however, some negative outcomes of the use of wind energy. The building of access roads and the construction of the turbine support systems disturbs the natural habitat of the land. Wind energy systems require large land areas because the turbines must be spaced widely apart to avoid interference with each other. Since the spinning blades may be dangerous to birds, they would not be suitable for location in habitat areas of endangered species. The most frequently voiced objection to wind turbines is based in esthetic considerations. Residents near wind farms claim that they are ugly and detract from the natural beauty of the area. In spite of these problems, wind energy is probably the most environmentally benign alternative source.

Geothermal Energy

Geothermal energy is the fourth major alternative energy source. Heat radiated from the interior of the earth can be captured for heating space or generating electricity. The heat that is most easily captured is that which accumulates in subterranean reservoirs or in rocks. High-temperature geothermal reservoirs contain water ranging from 400 to 700 degrees Fahrenheit; these tend to be concentrated in the continental margins ringing the Pacific Ocean, in southern Europe, and in Middle Asia. Hot-water sedimentary basins contain water at between 150 and 400 degrees Fahrenheit; these tend to be concentrated in the former Soviet Union, Australia, and the United States. Basins along the U.S. Gulf Coast average about 365 degrees Fahrenheit and occur at relatively shallow depths. While these temperatures are sufficient for low-temperature steam turbines, the water is often mixed with water heated by butane gas and the resultant steam is used in a conventional turbine. Finally, hot rocks consist of impermeable rocks layered over a heat source. The heat is captured either by injecting water or a low-boiling-point liquid over the rocks. The resultant heat is then used to operate the turbine.

Geothermal applications in the United States have been limited. Geothermal plants presently generate about 2,800 megawatts of power annually. The limited application is due in part to the fact that 75 percent of potential geothermal sites are on nationally owned land and the U.S. government has refused to lease the land for geothermal energy purposes. An additional problem is technological. The low-temperature turbines are inefficient. However, it has been estimated that as many as 23,000 megawatts could be produced with current technology from geothermal sources. Presently, only about 1 percent of the total heat in geothermal sources is used.

There are significant environmental effects of geothermal sources of energy. First, there is a large land requirement, particularly when all necessary supportive facilities, such as roads, pipelines, and the like, are taken into account. Furthermore, a number of geothermal sites are in fragile ecosystems. The geological characteristic of much of the land is also problematic. Some sites are on fault zones that are prone to earthquakes, and others are in volcanic areas. Second, the waste heat produced by a geothermal plant is higher than that of a conventional plant. Finally, the waste water produced has a high salt content. In most instances, the water is reinjected into the earth, potentially causing adverse environmental consequences. Geothermal energy, given present technology, is not an environmentally benign alternative source of energy.

Other Potential Energy Sources

There are other potential alternative energy sources still in the experimental stages. Some experimentation has been conducted on a type of geothermal energy that involves temperature gradation in the ocean. At present, the turbines have an efficiency ratio of only 6 percent, so it would take a very large turbine to generate any significant amount of energy.

The ocean also presents the possibility of energy from tides. A turbine can be emersed in the sea to derive energy directly from the tide, or can be placed in a "tidal dam" in an estuary or bay. France has a small tidal plant in operation that produces about 240,000 kilowatts, equivalent to the output of a small fossil fuel plant.

Considerable attention has also been given recently to the possibilities of an electric battery traction system. California in particular has emphasized the development of the electric car as an alternative to the internal combustion engine. However, given present technology, it is possible that the pollution associated with the production of batteries would be higher than that from the internal combustion engine.

Hydrogen fuels present another alternative fuel for the internal combustion engine. In some ways, hydrogen appears to be the most environmentally benign of all fuels. The only by-product of using hydrogen in the fuel cycle is water. However, the process requires the use of very high levels of energy from conventional sources. The expenditure of energy to produce hydrogen fuel may present higher levels of pollution than the simple use of fossil fuels.

A final possibility for alternative energy is cold water fusion. Considerable attention was drawn to the possibilities inherent in this "ultimate fuel" in the mid-1980s. Several laboratories announced successful fusion at low temperatures. The substantial scientific debate that occurred over whether fusion had actually occurred is reflective of the problems still associated with fusion as a potential energy source.

To some degree, each of these lesser sources of energy is still in the experimental stage; considerable development must occur before any one is a viable energy source. Also, their environmental impacts are difficult to assess at this point.

ENERGY CONSERVATION POLICY
IN AN ENVIRONMENTAL PERSPECTIVE

Energy conservation policy attempts to reduce harmful emissions by reducing the amount of energy that is used. Such policy can take several directions. The first is to encourage and strengthen market forces through changes in public policy. The second is to reduce energy use either by subsidizing that reduction or by regulating use so as to require reduction. A third approach is through public funding of energy research and development.

Market Forces

The indirect approach of encouraging development within the market is seen clearly in American policy response to developments within the electric power industry.

The generation of electric power has been a central concern of environmentalists from the beginning of the movement. The electric utility industry seemed successfully entrenched in a privileged position protected by state regulatory bodies—which in some states often functioned to protect the interest of the utilities. Political scientists have long used them as examples of "captive agencies," that is, agencies controlled by the interest they are established to regulate. The traditional relationships between utilities and regulatory agencies have changed in response to several important developments within the electric power industry. The first is that electric planning is no longer dominated by large-scale central power plants. Second, utilities have discovered that they can make money by encouraging their consumers to use less electricity.

Not only do large-scale central power plants no longer dominate electric planning, but cancellations of nuclear and coal plants have far exceeded the start-up of new plants. Several factors have moderated the importance of the large central plant. The first is the construction of small-scale power projects. Approximately 800 such plants have been registered with the Federal Energy Regulatory Commission since 1980. A major factor in the emergence of small-scale plants was the 1978 Public Utilities Regulatory Policies Act, which directs utilities to interconnect with small-scale producers and purchase power from them at a fair market rate. This policy recognizes that the distribution of electricity may best be served on a monopoly basis but the production of electricity need not be. The Act rightly separates regulations concerning the production of electricity from policies concerning its distribution.

Another factor that moderates reliance on large-scale central projects is increasing use of *co-generation,* or the combined production of heat and electricity. The basic idea is that the high heat required for some production processes can also be used to generate electricity. Industries that have high heat requirements are the chemical, primary metals, ore-refining, food-processing, and pulp and paper industries.

Co-generation raises the energy efficiency of a plant significantly. For example, the overall efficiency of a plant that produces its steam for heat needed in the production process and purchases its electricity from a utility is 50 to 70 percent. Co-generation raises the efficiency ratio to between 80 and 90 percent, depending on the application. Such an increase in efficiency results in enormous cost savings to an industry with high heat requirements. Data indicate that 15,000 megawatts are currently produced in co-generation projects in the United States. About 200 new projects are under construction with an output of 6,000 megawatts. Co-generation is an important technology for reducing energy loss in the production process.

The second major development in the electric utility industry is something of a paradox. How can utility companies make money by reducing demand for electricity? The answer is that electric conservation programs allow the utility to avoid the high costs of constructing new plants. Some of the savings are passed on to consumers in the form of lower rates; the remainder is kept by the utility as a return on its investment in conservation. Among the conservation measures that are promoted by utilities are energy audits, incentives for energy-conservation features in new homes, and incentives to both individual and commercial customers for energy conservation. The range of conservation measures that can be taken is very broad, from the simple act of wrapping an insulating blanket around a home hot water heater to sophisticated radio control devices that regulate equipment such as heat pumps.

Integrated resource planning, as energy conservation programs are called, have important environmental consequences. Two programs are illustrative of these results (World Resources Institute 1993:67). Southern California Edison reported that savings in energy generation over the life of its program, which began in 1978, prevented emissions of 29,000 tons of nitrogen oxides, 24,000 tons of sulfur dioxide, and 18 million tons of carbon dioxide. Wisconsin Electric, a smaller utility, reported that its Smart Money Energy Program initiated in 1987 has prevented the emissions of 6,150 tons of sulfur dioxide, 2,150 tons of nitrogen oxide, and 1 million tons of carbon dioxide. Energy reduction programs do pay off, both in economic and environmental terms.

In spite of these advantages of energy reduction programs, state regulatory agencies have a mixed record in adopting policies that stimulate this market development. In 1990 only 23 states had regulations that allowed electric utilities to earn revenue through energy conservation programs. Given the obvious benefits from such programs, it is difficult to explain this inaction, except through a captive agency concept. The regulatory bodies in the inactive states would seem to be responding to vested interest more than to economic or environmental objectives.

Subsidies and Regulations

The second major approach to energy conservation is direct encouragement of use reduction through either subsidy or regulation. Subsidy programs have targeted residential, commercial, industrial, and transportation use of energy. In the United States the policy instruments used for this strategy have been tax credits, investment credits, production credits, and development bonds. Tax credits have been used to encourage home owners to take various actions that will conserve energy, such as improving insulation, installing more energy-efficient heating and cooling systems, and experimenting with alternative energy sources such as alcohol fuels. Investment credits were made available to business firms to encourage use of alternative sources of energy, including solar, wind, geothermal, ocean thermal, biomass, and hydroelectric sources. Investment credits were also available for co-generation equipment. Production credits were applied to projects designed to produce steam from wood and agricultural by-products. Industrial development bonds supported construction of facilities for producing alcohol from solid waste, as well as building and modernizing of small-scale hydroelectric plants.

Measures to encourage conservation through subsidies were very popular in the aftermath of the oil crisis of the 1970s. Legislation authorizing such programs included the Energy Policy and Conservation Act of 1975, the Energy Production and Conservation Act of 1976, the National Energy Conservation Act of 1978, the Energy Tax Act of 1978, the Emergency Energy Conservation Act of 1979, and the Energy Security Act of 1980. At the time of the Reagan administration change in policy, total incentives from all programs amounted to approximately $6.5 billion.

The major attempt at conservation through regulation was the Clean Air Act of 1970. The Act established fuel efficiency standards for automobiles, known as the Corporate Average Fuel-Economy (CAFE) standards. The CAFE standards were part of a detailed but flexible timetable for control of vehicle emission standards. The standards were delayed several times. Peculiarly, the Amendments limited alternative fuels to fleet applications, such as car and truck pools, except in California. In addition to the Clean Air Act, two other pieces of legislation encouraged conservation through regulation: the National Appliance Energy Conservation Act of 1987 with its 1988 amendments, and the Steel and Aluminum Energy Conservation and Technology Competitiveness Act of 1988.

Public Funding of Research and Development

Public funding of research and development is the third leg in energy conservation programs. Public funding in the energy sector is particularly important given the industry's reluctance to use its own resources until new technologies have been substantially developed. Prior to the 1980s, research funding priorities stressed conservation and renewable energy sources such as biomass and geothermal sources. Reagan administration priorities, however, reflected a distinct preference for centralized renewable energy that had to be supplied from a single large provider (magnetic fusion and high-energy physics) and supply-enhancing strategies (Worthington 1984:366). Between 1980 and 1983 the Reagan administration decreased Department of Energy funding of research for conservation by 64 percent, for solar and other renewables by 66 percent, for electric energy systems by 54 percent, and for electric storage systems by 61 percent. On the other hand, it increased DOE funding of magnetic fusion research by 28 percent, high-energy physics by 27 percent, and supply-enhancing research by 27 percent in the same period. The 1980s produced a significant shift in American energy policy away from government sponsorship of conservation measures toward sponsorship of supply-enhancing strategies.

A FLEDGLING ENVIRONMENTAL POLICY ON ENERGY

When viewed in a larger historic perspective, American energy policy reflects some important trends. In the initial years the focus and concern were almost totally with ensuring an adequate and dependable supply of energy. Since fossil fuels were the principal source of energy, the policy system in the United States is replete with supply-enhancement strategies targeted to fossil fuels. The most visible of those strategies is the depletion allowance that is a financial boon to oil, gas, and coal producers and a financial boondoggle to the American tax system.

The traditional focus gradually gave way to a focus on energy through the lens of a concern for the environment. This shift reached its zenith in the Carter administration and is reflected in the Carter energy program. It is not accurate to say that the Carter program was an environmental policy for energy, but a concern for the environment definitely permeated this policy.

The 1980s, particularly during the Reagan administration, saw a shift in policy back to a focus on supply-enhancing strategies. Considerable emphasis was placed on deregulation and reducing the national government's involvement in the energy field. However, it is important to note the *direction* of that policy change. The direction was not toward eliminating all public policy involvement in energy. The massive subsidies, tax credits, and production credits of the supply-enhancing strategies stayed in place. The government remained an active policy actor in the energy field supportive of energy supply. How is this change in policy emphasis to be evaluated?

The Reagan policy offers an opportunity, although on a limited basis, to evaluate the competing strategies of government intervention versus the market as the most effective regulator of energy production and use. Several factors enter into such an evaluation. One paradoxical factor relates to the political context within which each strategy can function. Conservation programs based in government intervention had been successful in reducing demand for energy and stabilizing energy prices after the oil shock of the 1970s (Kushler, Witte, and Ehlke 1992:57). This development lessened public concern for conservation policies. The political paradox is that the success of conservation policy created a political environment within which a significant change in policy could occur.

A second factor in evaluating the two strategies concerns externalities, a basic phenomenon long accepted as justification for government intervention. There are a number of externalities in the supply of oil. Certainly the environmental consequences of fossil fuel production and use is one of them. Others are the cost of defending Middle East oil supplies, the cost of oil stored for emergencies, the cost of energy imports in the balance of payments deficit, the higher cost of supply-enhancement technologies over demand-reduction technologies, and the cost to developing nations of the heavy use of energy by the United States (Gibbins and Givin 1989). These externalities are not reflected in the price of oil. Many of them are the result of policy preferences of the national government, particularly the preference for supply-enhancement policies over demand-reduction policies. The presence of these externalities means that the market does not function efficiently as the mediator of energy production and use in large part because the price of oil is artificially low. Ironically, then, policy preferences of an administration committed to market strategies may have undercut the potential for such strategies to have an effect on energy production and use.

One of the most interesting features of the evaluation of market strategies has to do with an analysis of the relationship between energy price and energy consumption. It might be expected that a decline in consumption would accompany an increase in price and that an increase in consumption would accompany a decrease in price. The conclusion to be drawn, then, is that energy conservation would best be accomplished by deregulation of the market so that energy prices would rise. However, energy consumption does not necessarily respond in this way to price (Byrne and Rich 1984:332). For example, there were periods in which the real price of electricity declined, and this decline was accompanied by a decline in residential consumption. The explanation is that there is an important difference between consumption tendencies and conservation tendencies. Conservation tendencies are influenced not so much by price as by other factors, such as the price of conservation options, the financing available, the information available to consumers, the number and kind of substitutes, and the nature of public and private policies (Byrne and Rich 1984:335). Because public policy is an important factor in consumer conservation tendencies, a shift in policy away from conservation is a form of self-fulfilling prophecy; it creates an environment that weakens the conservation tendency. After an intriguing analysis of this phenomenon, two analysts reached these important conclusions: "Conservation will remain systematically undervalued as long as markets and policies focus attention on swings in conventional prices and deny recognition of conservation as a supply option with its own prices and economics"; "If we learned from experience...we should conclude that the major opportunities for our energy future lie in an increasing reliance on decentralized energy options like conservation" (Byrne and Rich 1984:335, 342). Certainly one of the primary problems with the market strategy is that its proponents have consistently underestimated the importance of conservation tendencies, one of the most important factors in an environmental policy for energy.

The strategy of developing alternative energy sources is more difficult to analyze. However, several conclusions seem warranted. First, several alternative sources do offer promise of significant supply with far fewer adverse outcomes for the environment than traditional sources. Solar energy and biomass energy are two examples. Some of the dynamics associated with energy conservation strategies have affected these alternative sources. The success of conservation measures in reducing the energy crisis created a political environment for abandoning government-sponsored research on solar and biomass energy. The claim was that alternative fuel research was abandoned because the policy did not work. A more probable position is that the policy did not work because of the abandonment of research support (Crow, Boseman, Meyer, and Shangraw 1988). The policy system has undervalued research on alternative fuels in a serious way.

The second important point to be made about alternative fuels is that an environmental policy for energy depends in part on energy choices that include alternatives to conventional energy. Prior to the Carter administration and during the 1980s, the criteria that guided energy policy was the stability of existing energy sources. As long as public policy focuses on ensuring adequate and secure supplies of traditional energy, choices relative to a different "energy future" are very restricted. Perhaps more important, as long as energy is viewed through the lens of a commitment to conventional energy sources, decision makers will continue to arrive at the same positions they have in the past. The major obstacle to a different perspective is that any energy transition is likely to be accompanied by a major shift in political power and economic gain (Byrne and Rich 1984:341). There are powerful vested interests which resist any transition from the fossil fuel energy regime, a transition that would involve changes larger in scale than with any past energy transition.

This point is the basis for an important conclusion. The problems associated with the development of alternative energy sources are not primarily technological, though problems of technology exist. The problems are political and economic. An environmental policy for energy must recognize the enormous political and economic hurdles that will have to be cleared before alternative fuels are given serious consideration (Lovins 1977). Paradoxically, many of those hurdles are supported by government policies associated with supply enhancement. Public institutions are, indeed, semi-autonomous actors in the policy process. In this instance, they create obstacles to the choice of policies that serve both environmental and energy objectives.

Chapter 9

Land

The Thin Veneer of Life

The word *earth* has at least two quite different meanings. The *Earth* is the name of the planet in our solar system that is third in distance from the sun. The word *earth* is used also to refer to the material, or soil, that composes the surface of the globe. For most people, these two meanings are fused into one. The planet Earth is associated with the soil and the soil with the Earth. The problem with this view is that it distorts the fragile nature of the soil. It leads people to think that the soil is an unlimited resource that will be worn out only when planet Earth is worn out. The soil is, in fact, a thin veneer over rock, both solid and molten, that comprises most of the mass of planet Earth. The Earth's thin veneer of soil is being placed under increasing stress.

Stress on the land comes from a number of sources, two of them very important to environmental policy. The first is the stress on the soil from the rapid growth in world population. The earth is a closed system of finite resources, and increasing numbers of people put greater and greater stress on that closed system. A second source of stress is land use practices that result in soil degradation. Many of these practices are linked to elements in the public policy of most nations, others to traditional practices that have developed over centuries, and, surprisingly, some to well-intentioned reforms.

AN UNCERTAIN CONCEPT BUT AN ALL TOO COMMON TRAGEDY

The attempt to develop a concept that will capture the relationship between stress on the land and the capacity of the land to support life has a long history. The first serious attempt was made by a British economist, Thomas Malthus, in 1798. Malthus' law held that population would increase to a level such that the land could support the vast majority of people only at a subsistence level. Continued increase in population would result in widespread disaster in the form of famine and deprivation.

Subsequent development of Malthus' work led to formulation of the *carrying-capacity* concept. Advocates of this concept believed that the earth has within its biosphere definite "Limits to Growth," as a book sponsored by the Club of Rome argued. Consequently, continued increases in population would place such stress on the natural resource base that the biosphere would collapse. Population growth, then, loomed as a bomb over the biosphere, a prospect that was forcefully argued by Paul Ehrlich in *The Population Bomb*. Widespread famine and death were predicted to be the results of the population bomb. Some of the more alarmist works predicted that as many as one-fourth of the world's population would die from starvation between 1973 and 1983. The carrying-capacity concept had been applied in such a way as to result in rather specific predictions.

An Uncertain Concept

The fact that the specific predictions did not prove correct has cast considerable uncertainty on the concept of carrying-capacity. It is important to understand the source of that uncertainty. In other words, is the original premise of the carrying-capacity concept invalid or are the resultant predictions invalid because of flaws in the prediction method? It is clear from an examination of the carrying-capacity theorists and their critics that the latter is the case.

A number of important flaws existed in the prediction methodology of the carrying-capacity theorists. One of the most important was that predictions were based on the experience in countries that were characterized by a subsistence agriculture. Additionally, the agricultural patterns in those societies were assumed to be static. Factors such as land use patterns, technology of production, patterns of consumption, and employment patterns were assumed to be fixed. No allowances were made for climate variability or long-range soil degradation. Finally, nearly all the studies focused on the capacity of a society to produce food, that is, they focused on supply. None of the studies took into account the very important factor of household income, or the demand side of the equation. Other studies have concluded that the collapse of family income rather than the lack of food production is the primary cause of starvation (Sen 1981). All of these factors combined to cast considerable uncertainty on the carrying-capacity methodology.

What is to be made of that uncertainty? The first reaction was to assume that the carrying-capacity concept should be deemphasized and attention directed to other factors, such as household income, the ability to access food supplies, consumption patterns at various levels of income, and the mobility and technological sophistication of a society. One of the more significant insights of this line of thinking is the importance of environmental variability, such as that associated with global warming, to the ability of a society to feed its population. Ironically, for those arguing this point, population growth is one of the major factors contributing to environmental variability.

Another response to the challenge to the carrying-capacity concept was an attempt to refine the methodology. The most ambitious of these attempts was a study by the Food and Agricultural Organization (FAO), in cooperation with the International Institute for Applied Systems Analysis, to determine the population-supporting capacities of all the countries of the world, except those of east Asia (FAO 1984). A three-category "production system" was devised. A low-input production system was one that utilized manual labor and no fertilizers or pesticides, an intermediate production system used draught animals and some fertilizers and pesticides, and a high-input system had complete mechanization and full use of fertilizers and pesticides. The year 1975 was used as the measure of the "present" population and 2000 as the measure of "future" population. The United Nations medium-population projections were accepted as the most valid estimates of future populations. Estimates were then made on the production potential of fifteen major crops.

The conclusions drawn from the analysis are extremely interesting. The general conclusion was that the global carrying capacity is adequate for projected population in the year 2000, even at low input levels. This conclusion assumes that most of the potentially arable land will be used for food crop production rather than for livestock, forest, or developmental purposes. This assumption raises the very important concept of arable land per capita, which has been decreasing at a very high rate since 1950. In the period 1951-55, there was an average of 1.2 acres of arable land per capita, but by 1981–1985 it had dropped to 0.8 acres. This decrease in arable land per capita has been accompanied by an increase in consumption per capita. This dual development has forced the clearing of forest as a means of increasing available farmland and the more intensive utilization of available land. Thus a major outcome of increasing the quantity of arable land is deforestation. The expansion of arable land for crop production is likely to cause the loss of 180 million hectares of forest and rangeland by 2025 (a hectare is 2.47 acres). This is an enormous amount of land—444.6 million acres or 694,683 square miles, equivalent to the land mass of Alaska and Colorado combined. These developments raise the critically important question of environmental sustainability. If an adequate carrying capacity exists only with the maximum use of arable land for agricultural purposes, can this carrying capacity be sustained over time? In other words, although the population bomb has failed to go off as predicted, is it inevitable that it will go off eventually?

A more specific conclusion drawn from the FAO study has to do with the concept of critical countries. When the analysis focuses at the country level, a very different conclusion is reached than when it focuses on a global level. At the low-input level, 64 of the 117 countries were found to be unable to feed their projected populations at the year 2000. This result holds even when all arable land is assumed to be devoted to food production. At the intermediate production level 36 countries will be unable to feed their projected populations, and at the high-input level 18 countries will lack the productive capacity to feed their populations. An important factor modifying the seriousness of this finding is the general economic resource base of the country under analysis. An individual country may have small quantities of productive arable land but large quantities of fossil fuel reserves. The oil-rich Middle East countries are literally able to buy their way out of their food production deficiencies. They will experience trouble only if the major food-exporting nations are unable to maintain their export potential. Thus the situation in some countries is not as bleak as the initial data suggested for the year 2000.

The efforts to resolve the uncertainty in the carrying-capacity concept have only increased the uncertainty. The effort to discard this concept in favor of a broader, more encompassing method seems to have brought us full circle to a point close to the original starting place. Arguing that population growth is only one of many factors, this view introduced the concept of environmental variability as an important determinant of whether the world's population can be fed. But population growth is one of the major factors contributing to environmental variability. Is there a level of population beyond which environmental quality cannot be sustained if we are to feed the world's people? If so, what is that level? Such questions are very similar to those addressed by the carrying-capacity concept. On the other hand, the efforts to refine the carrying-capacity methodology have pointed to the importance of a broad range of factors affecting a society's capacity to feed its people. Thus the relationship between population and the capacity of the environment to support life remains essentially unclarified.

Is there a way to resolve some of the uncertainty surrounding the relationship between population and the environment? One helpful approach is a basic shift in focus similar to the perspective utilized in the discussion of the relationship between energy and the environment in

Chapter 8. The carrying-capacity concept has focused on population increases and what has to be done, relative to agricultural technology, to sustain that population. A more appropriate focus would be on the environment and what should be done to protect the ecological basis of life given increases in world population.

In a sense, such a focus would bow to the almost inevitable increase in world population. Nearly all studies suggest that population increase has a tremendous momentum and is essentially unresponsive to factors that would reduce it. In other words, to check population growth would require some extraordinary development such as an AIDS pandemic or the widespread acceptance of birth control methods that are presently unacceptable in many countries. Minor adjustments that are within the range of the possible, such as changes in the fertility or mortality rates, will not have significant impact on world population (World Resources Institute 1992: 76–77). Given these facts, world population by the year 2025 will likely be in excess of 8.6 billion, or 3 billion more people than now. As David Norse observed, "…the issue is not whether Earth can support a population of 8.6 billion or so in 2025—it will have to—but, rather, whether it can do so sustainably" (Norse 1992:9). What are the consequences for the environment of a projected population of 8.6 billion persons? How can the ecological basis of life be protected given such a world population?

An All Too Common Tragedy

Unfortunately, there is not much known about the relationship of population growth rates and environmental degradation. The paucity of knowledge led the United Nations General Assembly, in anticipation of the 1992 UN Conference on Environment and Development, to pass a resolution stressing the importance of addressing the relationship between demographic pressures, unsustainable consumption patterns, and environmental degradation (Resolution 42/216, December 1990). However, the resolution was passed only after substantial discussion. Third World countries are very suspicious of the importance attached to population growth by First World nations. In large part, this attitude is traceable to the concern of Third World decision makers that the developed nations will place the blame for environmental degradation on population increases. Third World countries insist that developed countries, with essentially stable populations, are the main culprits in environmental degradation. The situation, then, involves a two-pronged problem of lack of studies of the relationship between population increase and environmental degradation and an international community deeply divided over the appropriate research approach to take.

From what is known about population and the environment, it is clear that population growth and distribution patterns can increase the rate of environmental deterioration. Experience within nations, rather than empirical studies, clearly indicates that population increases and distribution patterns are closely associated with displacement of land from traditional uses and the degradation of the land.

Deforestation: Displacement of Land from Traditional Uses

Land in all societies is subject to multiple uses. Crop production, forest cover, grazing land, urbanization, and industrialization are the most important of those usages. Experience in many countries suggests that crop production wins out over other uses of the land in periods of rapid population increase, with the possible exception of urbanization and industrialization. As a result of the process, forests and rangelands are lost to crop production. Additionally, in times of increased economic stress, forest land is converted to crops that are exportable or bring higher prices, such as coffee, fruits, and cattle. In some instances, these converted areas are only marginally suited for the new crop. For example, between 1966 and 1983 over 100,000 square kilometers (38,600 square miles) of Brazilian tropical forest were burned to make pasture. The problem is that it takes a hundred times more pasture to support a single head of cattle in the Amazon region than in South Brazil, where conditions are more conducive to pasture (Reiss 1992:131). In spite of this fact, Brazil has created an agency known as the Superintendency for the Development of the Amazon (SUDAM), which has approved projects totaling 8.4 million hectares (32,432 square miles), making the agency-sponsored projects the most single important source of deforestation.

Population distribution patterns, particularly those associated with urbanization, also appear to be important. Recent Landsat data reveal that forest cover within 100 kilometers of India's major cities dropped by 15 percent or more in a single decade. The area around New Delhi lost 60 percent of its forest cover. Public policy often adds to the problem. For centuries most land in India was considered to be common property, but in the 1950s the government began to distribute millions of acres of common property lands to private owners, thereby forcing the nonproperty-owning poor to exploit smaller and more ecologically fragile areas.

Estimating the total loss of forest from all causes is extremely difficult to do. Data from different countries are not comparable and the quality of some of the data is very low. However, satellite imagery has improved the monitoring of forest loss. For example, the National Space Research Institute in Brazil used satellite imagery to estimate the extent of deforestation in the Amazon. These studies indicated a deforestation rate of 2.18 million hectares a year for a total cumulative deforestation in the Amazon of 41.5 million hectares as of 1990 (World Resources Institute 1992:119). The United Nations Food and Agriculture Organization estimated that the total deforestation rate in tropical forests was just under 17 million hectares a year in the early 1990s—a 50 percent increase over the early 1980s. When viewed from a global perspective, it is clear that tropical deforestation is the most critical problem area. As Table 9.1 indicates, total deforestation rates are relatively stable for most regions of the world, averaging less than one half of one percent.

Table 9.1   Forest Cover and Deforestation Rates

Regions	1980 Forest Area[a] (000 hectares)	Average Annual Deforestation, 1981–1985	
		Extent (000 hectares)	Percentage Rate
Africa	1,339,060	3,772	0.5
The Americas	2,017,067	5,702	0.4
Asia	668,415	2,003	0.4
Europe	178,340	(b)	(b)
USSR	929,600	na	na
Oceania	156,073	26	0.0

[a]Includes all forest types, closed forest, open forest, plantation forest, and other wooded areas.
[b]Europe had a slight net gain of forest cover as reported in OCED 1991:114.
Source: Calculated from data in World Resources Institute, 1992, pp. 286-287.

The relative stability masks some very important differences within specific nations and subregions. The most serious problems are in African, Asian, and American countries. African nations experiencing high rates of annual deforestation include the following: Algeria 2.3 percent, Gambia 2.4 percent, Guinea-Bissau 2.7 percent, Mauritania 2.4 percent, Niger 2.6 percent, Cote d'Ivorie 5.2 percent, Liberia 2.3 percent, Nigeria 2.7 percent, Malawi 3.5 percent, Rwanda 2.2 percent, Comoros 3.1 percent, and Mauritius 3.3 percent. Countries in the Americas with high rates of deforestation are Costa Rica 3.6 percent, El Salvador 3.2 percent, Guatemala 2.0 percent, Honduras 2.3 percent, Nicaragua 2.7 percent, Haiti 3.7 percent, Jamaica 3.0 percent, and Ecuador 2.3 percent. Asian countries with high annual rates are Nepal 4.0 percent, Sri Lanka 3.5 percent, and Thailand 2.4 percent (World Resources Institute 1992: 286–87). These high annual rates result in significant deforestation within a few years.

In addition to the rate of deforestation, some regions are experiencing problems with more qualitative aspects of the forest cover. While the United States has an essentially static forest cover, declining by 3.4 percent over the 1970–1988 period, there are problems with forest preservation.

Considerable political conflict has developed over the issue of old-growth forest in the Northwest region of the country. This conflict led to a "Timber Summit" in 1993 to search for ways to reconcile the differences between timber interests and environmental interests in the old-growth forests. In other areas of the country, forest of one type growth are being replaced by forest of another type. For example, there is increasing political conflict in the Piedmont region of the Southeast over the cutting of hardwood forest and replacement by pine forest. A perennial problem is the replacement of forests that have high scenic value with forests of less esthetic attraction. None of these developments is reflected in general rates of deforestation, yet they all should be of vital concern to an environmental policy on forests.

Soil Degradation

Along with the displacement of land from traditional forest usage, population increase and distribution patterns are associated with soil degradation. Ironically, without the negative impact of human activities, the thin veneer of soil not only is a renewable resource but also increases over time. In natural systems the rate of soil production is equal to or greater than the rate of removal. Both the depth and fertility of the soil increase over time. Human activities have constrained those natural processes and caused substantial soil degradation globally.

The United Nations Environment Programme sponsored a three-year study to assess the extent of soil degradation, by degree of degradation. Dubbed the Global Assessment of Soil Degradation, GLASOD, the study was coordinated by the International Soil Reference and Information Center in the Netherlands (Oldeman, Hakkeling, and Sombroek 1990). Four categories of degradation were established. *Light degradation* is soil in which part of the topsoil has been removed, widely spaced rills or hollows exist, or salinization has increased. The study found that 750 million hectares are lightly degraded. *Moderate degradation* is land on which all topsoil has been removed, shallow rills are less than 20 meters apart, moderately deep gullies are no more than 50 meters apart, and nutrient decline involves a marked reduction in organic matter. This is the most extensive form of soil degradation, affecting 910 million hectares of land. *Severe degradation* is soil deeply marked by gullies and hollows, with pasture land having less than 30 percent of its native vegetation and being characterized by severe nutrient depletion. Approximately 300 million hectares of land are severely degraded. *Extreme degradation* is soil on which no crop growth occurs and restoration is impossible. Extreme degradation is found on approximately 9 million hectares of land. Taking all categories of degradation into account, 1.9 billion acres of land are degraded, 1.2 billion of which are moderate to extreme in nature. Degraded land represents 17 percent of the earth's vegetated surface (Oldeman, Hakkeling, and Sombroek 1990:Tables 1–7).

Soil degradation results from four processes. Water erosion, also called surface or sheet erosion, is the washing away of topsoil by water. Since the topsoil is rich in nutrients, loss of topsoil makes the land less productive. Wind erosion is a similar process, occurring primarily in arid and semi-arid regions. Coarse soil is most susceptible to wind erosion, particularly when there has been overgrazing, deforestation, or fuel wood removal. The third process, chemical deterioration, can occur in several ways. Nutrients can be depleted by raising of crops on poor soil without sufficient manure or fertilizers. Conversely, the overuse of acidifying fertilizers can result in chemical deterioration. In many countries, farmers are unprepared to engage in the controlled use of fertilizers. Nutrient loss can occur also from salinization. Salt concentrations increase as a result of irrigation or the withdrawal of groundwater in such a way that sea water infiltrates an aquifer. Chemical deterioration can occur too as a result of environmental variability, especially with regard to urban waste, industrial discharges, and excessive or unwise pesticide use. The final process that results in soil degradation is physical deterioration. This is associated with soil compaction and waterlogging. The most frequent cause of soil compaction is heavy machinery. Human interference with natural drainage systems is the most frequent cause of waterlogging.

The most extreme form of degradation from all sources is *desertification*. For most individuals the term carries with it images of a desert consuming ever-increasing amounts of once-productive land through the advance of sand dunes. Actually, there has been substantial disagreement over the definition of desertification. Some analysts define it as any development of desert-like conditions in green areas. Others define it as the long-term deterioration of the productive capacity of the soil as a result of man's activities. After considerable developmental work, beginning in 1970, the UN Environment Programme in 1991 officially defined desertification as "...land degradation in arid, semiarid, and dry subhumid areas resulting mainly from adverse human impact" (Dregne, Kaggag, and Rozanov 1992: 72). Such a definition provides the basis for a more sustainable response to the problem.

Case studies of desertification have indicated that three human activities are the most important contributors to the process. First, overgrazing along with its attendant activities is the major cause of desertification in drylands. Attendant activities include the trampling associated with watering points and the concentrations of stock associated with feedlots. Second, the extension of crop production into unsuitable areas or a change to crop production patterns unsuited to the area contribute to desertification. These changes are often accompanied by other changes that increase the problem, such as the siting of roads and the emergence of various construction projects. Third is the increased consumption of woody vegetation. With population increase and urbanization, foraging for wood is more intense and also conducted over a wider range. This foraging often causes the germination of replacement vegetation to be delayed or prevented altogether. The most important causes of desertification, then, are not the hot siroccos blowing out of existing deserts, but the work of humans who are often unaware of the outcomes of their actions.

Estimates differ regarding the extent of desertification. There is fairly common agreement that deserts resulting from climatic conditions account for approximately 48,350,000 square kilometers or 36.3 percent of the earth's land surface. When soil and vegetation data affected by human activities are taken into account, 43 percent of the earth's land surface is desert. The difference in the two estimates, the first based on physical factors and the second on the outcomes of people's activities, is assumed to be the extent of human-made desertification. This area is approximately 9,115,000 square kilometers. Estimated annual loss to desertification is 58,000 square kilometers (Walls 1980:169).

The essential question, then, is whether or not all forms of soil degradation can be stopped and remediation efforts conducted to restore the land to its former productivity. To many analysts, the term *irreversibly degraded* is a tautology. What is degraded, they argue, can be rehabilitated. Whether or not this is true depends a great deal on the type of degradation and the willingness to pay rather high costs. Lightly degraded soils can be rehabilitated with such measures as crop rotation, fallow periods, and minimum tillage. The cost is a temporarily reduced production, something most policy systems find within their reach. With regard to moderately degraded land, rehabilitation requires more resources than the average farmer possesses. Thus national programs and financing are needed. Severely eroded lands appear to require a rehabilitation effort beyond the capacity of most developing nations (World Resources Institute 1992:113). Such efforts would require multinational technical and financial assistance. Furthermore, rehabilitation would require resources other than financial, and the diversion of those resources would have important outcomes. Finally, extremely degraded land is impossible to rehabilitate in any meaningful sense of restoring it to its former productivity. Such rehabilitation would require either an as yet unanticipated technological breakthrough or a financial commitment beyond the capacity of the community of nations. Remediation is possible, then, with some forms of soil degradation and should be included in policy objectives along with prevention.

LIFE ON THE SOIL: SPECIES AND THEIR SURVIVAL

The all too common tragedies of deforestation and soil degradation contribute to a third common tragedy—the destruction of the habitat of many living species. Most species are subject to both natural and human influences. By and large, they have adapted to natural forces. Where they have not, as with the dinosaurs and the collapse of the vegetation cover on which they fed, they have become extinct. Species have had a more difficult time, however, adapting to the various influences created by human activities.

A number of human activities threaten the existence of wildlife. Perhaps the most important are those that result in habitat loss or modification. The most obvious example is the clearing of forest for crop production. The phenomenon is much more varied than forest clearing, however. For example, the gain in the total forest cover in Europe would seem to be an improvement in habitat. However, this gain has been a result of tree farms consisting of coniferous trees planted in long rows and kept clear of underbrush. Such forests are relatively poor environments for wildlife, a concept referred to by the term *biotic poverty*. Thus, total forest cover may not be a good indicator of the quality of wildlife habitat.

Agriculture patterns also can be important. The movement from the "family farm" to the corporate farm in the United States resulted in an enlargement of fields and the elimination of hedgerows and fences that were important cover for wildlife. In many instances the enlargement of farms meant the conversion of wetlands to production and increased irrigation with its attendant consequences for wildlife habitat. In addition, in all countries the movement to more intensive farming has increased the use of fertilizers, pesticides, and fungicides. Chemical fertilizer use rose from 14 million metric tons in 1970 to 146 million in 1989. The leaching of these substances into the surface water system has affected the habitat of aquatic life. In advanced nations, structural changes in the water course have resulted in serious loss of habitat. The Florida Bay at the southern tip of Florida, for example, is seriously threatened by algae and is close to biotic poverty. Most data suggest that the reason for the threat is the diversion of fresh water from the Everglades, a direct result of public policy decisions to increase the amount of cultivated land by draining vast areas.

Exploitation is a second human activity that threatens many species. Such exploitation can be excessive, illegal, or both. There is an immediate threat of overexploiting the world's fishing waters. The commercial global catch of fish was 85 million tons in 1988 (OECD 1991:90). The United Nations Food and Agriculture Organization estimates that the total annual sustainable yield of fish is 100 million tons, only 15 million more than was taken in 1988. Assuming a continued increase in the harvest of fish, the

FAO estimates that the maximum annual sustainable yield of fish will be reached by the year 2000. Along with these aggregate numbers, many of the more valuable species of fish are already overexploited. Excessive exploitation seriously reduced the population of Alaskan king crab, the Atlantic red fish, and Peruvian anchovies, among others. Additionally, the aggregate world figures mask some significant regional problems. The OECD reports that landings from the Mediterranean, the Black Sea, and the Pacific northwest regions already exceed the estimated sustainable yield of those regions. The risks of overexploitation will probably continue to increase as a result of greater need for protein and continuing improvements in fishing technology.

Exploitation is often illegal. Kenya has had a 70 percent decline in its elephant population over the past ten years as a result of illegal poaching of ivory. The government has issued game wardens automatic weapons and ordered that poachers be shot on sight. From June 1989, when the policy went into effect, to October 1989, the rate of elephant killings had been reduced from three a day to about one a month. More than twenty poachers were killed in that time period (*U.S. News and World Report*, October 2, 1989:52). The exploitation of protected species often continues because of loopholes in the law. Whales have been exploited to a point where their populations are very low. The International Whaling Commission responded by placing a moratorium on the killing of whales, but this moratorium permitted Japan to take 300 whales a year for "scientific study." Since it is hard to envision Japanese research requiring 300 whales a year, the more plausible conclusion is that the loophole permits the continuance of commercial whaling.

Pollution and climate change are the third set of human influences that threaten species. The wide range of chemicals, solid wastes, and radionuclides released into the biosphere affect wildlife in both subtle and overt ways. For example, acid rain has resulted in biotic poverty in a number of lakes. OECD reported that over 13,000 square kilometers of lakes in Norway will not support fish and that the fish stock in an additional 20,000 square kilometers has been seriously depleted (OECD 1991:140). Air pollution also affects many species of trees. Global warming, should it occur, and human-induced changes in climate patterns, will affect wildlife in a significant and pervasive way.

These three human factors—habitat loss, exploitation, and pollution—combine to pose a serious threat to many species. However, it is difficult to measure the real extent of that threat. Surprisingly little is known about either plant or animal wildlife. At the most basic level, the total number of species is not known. Various estimates have been made, ranging from 5 million to 30 million. Such an astonishingly wide range is the result of several factors. The most basic reason is the simple fact that there has been little study of wildlife, particularly in the tropics, the most ecologically fertile area of the earth for both plant and animal species. A second factor is that a number of species are minute organisms such as microbes and small aquatic creatures. Most study has been conducted in the temperate zone and on economically important species, so there has been a substantial bias in favor of the interest of the developed nations and economic elites.

Relative to wildlife, then, one of the most basic needs is for reliable data. The approach most often employed is to concentrate on species that are thought to be threatened. Such an approach, however, is characterized by a major flaw: Many species become extinct without having been identified. Unbelievably, in a world characterized by knowledge explosion, we do not know how many species of wildlife exist or how many of those species become extinct each year.

Given these facts, the process by which estimates are made of threatened species is interesting. The most widely used methodology is called *the species area curve*. The relationship is calculated between the size of an area and the known species that exist in it. From this relationship, an estimate can be made of the percentage of species that will become extinct if a certain amount of the habitat is lost. This methodology was applied to an analysis of the tropical rain forest. Using the current rates of deforestation with the subsequent loss of habitat, the study estimated that 4 to 8 percent of species would be extinct by the year 2015 and 17 to 35 percent by the year 2040 (Sayer and Whitmore 1993). Extinction at that rate would result in the loss of 15 percent of the world's species over the next 25 years, mostly of species that have not been cataloged by taxonomists.

Most OECD countries relate the term *threatened* to a species' ability to breed and reproduce itself. A threatened species, then, lacks the habitat, food sources, or breeding conditions that would ensure a stable population in the future. The data reported by OECD countries are disturbing. Nations reporting over 40 percent of their mammal species as threatened include France, West Germany, Luxembourg, the Netherlands, Portugal, and Switzerland. France, West Germany, the Netherlands, Portugal, and Switzerland, countries with heavy bird populations, report over 30 percent of their bird species threatened. Data from the North American Breeding Bird Survey, one of the most extensive monitoring systems in effect, revealed that 20 species (of the 62 analyzed) experienced significant decreases in population while only 4 had increases. Austria, West Germany, and Luxembourg reported between 36 and 70 percent of their fish populations as threatened. Other countries reported less than 15 percent of the fish population threatened. Belgium, West Germany, and Switzerland reported 25 percent of their vascular plant species as threatened (all data from OECD 1991:134–135). These data suggest that the problem is significant in both temperate and tropical nations.

Species loss joins deforestation and soil degradation as problems of significant proportions. Policy response to these problems has been slow developing both at the international and national levels.

POLICY RESPONSE TO STRESS ON THE LAND

A new perspective on population policy seems to be emerging in the international community. There is a new concentration on the dual objectives of human development and protection of children's health. Relative to human development, achieving a healthy, educated, and stable population is the cornerstone of the policy of sustainable development—a chief component in the new ethics of the environment that will be discussed in the final chapter.

The *human development index*, initiated by the United Nations Development Program in 1990, attempts to measure a nation's progress toward sustainable development. It uses three indicators: life expectancy, literacy, and living standards (United Nations 1990:40). In a country-by-country analysis the index yields some interesting findings. First, there are wide differences between men and women on each index. Economic growth does not necessarily result in a better life for females in many countries. Second, in several countries uneven income distribution was found to affect human development adversely; economic growth simply translates into greater wealth for the few without raising the living standards of the masses. Conversely, one of the most effective means of sustainable growth is an equitable distribution of income. Finally, the analysis found that high levels of human freedom are closely associated with high levels of economic growth. Human freedom does not necessarily preclude government activity, however. Well-structured government social spending was found to offset inequalities in income distribution and as a result improve human welfare. These are significant findings. They suggest that sustainable economic growth measured in terms of broad human well-being can occur within any given rate of population growth.

The second element in the emerging perspective on population policy is an emphasis on children's health. The United Nations sponsored a World Summit for Children in 1990, with 71 countries participating. The World Declaration on the Survival, Protection, and Development of Children established ten goals. The goals were based in a recognition that children's health improves primarily as a result of improvement in living conditions (nutrition, hygiene, and sanitation particularly), improvement in the environment (water and sanitation particularly), and overall improvement in the economy. The relationship between poverty and children's health is strong in both Third World and industrialized nations.

Poverty and illness are linked even with reference to environmentally based illness. For example, most of the 12 million children in the United States who are at risk of lead poisoning are poor (National Commission on Children 1991:121). The linkage between poverty and illness is especially important given the distribution of the world's children. Of the approximately 1.7 billion children under the age of fifteen, 82 percent, or 1.4 billion, live in developing nations. Projections are that 1.5 billion children will be born worldwide in the 1990s, over 90 percent of them in developing countries. These numbers are significant because 97 percent of all deaths among children under five years of age and 99 percent of all deaths of mothers occur in developing countries (United Nations 1988:22). Environmental conditions associated with underdevelopment are the cause of most of the ill health among the world's children.

The emphasis on children's health may appear on the surface to be in conflict with the goal of a stable population. However, the opposite is the case—reducing deaths among children actually slows the rate of population growth. In technical population research terms, the change is from a high-mortality/high-fertility condition to a low-mortality/low-fertility condition. This change usually takes place when death rates among infants under five years of age drops to 100–150 per 1,000 births (UN Children's Fund 1991:43–45). While the reasons for this drop are not known, the most widely accepted explanation is that parents' desire for children is fulfilled when their babies survive. High mortality rates seem to fuel the concern for children's ability to survive until the parents reach old age, increasing the likelihood of having more children. One of the important developments in this regard is the fact that infant mortality rates in many countries have reached the point where further declines can be expected to be accompanied by significant reductions in fertility rates. The decline in birth rates is especially steep in those countries where a reduction in infant mortality occurs simultaneously with strong family planning programs.

The long-term well-being of the world's children depends on protection of the ecological basis of life, given increases in population. Concern for population growth rates, then, must be accompanied by policies designed to sustain the world's ecology and resources, yet agricultural policies in most countries have had the opposite effect.

Agricultural policy, particularly in the industrialized nations, is based on the dual objectives of promoting production and stabilizing farm income. The first objective means that the policy structure itself provides strong incentives for farmers to increase production by any means possible. Results of this policy include a significant increase in the use of fertilizers and pesticides, the farming of land only marginally suited for crop production, and mono-cropping, or farming practices that emphasize the subsidized crop. Similarly, the objective of stabilizing farm incomes has led farmers to plant large acreages of supported crops, to forego crop rotation practices that would reduce production, and to seek high yields through extensive use of fertilizers. The result of all these practices has been the continuance or acceleration of soil degradation.

There are indications that a new perspective on soil policy is emerging. An example is the U.S. Food Security Act of 1985. The Act created the Conservation Reserve Program, a two-phased program designed to take erodible land out of production. In the first phase, farmers were paid $49 an acre for planting their most erodible land in a cover crop. American farmers have responded actively, primarily by taking out of production marginal land that should not have been subject to cropping at all. Annual erosion of land has been reduced from 1.6 billion tons down to 1.0 billion.

The second stage of the Conservation Reserve Program is the development of erosion control plans for farms with highly erodible land. Farmers owning such land must have these plans approved by the Soil Conservation Service by 1995 or lose their eligibility for crop subsidies. Approximately 1.5 million farmers are in the process of developing such plans on a total of 134 million acres of land. This aspect of the program has the potential for reducing erosion by an additional 700 million tons per year. The Food Security Act of 1985 is an important break with past agricultural policy in all industrialized nations as the first instance when a major agricultural nation has made soil conservation a policy priority.

Other countries in addition to the United States have adopted innovative practices to foster soil conservation. The European Community, for example, has adopted a policy designed to protect fragile areas. It permits the designation of environmentally sensitive areas (ESAs). Cooperating governments, of which the United Kingdom, Germany, France, and the Netherlands are the most active, pay farmers to employ agricultural practices that maintain wildlife habitat and traditional landscapes. South Australia has adopted a program, called the *heritage agreement*, which requires farmers to obtain a permit before clearing additional land for crops or pasture. When the permit is refused, the farmer is paid for the attachment of a heritage agreement, called a *conservation easement*, to the farm title. This easement protects native vegetation on the property in perpetuity. A few nations have experimented with tax provisions to reduce soil degradation. Some of these abolish tax incentives for clearing land; others take the positive approach of providing tax incentives for planting land cover crops. Australia did both. These policy changes signal an important modification of agricultural policy in a number of countries. Given the extraordinary loss of soil worldwide, soil conservation should at least join production promotion and income stabilization as a policy objective.

The objective of reducing stress on the land is also served by reducing the rate of deforestation. There have been several important steps taken at the international level to address deforestation. The 1992 United Nations Conference on Environment and Development adopted a nonbinding statement of principles of forest management. While it recognized the right of nations to develop forests according to domestic needs, it also affirmed the principle that forests should be managed in a sustainable manner and it called on nations to develop plans for sustainable management. The principles supported the creation of a global forest fund to help developing nations pay for conservation measures. Most of the developing nations eligible for such funding have substantial tropical forest.

A second international effort is the Tropical Forestry Action Plan adopted by the United Nations in 1985. This plan attempts to slow the rate of tropical deforestation through the development of forestry management plans by tropical countries. Funding agencies are then encouraged to make their decisions on the basis of the forestry plans. Unfortunately, a comprehensive evaluation of TFAP concluded that its effect on deforestation was modest at best and "that most national plans, based mainly on forestry sector reviews, simply justify increased investment in the forestry sector—a focus too narrow to adequately assess the root causes of deforestation" (Winterbottom 1990:21). The results of such studies point to the need for additional international action, perhaps in the form of a convention on deforestation.

Within nations, there is an almost bewildering array of policies on lands and forests. Some nations have virtually no policy or very simplistic ones. Other nations have highly complex policies. The United States faced the issue of public lands from its first days as a nation. The development of its policy, however, is a case study in how not to manage public lands.

The primary objective of American policy on the public lands, from the Washington administration through the nineteenth century, was that of disposal. The major differences occurred over the most effective process for disposal. Thomas Jefferson wanted the public lands distributed to persons without land as a means of developing a strong cadre of independent farmers and to landless persons outside the United States as a means of attracting immigrants. Alexander Hamilton, on the other hand, argued for the distribution of land through various investors and stock companies, as a means of strengthening the fledging American economy. One of the basic tensions in American land policy, then, existed from the very beginning. Should land be used in such a way as to benefit the masses or is it to be controlled by economic elites to ensure its use for economic development purposes? Many of the issues surrounding national land policy today are still as much distributional as they are environmental in nature.

In the early twentieth century there was a significant shift in attitudes away from an emphasis on disposal to a focus on national retention of some public lands. A number of factors contributed to the interest in retention (Brubaker 1984:2–3). Among the most powerful was public reaction, fueled by highly visible preservationists, against unbridled exploitation of forests. The "cut and run" practices of many companies generated strong fears that the nation would soon be short of timber resources. In addition, many individuals, such as Theodore Roosevelt, feared the loss of great national scenic treasures. Second, many of the lands were withdrawn from the homesteading laws simply by default. No one claimed them since they were thought to be unfit for settlement. Ironically, many of these lands are grazing lands associated with the recent "Sagebrush Rebellion," a bitter struggle by cattlemen to retain their privileged use of public lands in the West. Finally, the United States bought land that was stripped, overexploited, and abandoned, largely because the states were unwilling to assume responsibility. Public lands that are the residual of the original public domain are referred to as *public domain lands*. Lands that were subsequently bought by the United States for whatever reasons are referred to as *acquired lands*. Taken together, they make the United States a significant landowner in the American economy.

The national government presently owns approximately 732 million acres of land—just under one-third of the total land area of the country. State and local governments own an additional 154.4 million acres, placing the total publicly owned lands at just under 40 percent of the land mass of the United States. The distribution of nationally owned lands is not even across the country. Most are in the West, with the largest component being in Alaska. The national government owns approximately 355 million acres of Alaska's 365 million acres. The United States owns 85 percent of the land in Nevada, 73 percent in Arizona and Utah, 65 percent in Idaho, 53 percent in Oregon, 52 percent in Wyoming, 45 percent in California, 44 percent in New Mexico, 38 percent in Colorado, 37 percent in Montana and 35 percent in Washington. By contrast, in none of the original thirteen states does the national government own more than 8 percent of the land area. Public land conflicts in the United States as a result have tended to be centered in the West.

Management of most of the national lands is divided among four agencies in two Departments. The Department of Interior has jurisdiction over the bulk of national lands. Within the Department, the Bureau of Land Management is responsible for 334 million acres, the Fish and Wildlife Service for 89 million acres, and the National Park Service for 74 million acres. The Forest Service within the Department of Agriculture has responsibility for 192 million acres. Several other departments, including Defense, Transportation, and Energy, have responsibility for the remainder of the national lands.

The major components of management policy for public lands are specified in four important statutes. The most important of these is the Multiple Use, Sustained Yield Act (MUSY) passed in 1960. As its name implies, lands subject to the Act must be managed for multiple uses that are sustained over time. The Act defined multiple use as "the management of all the various renewable surface resources of the national forests so that they are utilized in the combination that will best meet the needs of the American people; making...use of the land...over areas large enough to provide sufficient latitude for periodic adjustments in use to conform to changing needs and conditions." Sustained yield was defined in the Act as the achievement and maintenance in perpetuity of a high-level annual output of the various renewable resources of the national forests without impairment of the productivity of the land. The Act did not necessarily require the use of all resources. Finally, the Act provided that the management plan did not have to seek the combination of uses that would give the largest dollar return or the greatest unit output. At the practical level, the Act gave the Forestry Service considerable discretion to manage public lands under its jurisdiction. In this respect, it represents an acceptance by Congress of the proposition that land management is a technical issue best left to professional planners (Wondolleck 1988:29).

The process toward professional management of public lands was accelerated with the passage of the National Forest Management Act of 1976, which requires the development of "land resource management plans" for all national forests. It stipulates that the planning process be open to public involvement. In point of fact, the most extensive participation in the process is by groups interested in timber. The Act requires that the plans include attention to several factors, including physical suitability, economic suitability, diversity, rotation age and culmination of mean annual increment, nondeclining even flow, clear cutting, and below-cost sales. The physical suitability requirement is the most important from an environmental perspective; it prohibits tree harvest in areas where the soil, slope, or watershed conditions will be irreversibly damaged, where the land cannot be restocked within five years, or where streams, lakes, wetlands, and other bodies of water cannot be adequately protected. The economic suitability requirement restricts cutting to those lands where the timber can be harvested economically. The diversity requirement seeks to ensure that the species of trees in the harvest areas remain the same mix as before harvest. It also is designed to protect the diversity of plant and animal life in the forest. The rotation and mean annual increment requirements are designed to assure that trees reach an acceptable level of maturity before they are harvested; this maturity requirement varies considerably among the species of trees. The nondeclining even flow factor places limits on the harvest itself; the plan must establish an average sale per year and harvest must not exceed that average over a ten-year period. The Act does not establish an absolute prohibition against clear cutting; rather the land resource management plan must identify when clear cutting is the optimum method and the area blocks within which it will occur. The below-costs sales requirement presumably means restricting cutting on marginal lands; in reality, however, when full costing of timber operations on public lands is done, most timber harvesting is below cost to the national government.

The third act important to management of public lands in the United States is the Federal Land Policy and Management Act of 1976. This Act applied specifically to lands managed by the Bureau of Land Management. The Bureau had favored livestock and mining over other potential uses of the 334 million acres under its management, and Congress in essence mandated that it shift to a multiple-use, sustained-yield policy. In addition, the Bureau is required to develop resource management plans for the lands under its jurisdiction, addressing issues such as the acquisition and sale of land, future usages of the land, the long-term effects of any particular use, and the efforts made to coordinate Bureau activities with those of other agencies. Development of the plans has proven to be a very slow process and the Bureau is far from realizing the objective of comprehensive planning.

The fourth act, the National Environmental Policy Act of 1969, applies to both Bureau of Land Management and Forestry Service lands. This act requires an environmental impact statement for all new uses of public lands or for significant new actions that affect the land. However, there are ways for agencies to circumvent such a requirement. The agency can, for example, reach a finding of no significant impact (referred to in bureaucratic jargon as a FONSI) on the basis of an "environmental record." Additionally, the Act exempts "everyday action" from the requirement of an environmental impact statement. Distinguishing between everyday actions and actions that are significant enough to require an environmental impact statement is not easy. Unfortunately, it is an easy basis on which to avoid the environmental impact statement.

A quick review of these acts may leave the impression of a highly professional comprehensive approach to land management. Quite the opposite is the case. Land policy is fragmented among these four and many other pieces of legislation. Responsibility is divided among several agencies with little effective coordination between them. The result is a highly fragmented and politicized approach fraught with a number of basic problems. Only a few of these problems can be discussed.

One of the major problems has to do with sustaining the yield of the land. Actually, since significant amounts of the land were marginal when made a part of the public domain, the problem really involves improvement of the land. To improve grazing land controlled by the Bureau of

Land Management, Congress passed the Public Rangelands Improvement Act. Funds for the improvement were to be derived from fees charged to ranchers and from supplemental appropriations to be made by Congress. However, the fees that were established were seriously underpriced; leasing grazing rights on the public lands is much cheaper than on private lands. Many ranchers sublease grazing rights on public lands at as much as eight times the fee they paid (Fairfax and Yale 1987:140). Revenues from the fee system are grossly inadequate for any meaningful improvement. Additionally, Congress has not appropriated supplemental funds in most years since the Act was passed.

In other areas, public policy encourages the blatant exploitation of resources from the land. Policy on mining hard rock minerals on public lands was established in the General Mining Law of 1872. In effect, the Act declares that a person who discovers a mineral may mine it almost at no charge and with no competition. Under this policy, about 25 million acres of public lands are subject to mining operations that extract over $4 billion worth of minerals annually. Companies extracting the minerals are required to pay a small fee of $100 per year for improvements on the mine and pay a modest $5 or less per acre for the mineral rights (Coggins and Wilkenson 1987:420). When passed in 1872, the Act was designed to encourage individuals to bring resources from the western lands to the market. Today the system is a blatant exploitation of public resources by a few.

A third problem is the difficulty in establishing a comprehensive approach to land management. An excellent example of this problem is wildlife. One would assume that a major objective of any land policy would be to ensure the continuance of adequate habitat for wildlife. However, such was not the case with lands managed by the Forestry Service or by the Bureau of Land Management. In both instances, habitat preservation was a secondary goal within the multiple-use policy. Initial efforts at habitat preservation were piecemeal and designed to protect a single species. The Pelican Island Bird Reservation created in 1903 and the National Bison Range created in 1906 are examples. A number of such areas were created in subsequent years. However, it was not until 1966 that a consolidated and comprehensive system was established through passage of the National Wildlife Refuge Administration Act, which consolidated 90 million acres into a single system administered by the Fish and Wildlife Service. The primary management goal is the preservation, protection, and enhancement of fish and wildlife. It is important to note, however, that multiple use of the land within the system can be allowed, including livestock grazing, recreation, timber harvesting, and mineral development (Brubaker 1984:137). Providing protection for fish and wildlife is simply the "dominant use" on refuge lands. As a result, the refuge system does not adequately safeguard wildlife (World Resources Institute 1993:160).

On a broader level, the fact that public land management in the United States has not been effective in addressing the issue of species protection gave rise to efforts to formulate policy for endangered species. These efforts culminated in actions on both the international and national levels. At the international level, the Convention on International Trade in Endangered Species of Wild Fauna and Flora (CITES) was adopted in 1973. Under terms of this agreement, species in need of protection are listed in three Appendices. Species in Appendix I are rare and endangered, and trade in these species is prohibited. Those in Appendix II face a threat of extinction if trade is not strictly regulated. Appendix III, which affords the lowest degree of protection, contains species that are threatened if long-term trading practices continue. However, any nation can take out a reservation to an Appendix listing. Five African nations have taken out such a reservation on the ivory trading ban. Nine other African nations are not members of CITES. As a result of these and other factors, opinion varies substantially on whether the CITES has reduced poaching of the elephant and the illegal trade in ivory (Hosang 1992:66).

U.S. efforts to protect endangered wildlife led to the passage of the Endangered Species Act of 1973, which prohibited hunting, harassment, collection, or capture of any species determined to be threatened with or in danger of extinction. Additionally, all agencies that manage national lands have to ensure that their actions do not harm any plant or animal on the threatened or endangered list. On a program level, the Fish and Wildlife Service was required to implement a program to recover and enhance endangered species.

A fourth problem in U.S. public land management has to do with the inability to settle some of the most basic questions regarding land policy. This problem is illustrated in the national approach to wilderness. One of the most basic questions in public land policy is whether or not wilderness has intrinsic value. Certainly the question involves clear-cut differences in values of various factions. Naturalists argue that wilderness has intrinsic value and is a precious resource. Entrepreneurs argue that the naturalist's position is based on the assumption that human activity is bad. They believe that wilderness was made for people and people for the wilderness. Public policy has tended to adopt the position of the naturalists. The Wilderness Act of 1964 declared that "it is the policy of Congress to secure for the American people...an enduring resource of wilderness." The Act was opposed not only by timber interest groups but also by the Forest Service and the National Park Service. A similar policy objective was expressed in the Wild and Scenic Rivers Act of 1968. This Act established three categories of rivers: A wild river is to remain inaccessible and essentially wilderness; a scenic river is one that is accessible but is to remain undeveloped; a recreational river is accessible and may be developed. The United States is inching in the direction of vesting intrinsic value in wilderness.

Unfortunately, both the international policy system and national policy systems are only inching their way toward effective land policy. The thin veneer of life is under substantial and increasing stress. Ways need to be found to accelerate the development of land policy for a global ecosystem.

Chapter 10

Fractals, Butterflies, and an Ethic for a Global Ecosystem

Several themes have been the basis for the discussion throughout the book. The first is the necessity of thinking about the environment as a unitary global system. From our earliest experiences with geography, we are taught to organize regions and sections of the environment by categories. The result is very little emphasis on the interrelatedness of a unitary ecosystem. Unfortunately, research and analysis have taken this tack also, so little is known about the complexity of the global ecosystem. Second, we must think about environmental policy on a cross-national basis. Pollution does not respect national borders, but considerable policy is formulated within national borders. Nations can and should learn from each other. The international system must also develop the capacity to formulate and implement policy. The third theme is that effective environmental policy requires an intergenerational mode of thinking. Indeed, some environmental problems require a time frame that is outside the meaningful experience of most people and are relevant only as computer variables.

All these themes combine to suggest that the way the environment is viewed determines to a large extent what is seen. The perspectives that underlie the analysis give shape and form to the perception of problems. The values that underlie the analysis determine the definitions given to the problems and suggest solutions. Thus the development of appropriate perspectives and values is essential to the development of effective environmental policy. These two imperatives—the development of appropriate perspectives and the articulation of appropriate values—are the themes of this chapter.

FRACTALS AND BUTTERFLIES: A PERSPECTIVE FOR A GLOBAL ECOSYSTEM

The need for an adequate perspective for a global ecosystem brings us full circle to an important point made in the first chapter. The conceptual lens through which a person looks determines to a large extent what the individual sees. If we pull the various threads of previous chapters together, it is apparent that an adequate perspective for a global ecosystem involves both factors at a very general level of understanding and factors associated with more specific economic and political ways of conceptualizing reality. The factors associated with the general conceptual lens through which we look pose a choice between fundamentally different ways of seeing reality.

Straight Lines or Undulating Waves: A General Perspective

The traditional perspective through which reality is viewed is based on a belief in the linear nature of reality. According to this view, the response of any system is directly proportional to the inputs into the system. Thus change occurs in a straight line and incremental fashion in response to inputs. This change can be predicted by identifying the inputs and their effects on the system. Complex systems make prediction more difficult since there are more inputs and more effects, but even complex systems can be understood and change within them can be predicted if enough information can be gathered. This understanding includes an identification of cause-and-effect relationships that occur within the system.

The widespread acceptance of the linear view has had profound effects on how individuals think about the ecosystem and therefore the prescription of environmental policy. Among the results are two important beliefs. The first is the proposition that what science does not now know about the ecosystem, it will know someday when enough information is available. The gaps in understanding the ecosystem, in this view, are the result of inadequate information and not inadequacy in the linear perspective through which the system is analyzed. Second, better understanding of the ecosystem will be the basis of more effective control to accomplish human objectives. Science, then, is viewed in a very narrow utilitarian context as being in the service of human well-being, as contrasted with the well-being of all life forms or of the ecosystem itself. This view is what deep ecologists object to as an anthropocentric view of the world as opposed to a more defensible ecocentric view. Most individuals who hold to the linear view have argued that science is in the service of humans, not of the ecosystem or even of all life forms.

A more recent approach is a nonlinear view of reality. This view holds that dynamic systems are subject to change through either external influences or their own subtle internal feedback (Briggs 1992:19). In other words, dynamic systems are extremely sensitive to their initial conditions. Thus a very slight difference in starting position and in factors that influence the system make a very large difference in outcome. Unlike linear systems, which are logical, incremental, and predictable, nonlinear systems are dynamic, sensitive, and unpredictable. Dynamic systems, then, are "chaotic" in the sense that influences on them are effectively infinite so that it is impossible to gather enough information to understand them. Dynamic systems are composed of an infinite range of interacting factors that are extraordinarily sensitive to the most miniscule factor.

One of the most important pieces of work contributing to the development of the nonlinear perspective was that of meteorologist Edward Lorenz. The problem Lorenz was trying to understand was the fact that having more information on variables that affect the weather, such as temperature, air pressure, and the like, did not increase the accuracy of long-range forecasts. Therefore:

> ...the problem wasn't just that forecasting models always display limited precision. The problem is that no model, no matter how sophisticated, could ever obtain sufficiently accurate information to start with because weather itself is so dynamical, so sensitive to the "information" continuously circling inside it, that even the wings of a butterfly stirring in the forests of Brazil would have to be taken into account. Accurate long-term weather prediction...is therefore not just practically, but also theoretically impossible. (Briggs 1992: 57, 79)

One physicist concluded that dynamic systems are so sensitive to miniscule influences that they can be affected by the gravitational attraction of an electron on the other end of the universe (Briggs 1992:16).

The attempt to track the complex "chaotic" activity of dynamic systems led to the development of fractal geometry. Benoit Mandelbrot, a researcher with IBM who provided much of the initial development of fractal geometry, defined fractals as the images of the way a thing folds and unfolds, feeding back on itself and others. The fractal defines the infinitely self-referential quality of dynamic systems in repetitive and nonrepetitive patterns. Using fractal geometry, researchers found that even simple systems, such as a wave on the ocean, that appeared to be functioning in an orderly manner as a result of deterministic forces playing on it, actually exhibited random behavior when there was a change in one of its parameters. That is, dynamic systems seem to function in an orderly manner up to a certain point. The introduction of a variable beyond that point results in a permutation that is unpredictable, or "chaos." Determining the boundary between the predictable and unpredictable, the calm and the chaotic, is not possible. To gather enough information to know that specific boundary would require the ability to control the influence of the attempt to gather the information itself.

What is to be made of the two fundamentally different ways of viewing reality, the linear and nonlinear? Again it is not our purpose to reconcile differences among scientists. Our interest is in drawing what lessons we can from such differences with the objective of better understanding the ecosystem. With this in mind, there are several important lessons to be learned from the contrast between linear and nonlinear views.

Among the most important of these lessons is that our initial assertion that the ecosystem is a single interrelated complex system seems like an understatement. Both the linearist and nonlinearist recognize the interrelatedness and the complexity of the ecosystem and the many factors that must be understood to explain it. And both understand the phenomenon of feedback—that a number of factors, both external and internal, play back upon the system to produce change. Where the two perspectives depart is in the assumption of order and predictability on the part of the linearist and of chaos and unpredictability for the nonlinearist. It is this difference that gives rise to the second lesson to be learned from the two perspectives.

The second lesson is that we ought to consider the possibility that humans can introduce relatively small perturbations into the ecosystem that could result in environmental catastrophe. What is at stake here is the issue of boundaries—for the linearist the threshold between what is acceptable risk and nonacceptable risk, and for the nonlinearist the boundary between order and chaos. The difference between the two is one of degree. For the linearist, movement across the threshold produces incremental and predictable results. In effect, "X" more people would die of cancer from exposure to radioactivity beyond the threshold than would die of cancer before the threshold level was reached. For the nonlinearist, once the boundary between order and chaos is crossed, the results are nonincremental and unpredictable. In effect, the introduction of a relatively small factor—the flapping of a butterfly's wings in Brazil—can result in nonincremental catastrophic change.

A prudent approach would be at least to recognize that the nonlinearist may be right. Such a recognition would result in a caution derived from the possibility that humans cannot continue to release pollutants into the ecosystem indefinitely. For example, there may be a point where the boundary between order and chaos is reached in the release of greenhouse gases into the atmosphere. If so, it is certainly prudent, as the Intergovernmental Panel on Climate Change noted, to reduce the release of such gases when it is technologically and economically feasible to do so. In fact, both from the linearist's threshold view and the nonlinearist's chaos view, it is imprudent not to reduce the release of pollutants in any form into the ecosystem while it is feasible to do so.

A third lesson to be learned from the contrast between the linearist and nonlinearist view is the necessity of being realistic about what we know and what we do not know. It is certainly humbling to realize that there is a basic disagreement among scientists about the most fundamental of all aspects of understanding—how reality is to be viewed. Since this is the case, we should recognize that we look through a glass darkly relative to the complex, multifaceted, and interdependent physical environment that we call the ecosystem. It needs to be emphasized again that environmental policy must be developed and implemented in the context of substantial uncertainty. However, uncertainty, while it should keep us humble and tolerant of other views, should not paralyze the policy system. Rather, uncertainty should energize the policy system. It should excite all citizens, analysts, and policy makers about the opportunities to learn more about the ecological basis of life. It should give a sense of accomplishment to those in the policy system when they are able to inch the system forward toward protecting the ecological basis of life. In short, uncertainty should be the occasion for movement and a sense of accomplishment, not inactivity and despair.

In addition to the need to consider a change in the analytical way that the ecosystem is viewed, there are ideological elements that need to become common features of the world's peoples. Ideology refers simply to a systematic body of concepts about culture. Within culture, the concepts used to shape our view of reality about politics and economics are very important to our relationships with the ecosystem. In other words, the ecosystem is very sensitive to human actions that are determined in part by political and economic ideology.

The Relevancy of an Impossible Ideal: An Ideological Perspective

The crucial change that needs to take place in the ideological perspective is a recognition of what is at issue relative to the ecosystem. The basic question is: Is the goal of preserving the ecological basis of life at issue or are the means to accomplish that objective at issue? The beginning point of an adequate ideological perspective for a global ecosystem is the recognition that the objective of preserving the ecological basis of life is not at issue. The Fourth Environmental Action Programme of the European Community expresses this reality as follows: "[E]nvironmental protection policy and strict environmental protection standards are no longer an optional extra but a *sine qua non* for the quality of life which the Community's citizens expect" (Commission of the European Communities 1986:3). Preserving the ecological basis of life, then, has become essential to humankind.

Such a recognition would help clarify some rather muddled aspects of the public perception of environmental policy in all countries. There is a deep division among analysts on the nature, direction, and intensity of public opinion on environmental issues (deHaven-Smith 1991:1). However, when the issue is posed as the preservation of the ecological basis of life, there is near unanimous positive response to the necessity of such an objective. The response to Earth Day 1990 is indicative of this proposition. A study of the event worldwide concluded that it "united more people concerned about a single cause than any other global event in history" (Cahn and Cahn 1990:17). While Earth Day is not a perfect surrogate for commitment to preserving the ecological basis of life, reaction to it and to other environmental issues strongly indicates that there is functional unanimity on the question of preserving the ecological basis of life.

Recognition of the functional unanimity on preserving the ecological basis of life would place this objective in the center of societal concerns, along with other great objectives such as justice, freedom, and equality. The symbolic force of such a recognition would be profound and reverberate through the policy systems of all countries. An analogy is the American experience with equality. There are significant differences among the American people on the most effective means for accomplishing equality for all. And, as with all ideals, the right to equality is subject to denial and is in fact denied by some in the American policy system. Nevertheless, powerful strains are placed on the system when the ideal of equality is denied or its implementation weakened. In effect, the ideal has profound relevancy for the policy system. What is needed in the environmental area is a similar recognition that preserving the ecological basis of life is one of the core objectives of all humanity. Differences may exist on the most effective means for accomplishing environmental objectives. Some individuals and groups may continue to deny the validity of the objective. But powerful countervailing strains should be placed on the policy systems of all nations when the ideal of preserving the ecological basis of life is denied or implementation of programs designed to accomplish the ideal is weakened. The oscillation in policy cycles between policy activism and policy inertia, between strong enforcement and weak enforcement, should even out in the direction of sustained and determined effort to preserve the ecological basis of life.

Disagreement is the context within which concepts are refined and alternatives are clarified. There should be an ongoing dialogue over the most appropriate means for achieving policy objectives. The crucible of questioning and disagreement remains the most effective context for a policy system when the adoption of means is under consideration.

Acceptance of the functional unanimity on preserving the ecological basis of life would have significant outcomes for political ideology. The most important change would be in the perception of the responsibilities of political decision makers. In most nations, elected decision makers are required to swear to defend their nation's constitution. Since governments are among the world's largest polluters and since public policy can affect the level of pollutants, political decision makers should also be confronted with their responsibilities for the ecosystem. In every nation political decision makers should be required to swear to defend the ecological basis of life. By contrast, a high-level political official in the United States in the 1980s dismissed the risks associated with depletion of the ozone layer with the comment that people could simply wear hats or thicker sunscreen. Such a comment is an offense against all. It should be grounds for removal from office. The world can no longer afford political leaders who are casual or cynical about the ecosystem. More important, the world can no longer afford political leaders who will sell the long-term goal of preserving the ecological basis of life for short term political gain. The new political ideology must put a cap on the new cattle a politician in the ecological commons can add to her or his herd.

In addition to changing perceptions of the responsibilities of elected officials, a political ideology for a global ecosystem needs also to direct energy toward the construction of institutions requisite to effective environmental policy. This is particularly important at the international level. While several international organizations have superlative track records, given their authority and resources, there is no international organization capable of developing and implementing policy on general environmental issues. The proposal for an Environmental Council analogous to the Security Council certainly would be a move in the direction of appropriate institution building. A model for the relationship between the Environmental Council and member nations could be the European Community and its member nations. On matters of general concern, the Environmental Council should have jurisdiction, including some means of enforcement even against recalcitrant nation states. In matters of specific concern, the member nations should retain jurisdiction. Sufficient experience in international cooperation exists to inform the building of institutions that protect a global ecosystem.

All nations experience institutional problems in their policy systems. In many nations, environmental policy institutions are only in the rudimentary stages of development if they exist at all. Thus institution building is a critical first step toward policy in those nations. Even in nations with seemingly sophisticated institutional arrangements, problems exist. The United States has a complicated two-tiered organization of national and state agencies. There are acute problems in the relations between those two levels, particularly in regard to partial preemption strategy. Institutions are semi-autonomous actors in the policy arena. In order to protect the global ecosystem, it is critical to build effective and responsible institutions at all levels.

A new ideology for a global ecosystem must contain some new elements in thinking about economic reality. At least two such changes are critical.

The first change has to do with the determination of price in a market economy. Changes in the resource base and deterioration of the ecosystem are seldom factored into the costing of a product. Thus market prices for goods and services do not include the cost of resource depletion and environmental pollution. The resource base and the ecosystem are systematically undervalued in the market system, and such undervaluing encourages overconsumption. Undervaluing and overconsumption in combination are serious market failures that need to be corrected.

The most promising suggestion for such a change is the movement to "environmental accounting" (Ahmad, Serafez, and Lutz 1989). Classical economics uses the gross national product (GNP) as the measure of a nation's economic activity and well-being. Environmental accounting would also include changes in the resource base and pollution of the ecosystem in the measure of a nation's wealth. The inadequacy in the GNP is seen in the fact that while it may show a society to be well off, the society could be overexploiting its resources and seriously reducing its capacity to produce in the future. Concepts that are put forward to replace the GNP are such measures as "real net national product," "sustainable social net national product," and "index of sustainable economic growth." Whatever the term used, an economic ideology for a global ecosystem must take account of a society's capacity to provide material well-being in the future. The question of sustainable economic growth, then, is at the heart of an economic ideology for a global ecosystem.

The concept of sustainable growth has undergone substantial development in recent years (World Resource Institute 1993: 2). Unfortunately, that development has led to different meanings of the term to different people. Common to nearly all concepts, however, is the notion that present use of resources should not diminish future economic well-being (Repetto 1986: 15). The World Commission on Environment and Development, established by the United Nations, defines sustainable growth as development that "meets the needs of the present without compromising the ability of future generations to meet their own needs" (World Commission 1987: 4). The use of the word *development* instead of *growth* is indicative of a major expansion in the concept. *Sustainable development* is frequently used to refer to those improvements in social well-being, such as education and health care, that are viewed as essential to preserving a clean environment. The United Nations *Human Development Report* emphasizes this feature of sustainable development. Finally, increasing emphasis is placed on the need to include in the decision process local people affected by policy. In this sense, sustainable development has taken on a process meaning. Political freedom and participatory democracy are the key elements in that process.

Is sustainable growth possible? Some analysts deny that it is and argue that sustainable growth is actually a contradiction in terms (Daly 1990:5). At the heart of this position is the belief that economic growth that neither decreases natural resources nor increases the production of wastes simply cannot sustain an ever-increasing world population. In this view, two things are necessary. First, there must be constraints on human behavior, particularly reproductive behavior. Second, there must be a redistribution of wealth as a means of more equitably allocating the world's scarce resources. These two things, in combination with the economic growth that is possible, are the only steps that can be taken to avert disaster.

What is to be made of the difference between those committed to some type of sustainable growth and those who deny its efficacy? First, it should be obvious that development is a critical necessity in many areas of the world. By any standard, the continuation of poverty and deprivation in billions of people is unacceptable. Further, it should be obvious that some form of new development policy is necessary. In short, traditional approaches to growth and development simply have not worked. One of the new elements should be a recognition that development anywhere must take into account the global ecology and the needs of future generations. In the words of the World Commission on Environment and Development, the new development policy must include a concern for the "entire planet into the distant future." In this regard, there needs to be a recognition of the importance of biodiversity. In fact, a biodiversity index is a better indicator of a country's health from an ecological perspective than is the GNP. The new development policy must recognize that the usefulness of renewable natural resources must at least be kept constant. Use of such resources should not decrease their renewability. Additionally, common pool resources, such as water, air, and soil, should be used in a way that maintains a nondeclining stock. That is, not only must degradation of common pool resources be stopped but also action must be taken to restore the pool. Soil degradation is an obvious example. Finally, future policy must address the serious problems of equity in the use of world resources—fairness both between different nations of the world and between the present and future generations. So whether one accepts the efficacy of sustainable development policy or not, certain critical changes must occur in our beliefs about and approach to economics.

The second major change that must occur in economic ideology is in a nation's perception of its position relative to other nations. Traditional thinking has assumed that protecting the environment is an economic burden, a cost to a nation in terms of relative productivity and competitiveness. It was concluded that a nation would have to forgo the costs of environmental protection if it wished to remain competitive with other nations.

The concept of ecological modernization challenges this traditional ideology. Rather than seeing ecological protection as a burden on an economy, ecological modernists see it as an important source of economic growth. They argue that "environmental amenity is a superior good, the demand for pollution control is likely to increase, and there is therefore a considerable advantage for an economy to have the technical and production capacity to produce low polluting goods or pollution control technology" (Weale 1992:76). The European Community has made the most serious attempt at integrating this concept into their policy system. The Fourth Environmental Action Programme, for example, asserts that "the future competitiveness of Community industry on world markets will depend heavily upon its ability to offer goods and services causing no pollution and achieving standards at least as high as its competitors" (quoted in Weale 1992:77). An economic ideology for a global ecosystem must link future economic development to high standards of pollution control in the production process and to environmentally safe products.

JUSTICE FOR ALL: AN ETHIC FOR THE GLOBAL ECOSYSTEM

Changes at the level of ideology are important. Much more important, however, are changes in basic values relative to the global ecosystem. The traditional approach to the development of such values involves an attempt to further "ecological wisdom," often referred to by the term *ecosophy*. An examination of this effort is useful before we present a more general ethic for a global ecosystem.

Adherents of ecosophy seek a state of harmonious relationship with nature (Drengson 1990: 101). The positive expression of this value is ecocentric identification, or seeing humans as only one of many self-realizing beings. If humans are to mature and experience self-realization, they should respect biodiversity and have a commitment to protect all life forms. Expressed negatively, ecosophy argues that an individual should act in such a way as to "do as little harm as possible." The "oath" of those committed to ecosophy closely parallels that of medical doctors: Above all else do no harm. From this negative expression, adherents of ecosophy argue that human interference with the ecosystem has become excessive. A part of the ethical action that needs to be taken, they argue, is a reversal of a number of lifestyle, economic, and technological processes that threaten the ecosystem (Naess 1989). The emphasis on lifestyle changes led to the formulation of *green consumerism*, which was based on the principle of voluntary simplicity in lifestyle that maximizes experiences in nature (Devall 1988). Care with regard to both the quality and quantity of products consumed are important elements in simplicity of consumption.

These values of the ecosophy movement are certainly superior to the utilitarian "greatest good for the greatest number" (of humans, of course) that has dominated human values on the ecosystem in the West. The problem is that the ethical prescriptions associated with ecosophy are not general enough. An ethic for a global ecosystem needs to be informed by more general theories of justice. John Rawls describes truth and justice as the "first virtues of human activities" and therefore beyond compromise (Rawls 1971:4). Truth and justice are to have primacy over all else. Certainly justice is the appropriate starting point of an ethic for a global ecosystem.

The prevailing definition of justice was formulated by Aristotle. In the *Nichomachean Ethics* Aristotle defined justice as refraining from gaining some advantage for oneself by taking what belongs to another or denying to a person what is due him. "Giving every person his or her due" came to be the most widely accepted formulation of the concept of justice. But what is due a person? This question went essentially unanswered until the work of John Rawls. Rawls argued that what is due a person is derived from social institutions. To Rawls, "the justice of a social scheme depends essentially on how fundamental rights and duties are assigned and on the economic opportunities and social conditions in the various sectors of society" (Rawls 1971:7). For justice to be accomplished, the basic structures of society must be just.

What are the principles of justice for the basic structures of society? Rawls argues that two principles are fundamental. First there must be "equality in the assignment of basic rights and duties," and second "social and economic inequalities...are just only if they result in compensating benefits for everyone, and in particular for the least advantaged members of society" (Rawls 1971:14–15). Taken together, the two principles mean that it is unjust for some individuals to have less in order that others may prosper.

Rawls' two principles of justice are extremely important for an ethic suitable to a global ecology. Their implications for environmental policy are pervasive and so important that they should be the object of much careful thought. In the context of a general work on global environmental policy, several things need to be emphasized about justice as the starting point for an ethic of the environment.

First, Rawls emphasizes that justice is the normal condition under which human cooperation is possible. In other words, adherence to the two principles of justice is especially important when a workable agreement between everyone "touched by a concern" is necessary. It is now necessary that the 5 billion people who inhabit the globe come to agreement on the general outlines of policy protecting the ecosystem and that they cooperate in implementing that policy. The process of developing policy is wrenchingly difficult, and even once it is developed, cooperation in implementing it is not uniform across nations. One of the basic reasons for this difficulty is the absence of justice in the relations among nations.

As with environmental problems generally, the necessity of justice as the basis for international cooperation is subject to deniability. Some individuals argue that negotiations on environmental concerns should not be linked to issues of justice (Sebenius 1991:126), preferring instead a two-track approach—one track relating to environmental policy and the second to justice. The problem with this proposal is simple. The two tracks in fact have been delinked in the past without the desired level of progress on either track. As Henry Shue argues, "A separate international 'justice' track has...been available for a long time without any movement having occurred along it, in spite of loud and urgent cries from the South to the North in support of a New International Economic Order and various other proposals, none of which have been taken seriously by any of the richest nations" (Shue 1992: 377). Thus decision makers in the South cannot expect justice to be accomplished unless it is linked to a policy area that First World decision makers consider to be in their national interest. The environment is emerging as a policy area offering the opportunity both to accomplish a national interest and to do justice.

An ethic for the environment based on justice between nations strains the concept of justice almost to a breaking point. However there are some beginning points. The first is what Shue calls the "absolutely minimum requirement for justice." This requirement provides that "poor nations ought not to be asked to sacrifice in any way the pace or extent of their own economic development in order to help to prevent the climate changes set in motion by the process of industrialization that has enriched others" (Shue 1992: 394–395). The United Nations expresses this minimum require-ment of justice through the concept of *additionality*, which means that funds to Third World countries for environmental purposes should be in addition to whatever funds are provided for other purposes such as economic development grants. The objective is to ensure that sustainable develop-ment is not slowed by the environmental commitments of Third World nations. On a practical level, additionality means that if, in order to protect the environment, Brazilian rain forest must not be burned, then Brazilian rain forest must not be burned—but Brazilian well-being should not be set back as a result. If the Brazilian people are made worse off, the affluent in other nations benefit by making the poor in Brazil worse off and severe injustice is done.

A second factor in ensuring justice in the relations among nations fol-lows from the first. Justice requires that rich nations be willing to accept less good terms in negotiation than could have been achieved without con-sideration for justice. For rich nations to act exclusively on the basis of national self-interest does not further the cause of justice between nations. This is true for several reasons. First, as Shue observed, "we have lots of good reasons to think that the existing international distributions of wealth and resources are morally arbitrary at best and the result of systematic exploitation at worst" (Shue 1992: 386). In other words, the present distrib-ution of wealth between nations does not reflect justice among nations.

Second, rich nations are the source of most environmental degradation. The numbers are staggering and have been presented in previous chapters. As the source of degradation, rich nations must pay the cost of coping with that degradation if justice is to be served.

How likely are nations to stop acting exclusively on the basis of self-interest and start taking justice into account when making decisions? A start toward establishing a precedent for decision making on the basis of justice is found in the London Amendments to the Montreal Protocol on Substances that Deplete the Ozone Layer. But this international order is only a start, far from a general application of the requirements of justice between nations. However, the proximate nature of justice between nations should not be the occasion for despair. Rather, it should be the occasion for a clear and consistent call for justice in all the affairs of human beings.

As difficult as justice between nations is, justice between generations is even more difficult. Rawls concluded that intergenerational justice "...subjects any ethical theory to severe if not impossible tests" (Rawls 1971:284). At the same time, he recognized the need for intergenerational justice. He wrote, "The life of a people is conceived as a scheme of cooperation spread out in historical time. It is to be governed by the same conception of justice that regulates the cooperation of contemporaries. No generation has stronger claims than any other" (Rawls 1971:289). We come face to face again with a matter on which the most ambitious hope is to make a beginning.

The beginning of a concept of intergenerational justice requires the recognition that each successive generation is entitled to equality in the enjoyment of a clean environment. To put it negatively, no generation has the right to enjoy social and economic advantages at the expense of future generations. Enjoyment of wealth in the present at the expense of the well-being of future generations is unjust. One of the most important implications of this requirement is that the present generation, particularly those living in the First World, needs to examine carefully its patterns of consumption.

What is forgotten in the thinking about justice is the fact that consumption patterns represent choices. Such choices become widespread and are ultimately institutionalized in the social patterns of society. The choice of a mass consumption pattern has certainly become institutionalized in First World nations. However, it is relatively recent, probably no older than the Industrial Revolution. Western societies need to reexamine the question of whether the good life is associated with mass consumption, and the trigger for that reexamination should be the concern for justice between the present and future generations.

A second element in an adequate concept of intergenerational justice is the issue of the present state of the environment. While there are differences in the assessment of environmental degradation, it is difficult to dispute the proposition that environmental degradation has occurred. What, then, does justice require of the present generation vis-a-vis future generations?

The general principle governing the answer to that difficult question is again one derived from Rawls. Justice requires maximizing the long-term prospects of the least favored individuals extending over future generations. Thus the present generation is ethically bound to put aside a suitable amount of wealth to prevent further environmental degradation and to cope with the effects of present degradation. As with the practical aspects of most principles of justice, determining that "suitable amount" is very difficult. Rawls suggests that we imagine ourselves as parents, facing the question: How much of our wealth should we set aside to protect the environment for our children? The answer, from the perspective of justice, is the amount we would believe ourselves entitled to claim from our parents—plus an allowance for improvements in our descendants' circumstances. In essence, what is due a future generation is some improvement in their circumstance over that of previous generations. Those two factors—what we would reasonably expect from our parents and what is required to accomplish due improvements in the circumstances of future generations—establish what is just between generations. When such action is taken, Rawls claims, "no generation can find fault with another, no matter how far removed in time" (Rawls 1971:290). Intergenerational justice will have been achieved.

The categorical imperative of preserving the ecological basis of life is an essential part of any moral system. The key ethical requirement that should guide human actions relative to that categorical imperative is this: Conduct oneself in such a way that the quality of the environment in the future is no less than is expected for oneself in the present. All the world's people need to internalize that ethical necessity.

Bibliography

Ahmed, Yusef J., Salah El Serafez, and Ernst Lutz (eds.) (1989). *Environmental Accounting for Sustainable Development.* Washington, DC: The World Bank.

Allison, Graham (1971). *Essence of Decision: Explaining the Cuban Missile Crises.* Boston: Little, Brown.

Arrandale, Tom (1992). "The Pollution That Washes Off the Land." *Governing*, August 1992, 69.

Basta, Daniel J., and Blair T. Bower (1982). *Analyzing Natural Systems.* Washington, DC: Resources for the Future, Inc.

Bergesen, Helge Ole, Magner Noderhaug, and Georg Parman (eds.) (1992). *Green Globe Yearbook, 1992.* New York: Oxford University Press.

Bower, Blair T., Remi Barre, Jocher Kuhner, and Clifford Russell (1981). *Incentives in Water Quality Management: France and the Ruhr Area.* Baltimore: Resources for the Future, Inc.

Bower, B.T., C.N. Ehler, and A.V. Kneese (1977). "Incentives for Managing the Environment." *Environmental Science and Technology*, 11, no. 3, 250–254.

Bratton, Michael (1989). "The Politics of Government—NGO Relations in Africa." *World Development*, 17, no. 4, 569–587.

Briggs, John (1992). *Fractals: The Patterns of Chaos.* New York: Simon and Schuster.

Brookfield, Harold (1992). "The Numbers Crunch." *The UNESCO Courier,* January 1992, 25–29.

Brubaker, Sterling (1984). *Rethinking the Federal Lands.* Washington, DC: Resources for the Future.

Byrne, John, and Daniel Rich (1984). "Deregulation and Energy Conservation: Reappraisal." *Policy Studies Journal,* 13, no. 2, 331–343.

Cahn, R., and P. Cahn (1990). "Did Earth Day Change the World?" *Environment,* September 16–20, 1990, 36–43.

Caldwell, Lynton K. (1963). *Environment.* Garden City, NY: Anchor Books.

Chapman, Neil A., and Ian G. McKinley (1987). *The Geological Disposal of Nuclear Waste.* Chichester, England: John Wiley & Sons.

Cobb, Charles E., Jr. (1987). "The Great Lake's Troubled Waters." *National Geographic,* 172, no. 1, 2–31.

Coggins, G. E., and C. Wilkenson (1987). *Federal Lands and Resources Law.* Westbury, NY: The Foundation Press.

Commission of the European Communities (1986). *Fourth Environmental Action Programme.* Luxembourg: Office for Official Publications of the European Communities.

Corson, Walter H. (ed.) (1990). *The Global Ecology Handbook.* Boston: Beacon Press.

Crow, M., B. Boseman, W. Meyer, and R. Shangraw, Jr. (1988). *Synthetic Fuel Technology Development in the United States: A Retrospective Assessment.* New York: Praeger.

Daly, Herman E. (1990). "Towards Some Operational Principles of Sustainable Development." *Ecological Economics,* 2, 1–5.

Davis, David Howard (1982). *Energy Politics,* 3rd ed. New York: St. Martins Press.

Davis, Gary (1990). "Shifting the Burden Off the Land: The Role of Technical Innovations." In Bruce W. Piasecki and Gary A. Davis, *America's Future in Toxic Waste Management: Lessons from Europe.* New York: Quorum Books.

Davis, Gary, Donald Huisingh, and Bruce Piasecki (1987). "Waste Reduction Strategies: European and American Prospects." In Bruce

W. Piasecki and Gary A. Davis, *America's Future in Toxic Waste Management: Lessons from Europe*. New York: Quorum Books.

de Haven-Smith, Lance (1991). *Environmental Concern in Florida and the Nation*. Gainesville: University of Florida Press.

Denison, Richard A., and John Ruston (eds.) (1990). *Recycling and Incineration: Evaluating the Choices*. Washington, DC: Island Press.

Department of Energy (1990). *The Potential of Renewable Energy: An Interlaboratory White Paper*. Washington, DC: Department of Energy.

Devall, B. (1988). *Simple in Means, Rich in Ends: Practicing Deep Ecology*. Salt Lake City: Peregrine Smith.

Dietz, Thomas M., and Robert W. Rycroft (1987). *The Risk Professionals*. New York: Russell Sage Foundation.

Dregne, H., M. Kassas, and B. Rozanov (1992). "A New Assessment of the World Status of Desertification." *Desertification Control Bulletin*, no. 20, 6–18.

Drengson, A. (1990). "In Praise of Ecosophy." *Trumpeter*, 7, 101–103.

Dunlap, Riley E., and Angela G. Mertig (eds.) (1992). *American Environmentalism*. Philadelphia: Taylor and Francis.

Dunn, Michael J. (1992). "Letter to the Editor." *Insight*, April 27, 1992.

Economic Commission for Europe (1984). *Report of the Seminar on Low-Waste Technology*. Geneva: United Nations Economic Commission for Europe.

English, Mary R. (1992). *Siting Low-Level Radioactive Waste Facilities*. New York: Quorum Books.

EPA (1980). *Groundwater Protection*. Washington, DC: Environmental Protection Agency.

EPA (1983). *Surface Impoundment Assessment Report*. Washington, DC: Environmental Protection Agency.

EPA (1986). *Census of State and Territorial D Non-Hazardous Waste Programs*. Washington, DC: Environmental Protection Agency.

EPA (1988). *Report to Congress: Solid Waste Disposal in the United States*. Washington, DC: Environmental Protection Agency.

Fairfax, Sally, and Carolyn Yale (1987). *Federal Lands*. Washington, DC: Island Press.

FAO (1984). *Land, Food, and People*. Rome: UN Food and Agriculture Organization.

Federal Water Pollution Control Administration (1966). *Water Pollution Problems in the Great Lakes Area*. Washington, DC: U.S. Government Printing Office.

Feldman, Stephen (1977). "Waste Water Reclamation and the Water Economy in Israel: A Case Study." In Roger E. Kasperson and Jeanne Kasperson (eds.), *Water Re-Use and the Cities*. Hanover, NH: Clarke University Press.

Feliciano, D. V. (1987). *Safe Drinking Water*. Washington, DC: Library of Congress.

Firor, John (1990). *The Changing Atmosphere: A Global Challenge*. New Haven, CT: Yale University Press.

General Accounting Office (1989). *Export of Unregistered Pesticides Is Not Adequately Monitored by EPA*. Washington, DC: U.S. Government Printing Office.

Gibbins, J. H., and H. L. Given (1989). "Lessons Learned from Twenty Years of Energy Policy." *Energy Systems and Policy* 13, 9–19.

Goldberg, E. D. (1981). "The Oceans as Waste Space: The Argument." *Oceanus*, 24, no. 1, 2–9.

Haigh, Nigel (1992). "The European Community and International Environmental Policy." In Andrew Hurrell and Benedict Kingsbury (eds.). *The International Politics of the Environment*. New York: Oxford University Press, pp. 228–249.

Hamilton, Chris, and Donald Wells (1990). *Federalism, Power, and Political Economy*. Englewood Cliffs, NJ: Prentice Hall.

Hardin, Garrett (1968). "The Tragedy of the Commons." *Science*, 162, 1243–1248.

Heckstra, G. P. (1989). "Sea Level Rise: Regional Consequences and Responses." In N. Rosenburg, W. Easterling, P. Crosson, and J. Darmstadter (eds.), *Greenhouse Warming: Abatement and Adaptation*. Washington, DC: Resources for the Future, Inc.

Herzik, Erick B., and Alvin H. Mushkatel (1992). "Intergovernmental Complexity in Nuclear Waste Disposal Policy." *Policy Studies Review*, 10, no. 4, 139–151.

Hill, Michael (1982). "The Role of the British Alkali and Clean Air Inspectorate in Air Pollution Control." *Policy Studies Journal*, 11, no. 1, 165–174.

Honeysett, J. D. (1975). "The Packaging Industry and Social Waste Management." In N. Y. Kerov (ed.), *Waste Management, Control, Recovery, and Reuse.* Ann Arbor, MI: Ann Arbor Science Publishers, Inc.

Hosang, Joanna Boddens (1992). "Trade with Endangered Species." In *Green Globe Almanac 1992.* New York: Oxford University Press.

ICRP (1977). *Recommendations of the International Commission on Radiological Protection.* Oxford, England: Pergamon.

Idso, Keith E. (1992). "Greening the Planet," *The New American,* 8, no. 11, 10.

Isaac, J.D. (1978). "Hearings on Modification of Secondary Treatment Requirements for Discharge into Marine Waters: Testimony." U.S. House of Representatives, Committee on Public Works and Transportation. Washington, DC: U.S. Government Printing Office.

Kasperson, Roger E., and Jeanne X. Kasperson (1977). *Water Re-Use and the Cities.* Hanover, NH: Clarke University Press.

Kenski, Henry C. (1990). *Saving the Hidden Treasure: The Evolution of Groundwater Policy.* Claremont, CA: Regina Books.

King, Laurestan R. (1986). "Anticipatory Policy and Marine Resources." *Policy Studies Review,* 6, no. 2, 302–309.

Kiss, Alexander Charles (1991). *International Environmental Law.* Irvington-on-Hudson, NY: Transnational Publications.

Kushler, Martin, Patti Witte, and Sharon Ehlke (1992). "Are High-Participation Residential Conservation Programs Still Feasible?" *Policy Studies Journal,* 20, no. 1, 57–67.

Lehr, Jay H. (1985). "Calming the Restless Natives: How Ground Water Quality Will Ultimately Answer the Questions of Ground Water Pollution." In C. H. Ward, W. Giger, and P. L. McCarty, *Ground Water Quality.* New York: John Wiley.

Lester, James P., James L. Franke, Ann Bowman, and Kenneth W. Kramer (1983). "Hazardous Waste, Politics, and Public Policy: A Comparative State Analysis." *Western Political Quarterly,* 36, no. 1, 275–285.

Logan, S. H. (1990). "Global Warming and the Sacramento-San Joaquin Delta." *California Agriculture,* 44, 16–18.

Lovins, Amory B. (1977). *Soft Energy Paths: Toward a Durable Peace.* New York: Harper and Row.

Lowrance, William W. (1976). *Of Acceptable Risk.* Los Altos, CA: William Kaufman, Inc.

Lunde, Leiu (1990). *The North/South Dimension in Global Greenhouse Politics.* Lysaker, Norway: Fredtzol Nasen Institute.

Lundqvist, Lennart J. (1974). *Environmental Policies in Canada, Sweden, and the United States: A Comparative Overview.* Beverly Hills, CA: Sage Publications.

Lynn, Frances M. (1986). "The Interplay of Science and Values in Assessing and Regulating Environmental Risks." *Science, Technology, and Human Values,* 11, no. 2, 40–50.

Makhijani, Arjun, Amanda Bickel, and Annie Makhijani (1990). "Beyond the Montreal Protocol: Still Working on the Ozone Hole." *Technology Review,* May/June 1990, 52–59.

March, James G., and John P. Olsen (1984). "The New Institutionalism: Organizational Factors in Political Life." *American Political Science Review,* 78, 734–749.

McCabe, A., and M. Fitzgerald (1992). "Prospects for Monitored Retrievable Storage of High Level Nuclear Waste." *Policy Studies Review,* 10, no. 4, 167–179.

Melosi, Martin V. (1981). *Garbage in the Cities: Refuse, Reform, and the Environment 1880–1980.* College Station, TX: Texas A & M University Press.

Mitchell, R. C. (1989). "From Conservation to Environmental Lobbies." In M. S. Lacey (ed.), *Government and Environmental Politics.* Washington, DC: Wilson Center Press.

Mitchell, Robert C., Angela G. Mertig, and Riley E. Dunlap (1992). "Twenty Years of Environmental Mobilization: Trends among National Environmental Organizations." In Riley E. Dunlap and Angela G. Mertig (eds.), *American Environmentalism.* Philadelphia: Taylor and Francis.

Morganthau, Tom (1988). "Don't Go Near the Water: Our Dying Coasts." *Newsweek,* August 1, 1988, 42–47.

Mott, Laurie, and Karen Snyder (1987). *Pesticide Alert.* San Francisco: Sierra Club Books.

Naess, A. (1989). *Ecology, Community, and Lifestyle.* trans. D. Rothenberg. New York: Cambridge University Press.

National Academy of Sciences (1984). *Groundwater Contamination.* Washington, DC: National Academy Press.

National Commission on Children (1991). *Beyond Rhetoric: A New American*

Agenda for Children and Families. Washington, DC: U.S. Government Printing Office.

National Conference of State Legislatures (1982). *Summary of State Siting Laws for Hazardous Waste Facilities.* Denver, CO: National Conference of State Legislatures.

National Research Council (1990). *Managing Troubled Waters: The Role of Marine Environmental Monitoring.* Washington, DC: National Academy Press.

National Resource Council (1984). *Toxicity Testing: Strategies to Determine Needs and Priorities.* Washington, DC: National Academy Press.

Neal, Homer A., and J. R. Schubel (1987). *Solid Waste Management and the Environment: The Mounting Garbage and Trash Crisis.* Englewood Cliffs, NJ: Prentice Hall, Inc.

Norse, David (1992). "A New Strategy for Feeding a Crowded Planet." *Environment*, 34, no. 5, 6–11, 32–39.

OECD (1985). *The State of the Environment.* Washington, DC: Organization for Economic Cooperation and Development.

OECD (1991). *The State of the Environment.* Paris: Organization for Economic Cooperation and Development.

Office of Technology Assessment (1983). *Technologies and Management Strategies for Hazardous Waste Control.* Washington, DC: U.S. Government Printing Office.

Oldeman, L. R., R. T. A. Hakkeling, and W. G. Sombroek (1990). *World Map of Human Induced Soil Degradation: An Explanatory Note.* Wageningen, The Netherlands: International Soil Reference and Information Centre.

Piasecki, Bruce (1984). *Beyond Dumping.* New York: Quorum Books.

Piasecki, Bruce, and Gary Davis (1990). *America's Future in Toxic Waste Management: Lessons from Europe.* New York: Quorum Books.

Pijawaka, N. David, and Alvin H. Mushkatel (1992). "Symposium on the Development of Nuclear Waste Policy: Siting the High Level Nuclear Waste Repository." *Policy Studies Review*, 10, no. 4, 88–89.

Porter, Garreth, and Janet Welsh Brown (1991). *Global Environmental Politics.* Boulder, CO: Westview Press.

Rawls, John (1971). *A Theory of Justice.* Cambridge, MA: Harvard University Press.

Reiss, Bob (1992). *The Road to Extremes*. New York: Summit Books.

Repetto, Robert (1986). *World Enough and Time*. New Haven, CT: Yale University Press.

Richard, J. J., and G. A. Junk (1981). "Polychlorinated Biphenyles in Effluents from Combustion of Coal/Refuse." *Environmental Science Technology*, 15, no. 9, 1095–1100.

Roxburgh, I. S. (1987). *Geology of High-Level Nuclear Waste Disposal*. London: Chapman and Hill.

Sadik, Nafis (1988). *The State of World Population*. New York: World Population Fund.

Samuelson, Robert J. (1992). "The End Is Not at Hand." *Newsweek*, June 1, 1992, 43.

Sayer, J., and T. Whitmore (eds.) (1993). *Tropical Deforestation and Species Extinction*. London: Chapman and Hall.

Schmandt, Jurgen, Ernest T. Merdon, and Judith Clarkson (1988). *State Water Policies*. New York: Praeger.

Sebenius, James K. (1991). "Designing Negotiations toward a New Regime: The Case of Global Warming." *International Security*, 15, 126–128.

Sen, A. (1981). *Poverty and Famines: An Essay in Entitlements and Deprivation*. Oxford, England: Clarendon Press.

Shue, Henry (1992). "The Unavoidability of Justice." In Andrew Hurrell and Benedict Kingsbury (eds.), *The International Politics of the Environment*. Oxford, England: The Clarendon Press.

Smith, V. Kerry (1976). *The Economic Consequences of Air Pollution*. Cambridge, MA: Ballinger Publishing Co.

Smith, J. B., and D. A. Tirpack (eds.) (1989). *The Potential Effects of Global Warming on the United States*. Washington, DC: U.S. Environmental Protection Agency.

Spiller, Judith, and Alison Rieser (1986). "Scientific Fact and Value in U.S. Ocean Dumping Policy." *Policy Studies Review*, 6, no. 2, 389–398.

Stairs, Kevin, and Peter Taylor (1992). "Non-Governmental Organizations and the Legal Protection of the Oceans: A Case Study." In Andrew Hurrell and Benedict Kingsbury (eds.), *The International Politics of the Environment*. Oxford, England: Clarendon Press.

Stolwizk, Jan A. J. (1983). "Nuclear Waste Management and Risks to Human Health." In Charles A. Walker, LeRoy C. Gould, and Edward

Woodhouse (eds.), *Too Hot to Handle? Social and Policy Issues in the Management of Radioactive Wastes*. New Haven, CT: Yale University Press.

Tientenberg, T. H. (1985). *Emissions Trading*. Washington, DC: Resources for the Future, Inc.

Turner, Tom (1991). "The American Military vs. The American Land." *Wilderness*, Fall 1991, 10–15, 31.

United Nations (1988). *Mortality of Children under Age 5: World Estimates and Projections*. New York: United Nations.

United Nations (1990). *Human Development Report*. New York: Oxford University Press.

UN Children's Fund (1991). *The State of the World's Children*. New York: Oxford University Press.

UN Environment Programme (1985). *Radiation, Doses, Effects, Risks*. Nairobi: United Nations Environment Programme.

UN Environment Programme (1988a). *Assessment of Urban Air Quality*. London: United Nations.

UN Environment Programme (1988b). UNEP News, April 1988.

UNSCEAR (1977). *Sources and Effects of Ionizing Radiation*. New York: UN Scientific Committee on the Effects of Atomic Radiation.

U.S. Department of Energy (1984). *Consumer Reaction to the Irradiation Concept*. Contract #DE-SC04-84AL24460.

van Duizvenbooden, W. (1985). "Effects of Local Sources of Pollution on Ground Water Quality in the Netherlands." In C. H. Ward, W. Giger, and P. L. McCarty (eds.), *Groundwater Quality*. New York: John Wiley & Sons.

Wagner, Travis P. (1990). *Hazardous Waste Identification and Classification Manual*. New York: Van Nostrand Reinhold.

Walker, Charles A., LeRoy C. Gould, and Edward J. Woodhouse (1983). *Too Hot to Handle? Social and Policy Issues in the Management of Radioactive Wastes*. New Haven, CT: Yale University Press.

Walls, James (1980). *Land, Man, and Sand: Desertification and Its Solution*. New York: Macmillan Publishing Co.

Water Resources Council (1980). *Bulletin 16*. Washington, DC: Water Resources Council.

Weale, Albert (1992). *The New Politics of Pollution*. Manchester: Manchester University Press.

Winterbottom, Robert (1990). *Taking Stock: The Tropical Forestry Action Plan after Five Years*. Washington, DC: World Resources Institute.

Wondolleck, Julia M. (1988). *Public Lands Conflict and Resolution: Managing National Forest Disputes*. New York: Plenum Press.

World Commission on Environment and Development (1987). *Our Common Future*. New York: Oxford University Press.

World Health Organization (1990). *Public Health Impact of Pesticides Used in Agriculture*. Geneva: World Health Organization.

World Resources Institute (1992). *World Resources 1992–93*. New York: Oxford University Press.

World Resources Institute (1993). *Environmental Almanac 1993*. New York: Houghton Mifflin.

Worthington, Richard K. (1984). "Renewable Energy Policy and Politics: The Case of the Windfall Profits Tax." *Policy Studies Journal*, 13, no. 2, 365–375.

Index